THE WORLD BIBLIOGRAPHICAL SERIES

This series, which is principally designed for the English speaker, will eventually cover every country in the world, each in a separate volume comprising annotated entries on works dealing with its history, geography, economy and politics; and with its people, their culture, customs, religion and social organization. Attention will also be paid to current living conditions – housing, education, newspapers, clothing, etc.– that are all too often ignored in standard bibliographies; and to those particular aspects relevant to individual countries. Each volume seeks to achieve, by use of careful selectivity and critical assessment of the literature, an expression of the country and an appreciation of its nature and national aspirations, to guide the reader towards an understanding of its importance. The keynote of the series is to provide, in a uniform format, an interpretation of each country that will express its culture, its place in the world, and the qualities and background that make it unique. The views expressed in individual volumes, however, are not necessarily those of the publisher.

VOLUMES IN THE SERIES

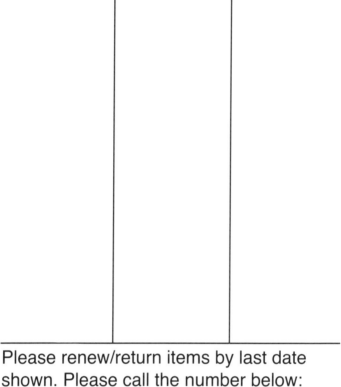

Please renew/return items by last date
shown. Please call the number below:

Renewals and enquiries: 0300 123 4049

Textphone for hearing or
speech impaired users: 0300 123 4041

www.hertsdirect.org/librarycatalogue
L32

Guinea-Bissau

WORLD BIBLIOGRAPHICAL SERIES

General Editors:
Robert G. Neville (Executive Editor)
John J. Horton
Robert A. Myers   Ian Wallace
Hans H. Wellisch   Ralph Lee Woodward, Jr.

John J. Horton is Deputy Librarian of the University of Bradford and currently Chairman of its Academic Board of Studies in Social Sciences. He has maintained a longstanding interest in the discipline of area studies and its associated bibliographical problems, with special reference to European Studies. In particular he has published in the field of Icelandic and of Yugoslav studies, including the two relevant volumes in the World Bibliographical Series.

Robert A. Myers is Associate Professor of Anthropology in the Division of Social Sciences and Director of Study Abroad Programs at Alfred University, Alfred, New York. He has studied post-colonial island nations of the Caribbean and has spent two years in Nigeria on a Fulbright Lectureship. His interests include international public health, historical anthropology and developing societies. In addition to *Amerindians of the Lesser Antilles: a bibliography* (1981), *A Resource Guide to Dominica, 1493-1986* (1987) and numerous articles, he has compiled the World Bibliographical Series volumes on *Dominica* (1987) and *Nigeria* (1989).

Ian Wallace is Professor of Modern Languages at Loughborough University of Technology. A graduate of Oxford in French and German, he also studied in Tübingen, Heidelberg and Lausanne before taking teaching posts at universities in the USA, Scotland and England. He specializes in East German affairs, especially literature and culture, on which he has published numerous articles and books. In 1979 he founded the journal *GDR Monitor*, which he continues to edit.

Hans H. Wellisch is Professor emeritus at the College of Library and Information Services, University of Maryland. He was President of the American Society of Indexers and was a member of the International Federation for Documentation. He is the author of numerous articles and several books on indexing and abstracting, and has published *The Conversion of Scripts* and *Indexing and Abstracting: an International Bibliography*. He also contributes frequently to *Journal of the American Society for Information Science*, *The Indexer* and other professional journals.

Ralph Lee Woodward, Jr. is Chairman of the Department of History at Tulane University, New Orleans, where he has been Professor of History since 1970. He is the author of *Central America, a Nation Divided*, 2nd ed. (1985), as well as several monographs and more than sixty scholarly articles on modern Latin America. He has also compiled volumes in the World Bibliographical Series on *Belize* (1980), *Nicaragua* (1983), and *El Salvador* (1988). Dr. Woodward edited the Central American section of the *Research Guide to Central America and the Caribbean* (1985) and is currently editor of the Central American history section of the *Handbook of Latin American Studies*.

VOLUME 121

Guinea-Bissau

Rosemary E. Galli

Compiler

CLIO PRESS

OXFORD, ENGLAND · SANTA BARBARA, CALIFORNIA
DENVER, COLORADO

British Library Cataloguing in Publication Data

Rosemary E. Galli
Guinea-Bissau. — (World bibliographical series, V. 121).
1. Guinea-Bissau – Bibliographies
I. Title   II. Series
016. 9883

ISBN 1-85109-108-4

Clio Press Ltd.,
55 St. Thomas' Street,
Oxford OX1 1JG, England.

ABC-CLIO,
130 Cremona Drive,
Santa Barbara,
CA 93117, USA.

Designed by Bernard Crossland.
Typeset by Columns Design and Production Services Ltd, Reading, England.
Printed and bound in Great Britain by
Billing and Sons Ltd., Worcester.

For Cesare and Katrin

Contents

Contents

Introduction

A small, coastal West African state, Guinea-Bissau achieved independence in September 1974 after an eleven-year war for liberation from Portuguese colonialism. Guinea-Bissau attracted international attention because of the force of personality and ideas of its nationalist leader, Amílcar Cabral. He was a brilliant thinker and strategist and charismatic leader whose magnetism is still felt inside and outside the country despite his assassination in 1973 (see Davidson, 1981; Chabal, 1983; McCulloch, 1983; Chilcote, 1991). With the help of a young and dynamic but small and inexperienced group of cadres, Cabral organized a party-state that operated more or less democratically, particularly in the southern regions of the country, in the early stages of the guerrilla struggle (see Rudebeck, 1974, for a balanced assessment of this experience; see also Davidson, Chaliand, Luís Cabral and Valimamad). Known as the Partido Africano da Independência da Guiné e Cabo Verde (PAIGC), the organization monopolized official politics into the 1990s.

Cabral inherited the experience of a generation of progressive African thinkers and rulers from Nkrumah and Nyerere to Sékou Touré, his host in Conakry for much of the independence struggle. He was able to go beyond their thinking to outline a political and economic strategy for his own country that brought him sympathy and the assistance of solidarity groups around Europe, Canada and the United States and from a number of governments including Sweden, Guinea-Conakry, the USSR, Czechoslovakia and China. This was based primarily on his and the party's ability to enlist the active support of a significant part of the rural population in Guinea and the party's stated position to define development in socialist, although not doctrinaire, terms.

Significant international assistance has been forthcoming from Western governments and multilateral organizations since independence despite the inability of the government under the leadership first of Luís Cabral – Amílcar's half brother – (1974-80) and then João

Introduction

Bernardo Vieira (1980-) to maintain the people's confidence, to stimulate the economy to pre-war levels of production and to support itself from national revenues. Andreini and Lambert are witness to the good intentions of the first government to lay the foundations for a socialist, if not democratic, society. Galli and Jones show that good intentions were not enough. They lay blame for the loss of PAIGC political and economic credibility among Guineans on the following factors: the reconstitution of a highly bureaucratic state; its adoption of a model of development out of tune with the needs of the country's majority; and the failure to organize the majority in a meaningful way, that is, to a lack of democracy (see also Rudebeck).

There are significant differences among authors in explaining this state of affairs. Lopes, in an early work from 1982, and Basil Davidson (1981) attribute the bureaucratization of government to the PAIGC's lack of experience in government and in not planning for the post-war future. Its lack of trained people and consequent alliance with the 'non-revolutionary bourgeoisie' in the colonial administration predisposed it to adopt a similar style of administration. In another work, Lopes sees the model of development deriving from the 'modern state rationality' adopted by the PAIGC which he contrasts with peasants' own 'ethnic rationality'.

In a later work, Lopes (1988) blames the government's lack of identification with the majority of people in the country and the lack of socialism on unfavourable world economic and political conditions. Guinea-Bissau was, however, no different from the rest of Africa. Lopes argues that these countries could not embark on an autarchic path. They had to seek development assistance from capitalist governments. Galli and Jones and Hermele and Rudebeck, however, see this as a matter of political choice. Governments and development agencies form a political alliance whose interests clash with those of the majority of producers in the country.

Some interpretations perceive the conflict between the government and peasants as a struggle between modernity and traditionality (see, for example, the various World Bank publications and the first development plan and other publications of the Ministério de Coordenação Económico e Plano). Other writers indirectly reinforce the image of Guinean cultivators as isolated and subsistence-minded by assuming that they were hardly touched by colonialism (Chabal, Ziegler) or were cut off from the world economy (Schiefer). Still others go so far as to posit a separate peasant mode of production (Forrest) and to see the struggle between rural producers and the state as ethnically based (Bollinger, Forrest).

Galli and Jones, on the other hand, explain the contradiction as historical, material and institutional rather than simply psychological or cultural. They show that the PAIGC adopted political forms and economic policies very similar to those of the former administration and that these aimed at maintaining a tight control over rural populations in order to exploit them; that is, to raise the revenues necessary to maintain the state and to begin a process of industrialization. However, the government provided very little in return. It did not help rural peoples rebuild their villages, nor did it provide the roads, transport, agricultural research, extension, inputs, production tools, consumer goods and so on that people needed. The developmental model was essentially statist and mercantilist (Galli, 1989).

Galli and Jones also show that the policy interventions in education, health and rural development have largely reinforced the social and material divide between educated urban classes and rural populations. Under pressure from the Swedish, US and French development agencies and from the World Bank and IMF, the current leadership has modified the developmental model but not yet the style of government. President João Bernardo Vieira has, however, announced constitutional reform and elections, possibly on a multiparty basis, before the end of his current term of office (1989-94).

Historical background

The lack of visible economic and social progress during the Luís Cabral years and the early years of government under Vieira has often been blamed upon an 'uncooperative, irrational, traditional' peasantry as noted above. The historical section of the bibliography gives the lie to this image.

The history of Guinea – as of all Africa – is a history of continual movement of both goods and people, the result of both increasing and decreasing economic opportunities, that is, trade and war. The integration of the northern and eastern parts of what is now known as Guinea-Bissau by the Mande peoples into the trans-Saharan trade is thought to have driven some inhabitants to settle along the coast. (There are a number of theories about how these settlements occurred; see, for example, Wright and Rogado Quintino.) The most numerous group of the over twenty in contemporary Guinea-Bissau – the Balanta Brassa or simply Brassa – learned to tame the sea by fashioning earthen dikes in order to cultivate rice. Rice, salt, palm wine and other crops were traded in a flourishing local economy (Rodney). Balanta techniques were not only celebrated during colonial times by such authors as Quintino but, as the section on agriculture shows, are the continuing subject of research (see Birkholz, Ribeiro and others).

Introduction

During the slave trade, the Kaabu empire, an offshoot of the Mali empire dominated the northern part of the country while the Beafada kingdom dominated central-southern parts (Hawkins). An area that *never* succumbed to centralized political power were the islands populated by the Bijagós who often raided the coastal peoples. Mandingas of Kaabu, Beafadas and Bijagós were the most prominent slave traders, trading mainly with Portuguese, Afro-Portuguese and Cape Verdean intermediaries who settled along the coast. The slave trade spawned a mixed-race group of Afro-Europeans who formed a new social formation all along the Upper Guinea Coast (Carreira, Brooks and Barreto). That part of the coast under Portuguese influence was called the Rios de Guiné do Cabo Verde or Rivers of Guinea of Cape Verde, which name I have used to denominate the second period of history in the bibliography.

From the fifteenth century onwards, Fula peoples from the Futa Djalon migrated as pastoralists. By the second period of the slave trade, they too had become prominent in the trade. Conversion to Islam became an important factor in this history and there were wars not only between Islamized and animist groups but also between the Islamized groups. Hawkins and Rodney agree that commercial as well as political control over the north of the country was at stake. Rodney argues that the capture of slaves was a primary motivation. In the series of wars, Kaabu disintegrated, the Beafada kingdom went into decline and many coastal rulers converted to Islam.

The 'legitimate' trade in groundnuts that flourished in the nineteenth century brought Afro-Europeans, Cape Verdeans and the French into commercial prominence. Manjaco and Brame peoples in particular migrated to form a labour force on the plantations which started on the islands of Bolama and Galinhas and along the Rio Grande de Buba. The Brames later became small plantation owners themselves. Mandingas were also involved as a labour force. Large French trading companies (CFAO, SCOA) were the main outlets for this trade and dominated the export economy of Guinea (see Roche and Honório Pereira Barreto). It was against this economic background that Portugal decided to try to conquer Guinea. Pélissier (1989) brings this story to life.

I have arbitrarily dated the third period in history – the period of Portuguese Guinea – from 1879, the year that Portugal detached Guinea from the administrative system centred in the Cape Verde islands and governed it as a separate province. Pélissier shows that the Portuguese, however, did not really govern the territory until well into the twentieth century. In agreement, I have deliberately concentrated the focus of this section on the Salazar–Caetano régime of the *Estado Novo* or New State because it had the greatest impact upon the social and political organization of Guineans and a lasting influence on those who led the nationalist movement. The final historical period, that of the national liberation struggle, has received the greatest attention from scholars, and the reader will notice that most of the historical works in English are on this period.

The historical section of the bibliography thus focuses on the role of trade and war in the political organization of the country. *Precolonial history* – as we know it – was dominated by the trans-Saharan trade organized mainly by Mande and other traders. The slave trade accounted for the rise of new groups and states in the area called the *Rios de Guiné*. The dominance of the French in the groundnut trade and the Germans in the rubber trade may not have been the deciding factors but formed the backdrop to Portugal's renewed efforts to secure a position in West Africa. There was nothing static about the resistance of Guineans to the military operations to establish *Portuguese Guinea* just as there had been nothing 'traditional' about their response to new markets. Instead, Guineans fought the Portuguese not once but many times in order to keep trading and political options open. The last section is on the final *national liberation struggle*.

Economic conditions

Squeezed in between Senegal on the north and east and Guinea-Conakry on the east and south, Guinea-Bissau is mainly a swampy marshland extending over 36,125 square kilometres. Its close to one million inhabitants are mainly agricultural producers, although a significant part of the active labour force migrates to work in a number of activities in neighbouring countries and abroad. The largest urban area is Bissau, the capital city, claiming between 15 and 20 per cent of the population. There are much smaller regional capitals.

Most people live in extended families of eight or more people, in villages ranging between 100 and 1,000 people. They grow a variety of crops but rice is the nearly universal staple. Hochet (1983) has the best overall description of how Guineans have adapted agriculture to their environment. Coastal peoples regulate the ebb and flow of the sea which daily bathes the land up to 100 kilometres. Inland, savannah peoples depend mainly on rain-fed crops including rice and a variety of millets, maize, sorghum and other secondary cereals. Sweet potatoes, some vegetables and manioc are also grown, the latter as a crop of last resort. All peoples have small animals and most raise cattle for ceremonial and other purposes.

There is pressure on land in some areas but it is generally

estimated that the considerable arable land exists for expansion. It is significant, however, that the amount of land under cultivation has been less than in pre-war times. In some areas, this is due to a labour shortage. In many areas, there is both seasonal and permanent labour migration.

The major reason for migration has been a lack of economic opportunity in rural areas before and especially since independence. People's reactions were manifest in the noteworthy number of Guineans who remained in Senegal after the war's end instead of going home; in the significant proportion of youth who continue to migrate to the capital city, Senegal and other countries; in the cutting back on rice production and sales on Guinean markets in the 1970s to mid-1980s; and in the smuggling of production across the country's borders.

As noted above, the lack of economic opportunity was related to the mercantilist model of development adopted by the country's new rulers. Trade policy was similar to the strategy adopted by the Salazar régime from 1928 in the colonies. In Portuguese Guinea, the goal had been to turn groundnut and other commodity production toward provisioning Portuguese rather than French and other European industries. In the 1950s, Guinean production provided one-third of Portugal's vegetable-oil requirements, accomplished through efforts to centralize control over imports and exports through large trading houses even though never fully realized. The colonial administration also turned towards stimulating new crops, setting up government trading posts to complement the operations of the large companies, taxing and otherwise obliging peasants to grow export crops and so on.

Luís Cabral's government turned the largest Portuguese commercial companies into a government-controlled trade monopoly, renamed the Armazéns do Povo and SOCOMIN, deliberately undermining small private traders. The monopoly set prices for imports as well as exports. It also set prices on local markets. After an initial price rise for basic crops, however, the terms of trade for agriculture fell dramatically. Production for the state agencies likewise fell.

Unlike the Portuguese strategy, the Cabral régime designed commercial and exchange rate policy in order to encourage industrialization in Guinea itself. However, there was little articulation between the industries set up and agriculture. This, too, was responsible for the loss of confidence between peasants and the government during the first ten years of independence.

Guinea-Bissau has the potential to be self-sufficient in basic foods and to produce surpluses for export, the value of which are dependent on international markets. It is also a primary producer of wood and fish for export, both of which could prove sources of national wealth in the short and medium term. The problem is that Guinea does not yet have a national capacity to exploit these resources rationally and is dependent upon private individuals, especially foreign investors and fishermen who, at present, mine these resources irrationally. Drilling for oil is underway to determine the exploitability of this resource, most probably in the long-term. There are, however, border conflicts with Senegal which involve both the off-shore oil fields and fishing rights (see the section on foreign relations).

In 1987, after years of economic stagnation and decline, the government reversed its development strategy and opened trade, industry and agriculture to private enterprise.

Politics

Since its founding in 1956, the Partido Africano da Independência da Guiné e Cabo Verde (PAIGC) (originally known simply as Partido Africano da Independência or PAI) has been subject to factional strife. In the 1950s, its founders belonged to a number of groups which combined and split over differences in position. By the end of the 1950s the founders had distinguished themselves by their decision to take up armed struggle against Portugal and to fight simultaneously for the liberation of Cape Verde and Guinea-Bissau.

From 1964, the top leadership was dominated by three Cape Verdeans – Amílcar Cabral, Luís Cabral (Amílcar's half-brother) and Aristides Pereira (who became the president of Cape Verde after independence). Despite Amílcar Cabral's unifying presence, resentment built up within the party and especially among the military over the prominent role of Cape Verdeans. In the 1970s, there was also frustration over the length of the war. Some of this sentiment surfaced with the assassination of Amílcar Cabral. The feelings against Cape Verdeans resurfaced within the party and the public at large during the seizure of power by the army in 1980 which turned over leadership to João Bernardo Vieira (known affectionately by his *nom de guerre*, 'Nino'). Relations with Cape Verde went from the previous commitment to unify the two countries gradually to almost complete rupture. However, time, patient negotiation and the intervention of other lusophone African countries restored normal, even friendly relations. There continue to be Cape Verdeans in government and other important positions.

The party went into decline as the principal centre of power under Luís Cabral. This was partly due to his domineering personality, his lack of respect for party collegiality and the growth of the state apparatus. Even though top positions in government were occupied mostly by party officials, Cabral kept many of the previous colonial administrators. Moreover, he and his cohorts expanded government, which kept many of the features of the colonial administration, and recruited as personnel urban-educated individuals not attached to the party. When Cabral appointed outsiders to high ranks in the army, the lower ranks rebelled. The government and the army rather than the party became the subjects and objects of power struggles, which were reflected in party councils.

By the 1980s, government factions formed along lines influenced by major 'donor' governments and agencies. In the 1970s, the principal division had been between those supported by socialist governments such as the USSR, Cuba, North Korea, the German Democratic Republic and those supported by Western governments and agencies such as France, the United States, Portugal, and the World Bank. The decisions announced by the Third Party Congress held in 1977 mirrored the initial triumph of 'socialist' forces. In the 1980s the balance began to change.

There were also those, such as the Western-oriented Foreign Minister and Prime Minister Victor Saúde Maria, who were notorious for using their ethnic affiliations to build a clientele. On the other hand, Paulo Correia – on the left wing – was accused of fomenting rebellion among the Balantas. By the mid-1980s, the faction favoured by the World Bank and the International Monetary Fund became predominant. This was reflected in the positions on liberalization of the economy taken by the Fourth Party Congress held in 1986. It was also reflected in the announcement in 1989 of the intention to proceed towards a liberalization of politics. At the party congress, announced to take place in November 1990, major decisions are expected regarding an opening of the political system. In the interim, President Vieira refused to open negotiations with a self-styled opposition group, the Movimento-Bafatá, headquartered in Lisbon.

Economic liberalization

The decision to end state control over commerce began hesitatingly in 1986. It was reinforced by the agreements negotiated within the framework of a structural adjustment programme (1987-88) with the World Bank and the International Monetary Fund. This included a pledge by the World Bank to negotiate balance-of-payments support loans and grants and to help Guinea-Bissau renegotiate its foreign debt.

The most positive results of liberalization have been the rise in agricultural producer prices, particularly significant in the rice and

xviii

cashew nut sectors where both have responded with a significant growth in production. Another important aspect of this phenomenon has been the emergence of a middle stratum of farmers who have invested their own resources in land and equipment to produce mainly fruit crops for export. They, like other producers however, were being starved of credit, transport and other infrastructure needed to make the sector flourish (see Galli, 1990).

The negative side of liberalization has been an extraordinary rise in inflation between 1986 and 1990 which cast doubt upon hopes for a reversal of the terms in favour of agriculture (see Hermele and Rudebeck, 1990; Galli, 1990). This was connected to the unusually large influx of international finance which was directed towards an expansion of credit to the economy that resulted in the growth of a class of speculators. These were mainly government officials, their family and their friends who, besides obtaining credit, were also given large land concessions but who produced next to nothing. A merchant class also sprang to life but continued throughout the 1980s to be overshadowed by the Armazéns do Povo which still had the contacts, money, and infrastructure to dominate both import and exports. In 1990, the government took a decision to privatize the company – although this by itself did not guarantee more competitive market conditions.

The structural adjustment programme was renegotiated in 1989 for another three years, during which time the hope among international 'donors' was that the government would be able to stabilize the currency; put its financial house in order; raise tax revenues; pay the arrears on its debt service; rationalize the state; help those groups at risk under the structural adjustment programme; and begin rural and industrial development. However, the government faced the 1990s with no development plan.

About the bibliography

Because the majority of works written on Guinea-Bissau have been written in Portuguese and because the government has opted to retain Portuguese as the official language, I have chosen to use Portuguese proper names for people and places throughout the text. The classification of the works compiled herein corresponds to the standard one suggested by the Clio Press in its manual for contributors, but because of the paucity of works in the English language, many categories have only a few items, and others – such as geography and geology, flora and fauna, ethnic groups – consist mainly of Portuguese texts. I cannot pretend to have explored all the sources in these and other categories; rather my goal has been to indicate to the reader where to look for more materials. Whenever possible, I have given precedence to works written in English or French, languages which I feel are more accessible to the general reader.

There is a dearth of ethnographic and anthropological research in any language. In this context, the research sponsored from the 1940s through to the mid-1970s by the Centro de Estudos da Guiné Portuguesa (Centre for Studies on Portuguese Guinea) is noteworthy. It is perhaps fitting to highlight the remarkable efforts of the then governor of the province of Guinea, M.M. Sarmento Rodrigues, and several administrators – among them Avelino Teixeira da Mota, António Carreira and Fernando Rogado Quintino – in stimulating and supporting the work of the Centre. Teixeira da Mota, Carreira and Rogado Quintino are internationally recognized for their historical and ethnographic research and publications, ample evidence of which can be found in this bibliography. The Centre published the quarterly *Boletim Cultural da Guiné Portuguesa*, which is of inestimable importance for the information, scientific, artistic and literary, that it provides about Portuguese Guinea. I have chosen not to cite individual articles because to do so would have more than doubled the number of entries allowed. I have, therefore, cited only a few in cases where there was little else. Several of the bibliographies noted in the section on bibliographies provide a guide to the articles in the *Boletim*.

It is important and very exciting for me to note that this tradition of research is being carried forward by a generation of young Guinean scholars who have established the Instituto Nacional de Estudos e Pesquisa (INEP), the National Research and Studies Institute, which houses the Public Library (Biblioteca Pública), the Centre for Contemporary Historical Studies, the Centre for Socio-Economic Investigation and the Centre of Appropriate Technology – each of which publishes bulletins and journals (noted under the periodicals section) which provide *essential* information for the contemporary researcher. Above all, *Soronda: Revista de Estudos Guineenses* is comparable to the *Boletim Cultural da Guiné Portuguesa* in its coverage, quality of information and analyses. As with the *Boletim*, I have not annotated most of the individual articles of *Soronda* which are now being indexed in the *International African Bibliography*.

As well as encouraging and sponsoring local academic investigation, INEP receives foreign researchers and provides a base of operations. I had the privilege of using the Public Library for compiling purposes and found several thousand works in all languages pertaining to Guinea-Bissau. Another important resource for the researcher on contemporary Guinea-Bissau is the library of the Centro de Informação e Documentação, Amílcar Cabral (CIDAC), the Amílcar Cabral Centre of Information and Documentation. Many of the books, pamphlets and articles in Portuguese and some in other languages cited herein are obtainable there. Moreover, CIDAC has an important collection of documents, known as the *documentação cinzenta* (grey dossiers) after the colour of the boxes in which the materials are stored. I have cited all of these files under their titles in the bibliography as they existed in June 1990. New material is constantly being added at the Lisbon-based centre.

For the majority of works in English, French and German, I have relied heavily on the collections of Rhodes House and Queen Elizabeth House at Oxford University and the School of Oriental and African Studies of the University of London.

Acknowledgements

Naturally I have accumulated a large debt to a great many people during the past ten years of studying Guinea-Bissau. I would like to take this opportunity to cite and thank wholeheartedly those who were most helpful in the preparation of the bibliography: Carlos Cardoso, director of INEP and Raul Fernandes, acting director during my library stay for their generous encouragement; the library staff of the Public Library, especially Diamantino and Ines, for their patience; Tete Montenegro and Ana Maria Delgado of INEP for their friendship. I am exceedingly grateful to the CIDAC library staff, especially Helena and the director, Luisa Teotonio Pereira, for many years of sympathetic collaboration. Without the cheeriness and helpful suggestions of Allan Lodge and the entire staff at Rhodes House, I could not have finished the collection of materials so quickly. Bob Townsend and Gill Short of the Institute of Commonwealth Studies library at Queen Elizabeth House have once again graciously lent me their ears, eyes and hands. Many thanks to them and colleagues, Ron Chilcote, Patrick Chabal, George Brooks, Ursula Funk and Joshua Forrest for encouragement and help. I fear that I have not lived up to their expectations. Lars Rudebeck has been important to me over the years for the integrity, courage and clarity of his work. Many thanks as well to Dr Robert Neville and his staff at Clio Press for seeing me through this project, and especially after the fire at the University of the Azores in 1989 completely destroyed the first draft of this manuscript and I had to make a fresh start. I am grateful to Linacre College for more than mere hospitality.

Rosemary E. Galli
August 1990

Theses and Dissertations on Guinea-Bissau

Dennis Charles Beller. 'The Portuguese territories issue in the United Nations: an analysis of debates', PhD thesis, University of California, Los Angeles, 1970. 265p.

Laura Ellen Bigman. 'The political economy of the food question in lusophone West Africa', PhD thesis, Howard University, 1988. 271p.

Mariama Sarr Cessay. 'Literary initiatives in national development: a critical analysis', PhD thesis, University of Missouri, Columbia, 1987. 274p.

Joan Elizabeth Collemacine. 'A study of African literary expression in the Portuguese language: poetry and liberation', PhD thesis, Temple University, 1978. 255p.

Ivana Elbl. 'The Portuguese trade with West Africa, 1440-1521', PhD thesis, University of Toronto, 1986.

Roberto S. M. Fernandes. 'Portugal and its overseas territories: economic structure and policies, 1950-57', PhD thesis, Harvard University, 1960. 150p.

Ursula Funk. 'Rural political economy, gender systems and changing social relations in Guinea-Bissau', PhD thesis, Stanford University, forthcoming.

D. F. Heisel. 'The indigenous populations of the Portuguese African territories', PhD thesis, University of Wisconsin, Madison, 1965-66. 220p.

S. Mkandla. 'The thought of Amílcar Lopes Cabral of Guinea-Bissau: revolution in an "underdeveloped" country', PhD thesis, University of Kent at Canterbury, 1986.

Américo Montes Moreira. 'The role of Marxism in the anti-colonial revolution in black Africa (Guinea-Bissau)', PhD thesis, Boston College, 1989. 365p.

Stephen Madry Peck, Jr. 'Tense, aspect and mood in Guinea-Casamance Portuguese creole', PhD thesis, University of California, 1988. 476p.

Luigi Scantamburlo. 'The ethnography of the Bijagós people of the island of Bubaque', MA thesis, Wayne State University, 1978. 151p.

The Country and Its People

1 **Congresso comemorativo do quinto centenário do descobrimento da Guiné.**
(The conference celebrating the 500th anniversary of the discovery of
Guinea.)
Lisbon: Sociedade de Geografia de Lisboa, 1946. 2 vols.
The essays in these volumes cover most topics from ethnography and diseases to
colonial policy. There is even an essay on military policy by Teixeira Pinto (q.v.), who
is credited with pacifying the territory. The texts were written by most of the
prominent scholars on Guinea.

2 **Contribuição para o estudo do estado de nutrição dos povos da Guiné
Portuguesa. I.** (Contribution to the study of the nutritional state of the
peoples of Portuguese Guinea. I.)
Carlos dos Santos Reis. *Anais do Instituto de Medecina Tropical*, vol.
19, nos 1-4 (1962), p. 63-105.
Covers almost everything known about the country and population groups, information
which was used as a background for the mission's reports on the state of nutrition,
published in volumes 20 and 21 of the *Anais*.

3 **Guinea-Bissau: alfabeto.** (Guinea-Bissau: from A to Z.)
Edited by Carlos Lopes. Bologna, Italy: Grupo Volontariato Civile,
1984. 87p. (Collana: Terra e Terra Immagini).
Mainly a book of photographs, the text provides an overview of the country through
selected writings of its leaders and historians and through interviews with ordinary
people. The material is organized around ideas and concepts, arranged in alphabetical
order.

The Country and Its People

4 **Guinea-Bissau: politics, economics and society.**
Rosemary E. Galli, Jocelyn Jones. London; New York: Pinter and Columbia University Press, 1987. 193p. 2 maps. bibliog.

Although the focus is primarily on political economy, the authors place their argument in a broad historical and sociological context. Beginning with the thirteenth century, they look at trade patterns and how the Atlantic trade transformed Guinean society. Creole influence is traced in the independence movement and post-independence politics. Although the authors emphasize the importance of the relationship between PAIGC (Partido Africano da Independência da Guiné e Cabo Verde) leadership and rural peoples in the national liberation struggle and afterward, they also stress the influence of Salazarian New State policies and administration on the newly independent government. Galli and Jones record the economic decline of the country from the 1950s onwards and the precipitous decline after 1978. They analyse rural development, education and health policies up to the end of 1986.

5 **Guiné: apontamentos inéditos.** (Guinea: unedited notes.)
H. Augusto Dias de Carvalho. Lisbon: Agência Geral das Colónias, 1944. 239p.

This is an edition of a work written by the general at the turn of the century. The 'notes' give a wealth of data regarding what constituted Portuguese Guinea at the time. It was mainly a coastal enclave consisting of a few towns and their surroundings: Bolama, Bissau, Cacheu and the Casamance (soon to be ceded to France). The book gives an overall impression of the flora, fauna, ethnography and 'administration' of the territory. An equally if not more interesting work of a slightly earlier period is Luíz Frederico de Barros' *Senegambia Portugueza ou notícia descriptiva das differentes tribus que habitam a Senegambia Meridional* (Portuguese Senegambia or a descriptive note on the different tribes that live in southern Senegambia), published in Lisbon in 1878. For a view of the 'colony' at a slightly later stage, during the Republican period of 'administration', consult Carlos Pereira's *La Guinée Portugaise: subsides pour son étude* (Subsidiary notes for the study of Portuguese Guinea) (Lisbon: A Editora Limitada, 1914).

6 **Guiné Portuguesa.** (Portuguese Guinea.)
A. Teixeira da Mota, preface by M. M. Sarmento Rodrigues. Lisbon: Agência-Geral do Ultramar, 1954. 2 vols. 16 maps. bibliog.

The most complete and authoritative work on the Guinea of its time. Besides being a colonial administrator, the author was a distinguished historian and scholar. The information ranges from physical geography through ethnicities to animal traction. It is also one of the most sympathetic and sensitive works extant. There is a brief English summary.

7 **Guiné Portuguesa.** (Portuguese Guinea.)
L. A. de Carvalho Viegas. Lisbon: Sociedade de Geografia de Lisboa, 1936-40. 3 vols.

Once one has discounted the inaccuracies and colonial mentality embedded in this work by a former governor of the colony, one finds a very detailed account of the administration and the economy, and much ethnographic material.

8 **Introdução a geografia económica da Guiné-Bissau.** (Introduction to the economic geography of Guinea-Bissau.)
Comissariado de Estado da Coordenação Económica e Plano. Preface by Vasco Cabral, note by Ladislau Dowbor. Bissau: Imprensa Nacional, 1980. 148p. 6 maps.

An excellent introduction to the physical, demographic and economic geography of the country, the text also broaches the question of development strategy. It concludes with a chapter on integrated regional development which was the preferred strategy of its authors in the Commissariat for Economic Coordination and Planning. This is a basic resource for primary data on the country in the late colonial and early postcolonial periods.

9 **La Guinée-Bissau aujourd'hui.** (Guinea-Bissau today.)
Patrick Érouart. Paris: Les Éditions du Jaguar, 1988. 165p. map.

Mainly a book for the traveller or tourist, the text takes one on a complete tour of the country, including the Bijagós islands. There are 69 colour photographs.

10 **Para uma leitura sociológica da Guiné-Bissau.** (Toward a sociological reading of Guinea-Bissau.)
Carlos Lopes, preface by Samir Amin. Lisbon; Bissau: Editorial Economia e Socialismo, CRL, and Instituto Nacional de Estudos e Pesquisa (INEP), 1988. 392p. bibliog.

Lopes wrote the essays collected in the book between 1976 and 1986. Although essentially theoretical, the essays contain a great deal of information; for example, there is a bibliography on the ancient kingdom of Kaabu, part of the Mali empire and an important independent slave-trading power. There is an annotated chronology of the major events in the country between 1974 and 1983. In the last section, there is a compendium of general statistics on the country.

11 **Paysanneries en attente: Guinée-Bissau.** (Peasants in waiting: Guinea-Bissau.)
Anne-Marie Hochet. Dakar, Senegal: Environnement Africain, ENDA, 1983. 174p. 10 maps.

Presents a sociological study of the nineteen or so different farm systems the author found in Guinea-Bissau. By itself it is an indispensable introduction to Guinean social and productive organization and environmental awareness and inventiveness. It is based upon a series of short studies of the countryside commissioned by the Commissariat of Economic Coordination and Planning. The numerous studies are well worth consulting for their detail. They can be found in the library of the planning department. Hochet has more recently published another fascinating book, *Les paysans, ces 'ignorants' efficaces* (Those efficient 'ignorant' people, the peasants) (Paris: L'Harmattan, 1985) which is a direct complement, being a journal-like narrative of the author's encounters in the Guinean countryside. It lives and breathes the experiences of the people themselves and allows them to speak.

12 **Sowing the first harvest: national construction in Guinea-Bissau.**
Ole Gjerstad, Chantal Sarrazin.   Oakland, California: Liberation
Support Movement Information Center, 1978. 101p. map. bibliog.

Presents a picture of the newly independent country through the eyes of political activists who supported the struggle of the PAIGC. The authors spent three months in the country in 1975, during which time they interviewed many of the party/state leaders as well as middle- and lower-level cadres. Prominent in their well-written personalized account are Manuel dos Santos, then Minister of Information, Carmen Pereira and Fidélis Cabral de Almada, then Secretary of Justice. This small book captures well the early enthusiasm to improve the country felt by party militants from the bottom up.

Historical dictionary of the Republic of Guinea-Bissau.
See item no. 572.

Geography and Geology

13 *Anais*, vol. 1.
  Junta das Missões Geográficas e de Investigações Coloniais. Lisbon:
  Agência Geral das Colónias, 1946. 274p.

The entire issue of this first publication is on Portuguese Guinea. There are three articles on geography including J. Carrington da Costa, 'Meio físico da Guiné Portuguesa' (The physical environment of Portuguese Guinea); A. Sousa Torres, J. Pires Soares and H. O'Donnel, 'Alguns testemunhos geológicos da Guiné Portuguesa' (Some geological evidence of Portuguese Guinea); and Teixeira Marinho, 'Esboço do clima da Guiné Portuguesa' (A sketch of the climate of Portuguese Guinea). Volume 4, no. 2 (1949) of the *Anais* includes an article by Décio Thadeu, 'Notas sobre a geologia da Guiné Portuguesa' (Notes on the geology of Portuguese Guinea) which includes a map and bibliography. Volume 5, no. 3 (1950) has two articles on geography by Orlando Ribeiro.

14 **A study of some clay deposits of Portuguese Guinea.**
  Judite dos Santos Pereira. In: *Conferência Internacional dos
  Africanistas Ocidentais*, vol. 2. São Tomé: Scientific Council for Africa
  South of the Sahara, 1956, p. 205-13.

Gives the chemical analysis carried out on sediment gathered on the island of Bissau. In the same volume is another article by this author, 'A study of some laterite rocks of Portuguese Guinea' which gives the results of chemical and thermic analyses on these rocks.

15 **Conferência internacional dos africanistas ocidentais.** (International
  conference of West Africanists.)
  Junta de Investigações Coloniais. Lisbon: Ministério das Colónias,
  1950-51. 5 vols.

This is the transcript of the proceedings of the second of such conferences which was held in Bissau in 1947. The first volume contains geophysical works on West Africa including Guinea-Bissau. The second and third volumes are dedicated to biological sciences. Volumes 4 and 5 deal with social sciences.

16 **Fisiografia e geologia da Província da Guiné.** (The physical geography and geology of the province of Guinea.)
J. Carrington da Costa. Porto, Portugal: Imprensa Moderna, 1946. 94p. 2 maps. bibliog.
Presents a general picture of the physical geography and geology of the country.

17 **Geologia da Guiné Portuguesa.** (Geology of Portuguese Guinea.)
Joao Ernesto Teixeira. Lisbon: Junta de Investigações do Ultramar, 1968. 100p. map. bibliog.
Surveys the geology of the country.

18 **L'aménagement du terroir en Afrique occidentale.** (Patterns of land use in West Africa.)
Orlando Ribeiro. *Bulletin de la Société Royale de Géologie Egypte*, vol. 25 (1953), p. 165-77.
Features Guinea-Bissau in this overview of land use in West Africa. Ribeiro's work is also featured in the *Anais*, vol. 5 (1950) cited above (q.v.).

19 **Le gisement de phosphate éocène de Farim-Salinquinhé (République de Guinée-Bissau).** (The Eocene Farim-Salinquinhe phosphate deposit [Republic of Guinea-Bissau].)
J. R. Prian, P. Gama, C. Bourdillon de Grissac, J. Roger. *Chronique de la recherche minière*, vol. 55, no. 486 (1987), p. 25-54.
A highly technical article with photographs and numerous drawings of the various sites studied. The conclusion is that the deposit is not of economic interest in the short term but that it could be useful for direct application in agriculture.

20 **Notas sobre a geologia da Guiné Portuguesa.** (Notes on the geology of Portuguese Guinea.)
Judite dos Santos Pereira. *Boletim de Sociedade de Geologia Portuguesa*, vol. 2, no. 1 (1943), p. 5-24.
Surveys the geology of the country using as a point of departure the research of earlier French geologists.

21 **Portuguese Guinea.**
United States Board on Geographic Names. Washington, DC: Geographic Names Division, Army Map Service, 1968. 122p. map. (Gazeteer no. 105).
Contains 8,700 entries of locations in Guinea-Bissau. The names refer to places and geographical features such as woods, hills, bays and so on. They are the standard Portuguese names, some of which have since changed.

22 **Trabalhos da missão geo-hidrográfica da Guiné (1948-55).** (The works of
the geo-hydrological mission of Guinea (1948-55).)
Manuel Pereira Crespo.   Bissau: Centro de Estudos da Guiné
Portuguesa, 1955. 193p. 6 maps. bibliog.
Surveys the topography of the land and the waterways.

Flora and Fauna

23 **Actualidade veterinária da Guiné Portuguesa.** (Contemporary veterinary
services in Portuguese Guinea.)
João Tendeiro. Bissau: Centro de Estudos da Guiné Portuguesa, 1951.
204p. bibliog.
Details the various sicknesses affecting livestock in the colony as well as reporting the
state of veterinary medicine. There is also an account of livestock and dairy production
and an assessment of the possibilities of a leather industry.

24 **An anatomical study of timbers of the Portuguese Guinea.**
Manuel P. Ferreirinha, M. C. de Freitas. In: *Conferência Internacional
dos Africanistas Ocidentais*, vol. 3. São Tomé: Scientific Council for
Africa South of the Sahara, 1956, p. 107-14.
Diagnoses the macro- and microscopic aspects of the woods of *Erythrophloeum
guineense* G. Don., *Lophira alata* Banks ex Gaertn. f., *Cordyla africana* Lour., *Afzelia
africana* Smith., *Chlorophora regia* A. Chev. and *Pterocarpus erinaceus* Poir.

25 **Bichos de Guiné: caça, fauna, natureza.** (Animal life in Guinea-Bissau:
game, fauna, nature.)
Júlio de Araújo Ferreira. Tomar, Portugal: Jacinto Nunes, Ltda, 1973.
226p. map.
Gives the author's personal impressions of Guinean wildlife. This is not a scientific
work, but more a diary of his hunting trips.

26 Catálogo de uma colecção de aves da ex-Guiné Portuguesa existente no Museu de Zoologia 'Dr. Augusto Nobre': I – Non-Passeriformes.
(Catalogue of a collection of birds from the ex-colony of Portuguese Guinea in the 'Dr Augusto Nobre' Museum of Zoology: I – Non-Passeriformes.)
Anais de Faculdade de Ciências do Porto, vol. 60, nos 1-4 (1978), p. 3-22.

Catalogues this collection of birds and gives the Portuguese and African names as well as the scientific names. It details where the birds were sighted and other bibliographical references.

27 Contribuição para o estudo do problema florestal da Guiné Portuguesa.
(Contribution to a study of the forestry problem in Portuguese Guinea.)
José Amaral Tavares de Carvalho, Fernando J. Serrão de Faria Pereira Nunes. Lisbon: Ministério do Ultramar, Junta de Investigações Científicas do Ultramar, 1956. 192p. map. bibliog. (Estudos, Ensaios e Documentos no. 30).

Classifies two important forests in Farim in the north and in Catanhez in the south of the country. There is a summary in English at the back of the book.

28 Contribuições para o conhecimento da flora da Guiné Portuguesa.
(Contributions to the knowledge of the flora of Portuguese Guinea.)
E. Pereira de Sousa. *Anais*, vol. 1 (1946), p. 41-152.

This is the first article of eight which appeared regularly in the *Anais*. The second article appeared in volume 3, no. 3 (1948); the third in volume 4, no. 3 (1949); the fourth in volume 5, no. 5 (1950); the fifth in volume 6, no. 3 (1951); the sixth in volume 7, no. 2 (1952); the seventh in volume 11, no. 4 (1956); and the eighth in volume 12, no. 3 (1957).

29 Entomofauna of Portuguese Guinea and of the islands of São Tomé and Príncipe. II. Coleoptera.
M. Luísa Gomes Alves. In: *Conferência Internacional dos Africanistas Ocidentais*, vol. 4. São Tomé: Scientific Council for Africa South of the Sahara, 1956, p. 11-22.

Reports on several species of the families *Scarabaeidae*, *Buprestidae*, *Lucanidae* and *Cicindelidae*. In the same volume are articles on insects in the *Cerambycedae* and *Limexylonidae* families of *Coleoptera*, as well as those belonging to *Hymenoptera*, *Hemiptera* and *Malophaga*.

30 Essências florestais da Guiné Portuguesa. (Forestry resources in Guinea-Bissau.)
Brigada de Estudos Florestais da Guiné. Lisbon: Ministério do Ultramar, Jardim e Museu Agrícola do Ultramar, 1955-59. 17 vols.

The result of a survey of forestry resources conducted by the Brigade [of forestry studies in Guinea] from December 1953 to May 1954, these pamphlets describe some of the trees found in Guinea. The tree, *Khaya senegalensis*, described in vol. 1 and

9

Flora and Fauna

also known as *bissolim* is considered one of the most commercially exploitable. *Pterocarpaus erinaceus* is described in vol. 2, *Cordyla africana* in vol. 3, *Chlorophora regia* in vol. 4, *Afzelia africana* in vol. 5, *Erythrophloeum guineense* in vol. 6, *Parkia biglobosa* in vol. 7, *Daniellia oliveri* in vol. 8, *Prosopis africana* in vol. 9, *Detarium senegalense* in vol. 10, *Schrebera arborea* in vol. 11, *Cola cordifolia* in vol. 12, *Parinari excelsa* in vol. 13, *Lophira alata* in vol. 14, *Diallium guineense* in vol. 15 and *Borassus aethiopium* in vol. 16. There is also an introductory volume.

31 **Flora da Guiné-Bissau: Connaraceae.** (Flora of Guinea-Bissau: the Connaraceae.)
   Maria Cândida Liberato.   Lisbon: Junta de Investigações Científicas do Ultramar, Jardim e Museu Agrícola do Ultramar, 1980. 16p.

This is one of a long series of works of the same main title by the same author, at times in collaboration with other authors. The texts give a detailed description of the various families of plants, along with bibliographical references. Later works can be traced under the publisher's new name: Instituto de Investigação Científica Tropical, Jardim-Museu Agrícola Tropical.

32 **Relatório da Missão Zoológica e contribuições para o conhecimento da fauna da Guiné Portuguesa.** (The report of the Zoological Mission and contributions to knowledge of the fauna of Portuguese Guinea.)
   Fernando Frade, Amélia Bacelar, Bernardo Gonçalves.   *Anais*, vol. 1 (1946), p. 261-74.

This is the first of a series of reports by the Mission which appeared regularly in the *Anais*. The second appeared in vol. 2, no. 3 (1947). There were articles on marine mussels, on copepods, *Lycideos*, *Cicindelideos* and on *Batraquios aglossos*. The next report appeared in vol. 3, no. 4 (1948), and the next in volume 4, no. 4 (1949). The fifth report was in vol. 6, no. 4 (1951). In 1955, there were two issues of vol. 10, no. 4; the first was on the works of the Zoological Mission and the Centre for Zoology while the second was a catalogue of birds, 'Non-Passeriformes'.

An account of Sierra Leone and the Rivers of Cape Verde (1625).
See item no. 50.

Annuário da Província da Guiné do anno de 1925.
See item no. 83.

Anuário da Guiné Portuguesa.
See item no. 84.

Guiné.
See item no. 93.

History

General

33 **An economic history of West Africa.**
A. G. Hopkins. London: Longman, 1973. 296p. 17 maps. bibliog.
Provides an excellent resource for an overview of the economic development of the entire region.

34 **A note on the scholarly fraternity in lusophone Africa.**
David Birmingham. In: *Into the 80s: the proceedings of the 11th annual conference of the Canadian Association of African Studies*, edited by Donald I. Ray, Peter Shinnie, Donovan Williams. Vancouver, Canada: Tantalus Research, 1981. vol. 1, p. 218-23.
A brief report on the four stages of research and historical writing on lusophone Africa, this article will be of greatest interest to the budding historian. There is a bibliography of core secondary sources published as of 1981.

35 **Guiné-Bissau: História I and II.** (Guinea-Bissau: History I and II.)
Lisbon: Centro de Informação e Documentação, Amílcar Cabral (CIDAC), 1990.
The first dossier contains five documents including Joye Bowman Hawkins' work (q.v.) and Carlo Lopes' manuscript on the transition from national liberation movement to statehood (q.v.). The second file contains articles mainly on the national liberation movement but also an article by George Brooks on historical perspectives on Guinea-Bissau from the fifteenth to the nineteenth centuries.

36 **Guiné-Bissau: zwischen Weltwirtschaft und Subsistenz.** (Guinea-Bissau: between the world economy and subsistence.)
Ulrich Schiefer. Bonn, West Germany: Informationsstelle Südliches Afrika e.V., 1986. 261p. 22 maps. bibliog.

A history of the integration of the Upper Guinea Coast into the world economy from the 'discoveries' to 1980. One of the themes is the resistance of indigenous societies and their 'subsistence' societies to such incorporation. There is a brief summary of the chapters in English.

37 **História: a Guiné e as ilhas de Cabo Verde.** (History: Guinea-Bissau and Cape Verde.)
PAIGC. Paris: UNESCO, 1974. 182p. 17 maps.

The official history of the two countries from precolonial times until independence in 1974-75.

38 **História da Guiné 1418-1918.** (History of Guinea 1418-1918.)
João Barreto, preface by Col. Leite de Magalhães. Lisbon: author's edition, 1938. 452p.

Obligatory reading for any student of Guinean history, this is the most general work on the influence of the Portuguese and Cape Verdeans on the Guinean coast. Barreto repeats the colonial myths that if the Portuguese had strengthened their military and administrative positions in the Upper Guinea Coast, they would have held on to it. Barreto, however, also adopts the viewpoint of the colonials engaged in trade and stimulating production when he criticizes the monopolistic commercial policies of the various Portuguese administrations.

39 **La Guinée Portugaise au XXe siècle.** (Portuguese Guinea in the twentieth century.)
Jean Mettas. Paris: Agence de Coopération Culturelle et Technique, 1984. 114p. 17 maps.

Documents the history of the country during this century beginning with the peoples' resistance to colonization through the national liberation struggle. Mettas uses both oral and written sources.

40 **The Portuguese seaborne empire, 1416-1825.**
C. R. Boxer, preface by J. H. Plumb. London: Hutchinson, 1977. 380p. 7 maps. bibliog.

This is the classic text on Portuguese overseas 'discoveries' and colonization. See also B. D. Diffie and G. D. Winius, *Foundations of the Portuguese Empire, 1415-1580* (Minneapolis: University of Minnesota Press, 1977). Chapter 6 describes the explorations of Guinea-Bissau and the Cape Verde islands.

41 **The western Atlantic coast.**
Jean Boulegue, Jean Suret-Canale. In: *History of West Africa*, vol. 1, edited by J. F. Ade Ajayi, M. Crowder. London: Longman, 1985, p. 503-30.

Provides a good introduction to the area as it existed when the Portuguese arrived.

42 **UNESCO general history of Africa.**
UNESCO International Scientific Committee for the Drafting of a
General History of Africa. Paris; London; Berkeley, California:
UNESCO, Heinemann and University of California Press, 1981- .
Volumes 1-4, 6, 7.

There will be eight volumes in all. Each volume has a different editor. Most of the
articles are very general but they allow the reader a broad grasp on the development of
society, agriculture, iron-working, cultural contacts in precolonial history. There are
also articles on the decline of Mali and of Kaabu.

Guinea-Bissau: politics, economics and society.
See item no. 4.

Anuário da Guiné Portuguesa.
See item no. 84.

**Ecological perspectives on Mande population movements, commercial networks
and settlement patterns from the Atlantic Wet Phase (ca 5500-2500 BC) to the
present.**
See item no. 191.

Historical dictionary of the Republic of Guinea-Bissau.
See item no. 572.

Precolonial history

43 **Beyond migration and conquest: oral traditions and Mandinka ethnicity
in Senegambia.**
Donald R. Wright. *History in Africa*, vol. 12 (1985), p. 335-48.

Disputes the accepted theory that the incorporation of the Senegambia into the Malian
empire was accomplished through conquest. Wright sees it as having resulted from a
long process of cultural transferral similar to that occurring today.

44 **Dinah Salifou: roi des Nalous.** (Dinah Salifou: king of the Nalus.)
Thierno Diallo. Paris: ABC, 1977. 95p. (Grandes Figures Africaines).

The Nalu kingdom touched the southern part of what has become Guinea-Bissau. This
interesting history shows the interchange of people along the coast which helps one
understand the colonial conquest in the last quarter of the nineteenth century. The
book reads like a novel. There is an interesting comparative chronology at the end of
the text showing important events in the rest of Africa and the world.

45 **Fulas e Beafadas no Rio Grande no século XV: achegas para a
etnohistória de África Ocidental.** (Fulas and Beafadas in the Rio Grande
during the fifteenth century: notes for a West African ethnohistory.)
A. Teixeira da Mota. *Memórias da Academia das Ciências de Lisboa,
Classe de Ciências*, vol. 14 (1970), p. 259-77.

Describes the extensive Beafada kingdoms covering one-third of what is now Guinea,
but the group is now a very minor one. The article also covers Fula migration from the
Futa Djalon to the northeast of what is now Senegal. Under Dulo Demba, the Fulas
clashed with the Beafadas during the years 1450-60 and were beaten back.
Nevertheless, smaller groups of Fulas continued to migrate and settle peacefully among
the Beafadas as well as among the Mandingas in the kingdom of Kaabu to the north of
the Beafadas.

46 **Les Kaabunke: structures politiques et mutations.** (The Kaabu empire:
political structures and changes.)
Carlos Lopes. PhD thesis, Université de Paris, Paris 1-Panthéon,
Sorbonne, Faculté des Lettres et Sciences Humaines, 1988. 276p. 17
maps. bibliog.

Presents an historical argument for a Guinean nationality based on the political and
economic space defined by the ancient empire of Kaabu. This is an excellent resource
on the political aspects of this civilization. It focuses primarily on its unifying force in a
region composed of multiple peoples and societies. Lopes demonstrates the continuity
of this civilization in contemporary life thoughout the Senegambia region.

47 **Monjur: o Gabú e a sua história.** (Monjur: the history of Gabú.)
Jorge Vellez Caroço. Bissau: Centro de Estudos da Guiné Portuguesa,
1948. 269p. bibliog.

Recounts the history of the region of Gabú from precolonial times – when it was part
of the Mandinga kingdom of Kaabu – through to colonial times. Also included is an
account of the Fula kingdom of Firdu and its relations with Gabú as well as the
eventual immigration of Fulas into the territory and their seizure of power. Monjur
Meta Balo was the chief of the area from 1906 to 1927. The author attempts to restore
the prestige of the great chief.

48 **The epic of Kelefa Saane as a guide to the nature of precolonial
Senegambian society – and vice versa.**
Donald R. Wright. *History in Africa*, vol. 14 (1987), p. 287-309.

Kelefa Saane was born in one of the client states of Kaabu, Badora, which lay along
the middle Geba river in Guinea-Bissau. He is often sung about in the songs which tell
the history of the region. Saane was a great warrior in the tradition of the Mandinga
aristocracy. The article explains Kaabu social structure and makes the important point
that ethnicity was highly mixed so that identity came more from lifestyle or place in the
social structure than from blood or parentage. Then as now '. . . kinship rather than
ethnicity was the concrete foundation of all levels of society'.

História: a Guiné e as ilhas de Cabo Verde.
See item no. 37.

The western Atlantic coast.
See item no. 41.

UNESCO general history of Africa.
See item no. 42.

History of the Upper Guinea Coast, 1545-1800.
See item no. 62.

Kola trade and state-building: Upper Guinea Coast and Senegambia, 15th-17th centuries.
See item no. 64.

Slavery and slaving in the Portuguese Atlantic (to about 1500).
See item no. 73.

Ecological perspectives on Mande population movements, commercial networks and settlement patterns from the Atlantic Wet Phase (ca 5500-2500 BC) to the present.
See item no. 191.

Manding: focus on an African civilization.
See item no. 193.

The period of the Rios de Guiné

49 **African memoranda: relative to an attempt to establish a British settlement on the island of Bulama, on the western coast of Africa, in the year 1792 . . . .**
Philip Beaver.   London: C. and R. Baldwin, 1805. 415p. map.
This is the fascinating account of Beaver's expedition to the Bijagós islands and his settlement in Bolama. He also describes the people of Guinea and the societies he found in the various European enclaves he encountered. Andrew Johansen, *A geographical and historical account of the island of Bulama with observations on its climate, productions, &c.* (London: Martin and Bain, 1794) is much shorter and perhaps more accessible. It records the formation of the Bulam Association in 1791 and its settlement on Bolama under the direction of Beaver. The tract is based on the communications of Beaver to the Association and on interviews with some of the surviving colonists.

50 **An account of Sierra Leone and the Rivers of Guinea of Cape Verde (1625).**
André Donelha, edited and introduced by A. Teixeira da Mota, with notes and English translation by P. E. H. Hair. Lisbon: Junta de Investigações Científicas do Ultramar, Centro de Estudos de Cartografia Antiga, 1977. 377p. 13 maps. bibliog.

This is a bilingual Portuguese–English edition of the classical texts written by the Cape Verdean author. A basic resource for the history of the Upp. Guinea Coast including the Rivers of Guinea, it is a compilation of what the author saw on three trips to the area and what he was told. He describes the geography, peoples, flora and fauna.

51 **A Nhara of the Guinea-Bissau region: Mãe Aurélia Correia.**
George E. Brooks. In: *Women and Slavery in Africa*, edited by Claire C. Robertson, Martin A. Klein. Madison, Wisconsin: University of Wisconsin Press, 1983, p. 295-319.

Reports the facinating account of one of the African and Euro-African women who acted as intermediaries in the Atlantic trade along the Upper Guinea Coast from the seventeenth to the nineteenth centuries. Mãe Aurélia was the wife of Caetano José Nozolini, a very successful trader in the Bissau area. They evidently divided the slave and 'legitimate' trading businesses between them. Although little is known about her origins, there is no doubt that she commanded great influence and wealth in the area independent of her husband. They made a formidable team in the 1840s and their mark is still evident in the Bissau of today. The article gives a lot of information about the society of the Upper Guinea Coast in general.

52 **Crónica dos feitos de Guiné.** (Diary of the facts of Guinea.)
Gomes Eanes de Zurara. Lisbon: Agência Geral das Colónias, Divisão de Publicações e Biblioteca, 1949. 2 vols.

This is a classic text describing the 'discovery' of the area by Portugal. The reader is warned that the text is written in archaic Portuguese. There appears to be a 1963 English-language reprint of the work entitled *Chronicle of the discovery and conquest of Guinea*. A commentary on the work by Marian Malowist, 'Some aspects of the early colonial expansion as presented by Zurara in the Chronicle of Guinea', *Africana Bulletin* (Warsaw), no. 25 (1976) deals mainly with the motivation behind the explorations but it is evident that the search for gold was uppermost. A biography of Zurara appears in Antonio J. Dias Dinis, *Vida e obras de Gomes Eanes de Zurara* (Life and works of Gomes Eanes de Zurara) (Lisbon: Agência Geral das Colónias, 1949).

53 **Description de la côte occidentale d'Afrique (Sénégal au Cap de Monte, Archipels) par Valentim Fernandes.** (Description of the west coast of Africa [Senegal to Cap Mount, archipelagos] by Valentim Fernandes.)
T. Monod, A. Teixeira da Mota, R. Mauny, preface by M. M. Sarmento Rodrigues. Bissau: Centro de Estudos da Guiné Portuguesa, 1951. 147p. 5 maps. bibliog. (no. 11).

Written in the sixteenth century, the text, which is considered a classic, recounts the 'discoveries' of West Africa. This edition of the third, fourth and fifth parts of Fernandes' work is bilingual, from the original Portuguese to French. The different

16

parts treat the geographical areas of the title, the Rios de Guiné do Cabo Verde and the islands of Cape Verde, São Tomé and Ano Bom. The work relates what was known about the various peoples living in these areas.

54 Documentos para a história das ilhas de Cabo Verde e "Rios de Guiné" (Secúlos XVII e XVIII). (Documents for a history of the Cape Verde islands and the 'Rivers of Guinea' [17th and 18th centuries].) António Carreira. Lisbon: author's edition, 1983. 306p. 4 maps.

This is yet another collection of indispensable documents for a history of the slave and groundnut trade in Guinea and Cape Verde. There is an introductory note.

55 Duas descrições seiscentistas da Guiné. (Two sixteenth-century descriptions of Guinea.) Francísco de Lemos Coelho, introduction and historical notes by Damião Peres. Lisbon: Academia Portuguesa da História, 1953. 266p.

Another edition commissioned in commemoration of the 500th anniversary of the Portuguese 'discovery' of Guinea, these two descriptions were written in 1669 and 1684 by the merchant, captain and adventurer, Coelho. These works give a good insight into the political and economic organization of the people he encountered in trading along the Upper Guinea Coast. They also describe the geography of the area, particularly the navigable rivers, from the point of view of the trader.

56 Economic change in precolonial Africa: Senegambia in the era of the slave trade. Philip Curtin. Madison, Wisconsin: University of Wisconsin Press, 1975. 342p. 22 maps.

Although focused mainly on The Gambia, this work gives a general overview of the impact of the Atlantic trade on the lives of the peoples of the entire region. See also J. D. Fage, 'Slavery and the Slave Trade in the Context of West African History', *Journal of African History*, vol. 10, no. 3 (1969), which develops the thesis that slavery was not endemic to West African society. Fage argues that rulers and merchants reacted rationally to the European demand for slaves and used it to reinforce economic and political developments in their regions.

57 Esmeraldo de situ orbis. (About the emerald place of the world.) Duarte Pacheco Pereira, translated from the Portuguese into French, introduced and edited by Raymond Mauny. Bissau: Centro de Estudos da Guiné Portuguesa, 1956. 3 maps. bibliog. (Memórias: no. 19).

This bilingual edition, in Portuguese and French, is one of the earliest works on the Upper Guinea Coast written at some time between 1505 and 1508 by one of the original explorers. It was written as a guide for those navigating the area but it also describes the people and the trade conducted in the area. In this last respect, it is much less interesting than the works of Cadamosto, Coelho or Álvares d'Almada. 'A commentary on Duarte Pacheco Pereira's account of the lower Guinea coastlands in his *Esmeraldo de Situ Orbis*, and on some other early accounts', *History in Africa*, vol. 7 (1980) by J. D. Fage concentrates on the Lower rather than the Upper Guinea Coast.

58 **Europeans in West Africa, 1450-1560.**
Translated and edited by John William Blake. London: Hakluyt
Society, 1942. 2 vols. (Second Series no. 87).
Of general interest, the two volumes present documents relating to the Portuguese,
Spanish and English expeditions to the Upper Guinea Coast.

59 **Gonçalo de Gamboa de Aiala, Capitão-mor de Cacheu, e o comércio
negreiro espanhol (1640-50).** (Captain-Major Gonçalo de Gamboa de
Aiala of Cacheu and the Spanish slave trade [1640-50].)
Maria Luisa Esteves. Lisbon: Instituto de Investigação Científica
Tropical and INEP, 1988. 131p. bibliog.
Contains mainly documents of the period from the Arquivo Histórico Ultramarino.
The narrative summarizes the activities of the Captain-Major in securing the area for
Portugal.

60 **Guinea-Bissau in Anglo-Portuguese relations 1860-70: a study in the
diplomacy of colonial acquisition.**
Richard A. Olaniyan. Ile-Ife, Nigeria: University of Ife Press, 1984.
117p. map. bibliog.
Describes the contest between Great Britain and Portugal over the island of Bolama
which was arbitrated by the US president, Ulysses S. Grant, in favour of Portugal.
Olaniyan has written a PhD thesis on the subject: 'The Anglo-Portuguese dispute over
Bulama: a study in British colonial policy, 1860-70', Georgetown University, 1969-70.
A fuller study was published by the University of Ife Press in Nigeria in 1984.

61 **Histoire de la Casamance: conquête et résistance, 1850-1920.** (History of
the Casamance: conquest and resistance, 1850-1920.)
Christian Roche. Paris: Éditions Karthala, 1985. 2nd ed. 362p. 28
maps. bibliog.
Once a Portuguese and Luso-African enclave, the Casamance was ceded to France by
Portugal in 1886. Yet it still shelters numerous immigrants from Guinea. This excellent
historical work discusses the history of the region and its economy in the colonial
period. Roche concludes that the Europeans should have been able to conduct trade
without conquest. The history deals at great length with the resistance to colonialism.

62 **History of the Upper Guinea Coast, 1545-1800.**
Walter Rodney. Oxford: Clarendon Press, 1970. 270p. 5 maps. bibliog.
This is essential reading for all those who want an historical and political economic
view of the region beginning at the time of the Portuguese 'discoveries' and settlement.
Relying heavily on the documentation of the earliest Arab and European explorers and
settlers, Rodney brings to life the daily activities of the coastal peoples and settlers, the
interactions between them and among them, and the impact of the slave trade on their
lives and social formations.

63 **Honório Pereira Barreto.**
Jaime Walter. Bissau: Centro de Estudos da Guiné Portuguesa, 1947.
183p. map.

A biography of this most remarkable Guinean who was governor of the Rios de Guiné do Cabo Verde in the nineteenth century, this edition includes documents from Barreto's period of governorship as well as the very important and revealing report written by him: *Memória sobre o estado actual de Senegambia Portugueza, causas de sua decadência e meios de a fazer prosperar* (Memoir on the present state of Portuguese Senegambia, the causes of its decline and ways to make it prosper) (1843). There are a number of other monographs on Barreto including Teixeira da Mota's *Um luso-africano: Honório Pereira Barreto* (A Luso-African: Honório Pereira Barreto) (Lisbon: Sociedade de Geografia de Lisboa, 1959) and Joaquim Duarte Silva's *Honório Pereira Barreto* (Lisbon, 1939).

64 **Kola trade and state-building: Upper Guinea Coast and Senegambia, 15th-17th centuries.**
George E. Brooks. Boston, Massachusetts: African Studies Center, 1980. 37p. 5 maps. (Working Papers no. 38).

This extremely important and fascinating history shows that kola trade between the coastal areas of Guinea and the savannah areas of the interior is of ancient date, that Guinea was the site of trade between the Beafadas, Banhans and Mandingas in precolonial times and that the Portuguese also engaged in this lucrative commerce from the earliest moments of their penetration into West Africa.

65 **La traite portugaise en Haute Guinée, 1758-97: problèmes et méthodes.**
(Portuguese trade in Upper Guinea, 1758–97: problems and methods.)
Jean Mettas. *Journal of African History*, vol. 16, no. 3 (1975), p. 343-63.

Studies the Portuguese slave trade along the coast during the eighteenth century when Bissau supplied labour to the company of the Marquês de Pombal, the Companhia Geral de Grão Pará e Maranhão (see also António Carreira). Mettas shows that the company traded not only with Bissau but also with Cacheu in northern Guinea and to a much lesser extent with Luanda and Benguela in Angola. This is a very interesting and detailed account.

66 **Luso-African commerce and settlement in the Gambia and Guinea-Bissau region.**
George E. Brooks. Boston, Massachusetts: African Studies Center, 1980. 19p. 3 maps.

Traces the origins and influence of Luso-Africans, Euro-Africans and Cape Verdeans and their interrelationships in the developing Atlantic trade from the sixteenth to the nineteenth centuries.

67 **Notas sobre o tráfico português de escravos: circunscritos a costa ocidental africana.** (Notes on the Portuguese slave trade along the West African coast.)
    António Carreira.   Lisbon: Universidade Nova de Lisboa, Ciências Humanas e Sociais, 1978. 72p. map. bibliog.

Cites and summarizes many of the classic texts on the subject. There is also original research from the Angolan archives. Carreira also published two other works on this subject with the Junta de Investigações Científicas do Ultramar: *O tráfico português de escravos na costa oriental africana nos começos do século XIX* (The Portuguese slave trade on the east coast of Africa at the beginning of the nineteenth century) (no. 12, 1977) and *O tráfico de escravos nos Rios de Guiné e Ilhas de Cabo Verde (1810-50)* (The slave trade in the Rivers of Guinea and the Cape Verde islands, 1810-50) (no. 14, 1981). A more specialized work is *As companhias pombalinas de navegação, comércio e tráfico de escravos entre a costa africana e o nordeste brasileiro* (The pombaline companies shipping and trading slaves between the African coast and Northeast Brazil), published in Bissau by the Centro de Estudos da Guiné Portuguesa in 1962. This work centres on the activities of the Companhia Geral de Grão Pará e Maranhão and the Companhia Geral de Pernambuco e Paraiba, both of which were founded by the Marquês de Pombal.

68 **Os portugueses nos Rios de Guiné (1500-1900).** (The Portuguese in the Rivers of Guinea (1500-1900).)
    António Carreira.   Lisbon: author's edition, 1984. 205p. 2 maps. bibliog.

An indispensable work for those interested in the beginnings of creole culture and society along the Upper Guinea Coast, this book documents the living record of Portuguese trade and settlement. Carreira uses the Arquivo Histórico Ultramarino and imposes order on the confusion of documents existing there. There are seventy pages of original documents.

69 **Peanuts and colonialism: consequences of the commercialization of peanuts in West Africa, 1830-70.**
    George E. Brooks.   *Journal of African History*, vol. 16, no. 1 (1975), p. 29-54.

Documents the dominance of the French and Senegalese traders in the peanut trade in the Senegambia including the Rio Grande area of present-day Guinea-Bissau.

70 **Portuguese adaptation to trade patterns: Guinea to Angola (1443-1640).**
    Eugenia W. Herbert.   *African Studies Review*, vol. 17, no. 2 (1974), p. 411-23.

Presents an overview of how the Portuguese exploited local conditions all over the west coast of Africa in order to trade. Each area is described in turn. Herbert outlines the gold trade with Mandinga traders in the area now known as Guinea-Bissau. She uses Fernandes (q.v.) and Pacheco (q.v.) as main sources.

71 **Race relations in the Portuguese colonial empire, 1415-1825.**
C. R. Boxer. Oxford: Clarendon Press, 1963. 130p.
This work should be read in contrast to official statements on the treatment of Africans, such as Moreira (q.v.), Spínola (q.v.), and Sarmento Rodrigues (q.v.).

72 **Reply of the Portuguese government to the case in support of the claim of Great Britain to the island of Bolama on the western coast of Africa and to a certain portion of territory opposite to that island to be laid before the President of the United States of America as the arbiter selected to decide the question.**
Lisbon: National Printing Office, 1869. 194p.
This document in both Portuguese and English lays out the Portuguese claim to Bolama and includes supporting documents. It is a reply to the British claim. There are references to the British capture and arrest of João Marques de Barros, the then leading official of Bissau; the British destruction of Nozolini's property; and Philip Beaver's unsuccessful attempt to found a colony (q.v.).

73 **Slavery and slaving in the Portuguese Atlantic (to about 1500).**
Anthony Luttrell. In: *The transatlantic slave trade from West Africa: proceedings of a seminar.* Edinburgh: Centre of African Studies, University of Edinburgh, 1965, p. 61-79.
An interesting introduction to the topic, the paper focuses on the changing image of the slave and Portuguese attitude toward slaves as the trade evolved. Luttrell sees Portugal as a chivalric warrior state that became a commercial state with the development of the Atlantic trade. As a consequence, Africans suffered – they were no longer considered captures as a result of war or raids but commodities to be used in trade. Luttrell takes his reading from the works of Zurara (q.v.) and Cadamosto (q.v.). See also Malyn Newitt's 'Prince Henry and the origins of Portuguese expansion', in *The first Portuguese colonial empire*, edited by Newitt and published by the University of Exeter in 1986.

74 **Some minor sources for Guinea, 1519-59: Enciso and Alfonce/Fontineau.**
P. E. H. Hair. *History in Africa*, vol. 3 (1976), p. 19-46.
For those wanting to do research on the early years of European exploration, this article could serve as a brief introduction to some of the early texts.

75 **Subsídios para a história de Cabo Verde e Guiné.** (Notes for a history of Cape Verde and Guinea.)
Christiano José de Senna Barcellos. Lisbon; Coimbra, Portugal: Imprensa Nacional and Imprensa da Universidade, 1899-1913. 7 vols.
This is a very detailed history and is particularly valuable for tracing major figures in the overlapping creole society of the two regions.

76 **The establishment of the colonial economy in Guinea-Bissau: the colonial state, trade and agriculture, 1815-1925: a historical outline.**
H. Shoenmakers. *Les Cahiers du CEDAF*, nos 2, 3, 4 (1986), p. 3-29.
A very brief outline of the beginnings of the colonial economy, the article focuses on the transition from the slave trade to groundnut exportation and on the role of the state in trade. Shoenmakers continues his work on the state in 'Old men and new state structures in Guinea-Bissau', *Journal of Legal Pluralism and Unofficial Law*, nos 25-26 (1987). In this article, he announces a forthcoming publication, *State and rural development in Guinea-Bissau* from the Afrika Studiecentrum in Leiden, The Netherlands.

77 **The voyages of Cadamosto and other documents on Western Africa in the second half of the fifteenth century.**
Translated and edited by G. R. Crone, introduction by E. W. Bovill. London: Hakluyt Society, 1937. 147p. 3 maps. bibliog. (Second Series, no. 80).
This is the follow-up to the first volumes printed by the Hakluyt Society in 1896 and 1899 which translated the work of Azurara. The original volumes treated the works of the explorers of the 1440s. The present book carries on from that time and contains the texts of Alvise da Ca' da Mosta (a Venetian who sailed for Portugal), Antoine Malfante, Diogo Gomes and João de Barros. According to the editor, the voyages of these men should be understood as commercial ventures rather than voyages of discovery as the latter had already been accomplished by Nuno Tristão, Gil Eannes and Álvaro Fernandes. Cadamosto's works are valuable for the detail he gives of the inhabitants and their daily lives in the areas he visited. He is also known as one of the first Europeans to have described the trans-Saharan gold trade which the Portuguese were trying to divert to the African coast. He sailed as far south as the Rio Geba. João de Barros' account tells of the trading contacts of the Congo with West Africa.

78 **Tratado breve dos Rios de Guiné.** (Brief tract on the Rivers of Guinea.)
Capitão André Álvares d'Almada, edited by Luís Silveira. Lisbon: Governo da Colónia da Guiné, 1946. 88p.
This edition of the classic work written in 1594 was commissioned on the occasion of the 500th anniversary of the 'discovery' of Guinea by the Portuguese. It describes the many different ethnic groups encountered by the author in the area from the Senegal river to Sierra Leone. P. E. H. Hair has translated an edition of the work by A. Teixeira da Mota which is available from the University of Liverpool. He calls this an interim, makeshift version because he hopes that it will be edited into a trilingual edition as originally planned by Teixeira da Mota before his death in 1983.

79 **Yankee traders, old coasters and African middlemen: a history of American legitimate trade with West Africa in the nineteenth century.**
George E. Brooks. Boston, Massachussetts: Boston University Press, 1970. 293p. 3 maps. bibliog.
Describes commerce between the United States and the Windward Coast of Africa in the nineteenth century. The area known as the Rios de Guiné is featured in chapters 4 and 5. The main products traded from Bissau were hides, wax, ivory, gum copal, and specie. Peanuts became an important export from the 1840s.

História: a Guiné e as ilhas de Cabo Verde.
See item no. 37.

História da Guiné 1418-1918.
See item no. 38.

The Portuguese seaborne empire, 1416-1825.
See item no. 40.

The period of Portuguese Guinea

80   **Abdul Njai: ally and enemy of the Portuguese in Guinea-Bissau, 1895-1910.**
Joye L. Bowman. *Journal of African History*, vol. 27, no. 3 (1986), p. 463-79.
Describes the changing relationship of the Portuguese and Abdul Njai, originally a Senegalese trader, who commanded and recruited soldiers during the wars of occupation. Njai was one of the best known and most successful mercenaries used by the Portuguese. He was rewarded with a concession of the region of Oio. The Portuguese eventually deported him in 1919 because of his independent behaviour. See also Alex Trilling's *Abou Njie: an oral history* (Banjul, The Gambia: The President's Office, Oral History and Antiquities Division, [n.d.]).

81   **A estatística ante o movimento comercial da província no periodo de 1939-61.** (Trade statistics of the province in the period, 1939-61.)
Zeferino Monteiro de Macedo, notes by Tomaz Joaquim da Cunha Alves.   Bissau: Província da Guiné, Repartição Provincial dos Serviços de Economia e Estatística Geral, [n.d.]. 49p.
Gives an invaluable record of the government budget. Revenues were made up mainly of receipts from trade. The document shows the development of such exports as groundnuts (peanuts), rice, rubber, wax, palm kernel, palm oil and leather.

82   **A Guiné a saque: documentos e factos para a história.** (Plundered Guinea: documents and facts for its history.)
Valentim da Fonseca Campos.   Lisbon: Imprensa Africana, 1912. 55p.
Records the chaotic state of Republican administration of the colony. This pamphlet is especially useful for understanding the viewpoint of the small trader and for giving an insight into creole society. It is also a cry for more autonomy.

83 **Annuário da Província da Guiné do anno de 1925.** (The 1925 yearbook of
the Province of Guinea.)
Armando Augusto Gonçalves de Morães e Castro. Bolama, Guinea-
Bissau: Imprensa Nacional, 1925. 198p.
This is an excellent source of information on the colonial administration, on
commerce, the population and so on. It illustrates well the colonial mentality of the
time.

84 **Anuário da Guiné Portuguesa.** (The yearbook of Portuguese Guinea.)
Compiled by Fausto Duarte. Lisbon: Governo da Colónia, 1948. 810p.
2 maps.
Presents an invaluable picture of the colony at its most prosperous and Portuguese
moment. The text details much pertinent information on history, geology, administration, commerce, flora, fauna, agriculture, ethnic groups and other similar topics of
interest.

85 **A ocupação militar da Guiné.** (The military occupation of Guinea.)
João Teixeira Pinto. Lisbon: Divisão de Publicações e Biblioteca,
Agência Geral das Colónias, 1936. 205p. map.
Recounts the war of colonization against the various populations of Guinea-Bissau
such as the Balantas and Papéis. This is the account of the captain who is credited with
the pacification of the indigenous groups. There are also a number of documents from
the governor and various administrators and commanders. A balanced view can be
found in Bowman (q.v.) and Pélissier (q.v.).

86 **A questão do Casamansa e a delimitação das fronteiras da Guiné.** (The
question of the Casamance and the definition of Guinea's borders.)
Maria Luísa Esteves, preface by Maria Emília Madeira Santos, Carlos
Cardoso. Lisbon: Instituto de Investigação Científica Tropical and
Instituto Nacional de Estudos e Pesquisa, 1988. 291p. 2 maps. bibliog.
This is an extensive and comprehensive history of this strategically important area
which is still the site of border problems between Senegal and Guinea-Bissau. The
narrative ends in 1906, however, with the signing of an accord between France and
Portugal.

87 **As *elites* das províncias portuguesas de indigenato (Guiné, Angola,
Moçambique).** (Indigenous *élites* of the Portuguese provinces [Guinea,
Angola, Mozambique].)
Adriano Moreira. In: *Ensaios*, edited by A. Moreira, 3rd ed. Lisbon:
Junta de Investigações do Ultramar, Centro de Estudos Políticas e
Sociais, 1960, p. 33-58.
This is an essay on the issue of cultural assimilation – 'detribalization' in the author's
words – and the role of Roman Catholic missions in this process. He also discusses
ethnic minorities and their protection.

88 **Conferência dos administradores: actas das sessões realizadas em 1943, sob a presidência do governador da colónia.** (The administrators' conference: proceedings of the sessions held in 1943 under the presidency of the governor of the colony.)
Major de Artilharia Ricardo Vaz Monteiro.   Bolama, Guinea-Bissau: Imprensa Nacional, 1943. 159p.
Gives a good insight into the problems of the colony from the administrator's viewpoint. This was the period of greatest Portuguese impact. Two of the administrators at the time, António Carreira and Fernando Rogado Quintino, were among the most prolific writers on Guinea. At the conference, the administrators dealt with such issues as the export of rubber; the introduction of manioc, maize and other crops; changes in the civil code; instruction in the Portuguese language; the provision of clean water for the city of Bissau; taxes, etc. There are also published records of similar conferences held in 1941 and 1942 under a similar title. The 1941 *actas* were published in 1941 but those for 1942 bear neither date nor place of publication.

89 **Conflict, interaction and change in Guinea-Bissau: Fulbe expansion and its impact, 1850-1900.**
Joye Bowman Hawkins.   PhD thesis, University of California, Los Angeles, 1980. 295p. 3 maps. bibliog.
This is an essential resource for studying the events and peoples surrounding the colonization of the Senegambia with especial reference to Guinea-Bissau. The emphasis is on the fall of Kaabu, the several competing colonizations, and the rise and fall of Firdu and Fuladu. It is also an important economic history.

90 **Decree repealing the 'Estatuto dos Indígenas'.**
Lisbon: Ministry for Overseas Provinces, 1961. 14p.
Repeals the law which had legitimized the division of colonial society into *indígena* (native) and *civilizado* (civilized person). Native peoples were governed by 'traditional law' while civilized peoples were considered full citizens of Portugal under the constitution. A native could become civilized only by being educated in the Portuguese language and customs and by adopting these. The repeal eliminated this insidious distinction.

91 **Ensino rudimentar (para indígenas) em Angola e na Guiné Portuguesa.**
(Basic education [for natives] in Angola and Portuguese Guinea.)
Manuel Ferreira Rosa.   *Boletim Cultural da Guiné Portuguesa*, no. 24 (October 1951), p. 11-107.
Poses the question of whether there should be an apartheid system of education, one for whites and 'civilized' peoples and one for natives, or whether there should be a common education for all. The question was purely theoretical since indigenous education was confined to missionary schools. In any case, the author was of the opinion that the differences not only between Europeans and Africans but also among Africans warranted special education.

92 **Essential problems of urbanization in the Overseas Provinces: urban structures of integration and intercourse.**
Mário de Oliveira. Lisbon: Agency General for Overseas, 1962. 56p. 8 maps.
Focusing on Bissau, this progagandistic essay outlines a purely hypothetical urban policy which the author terms 'multiracial'. There is a great deal of information on Bissau as a city, however, including detailed maps.

93 **Guiné. (Guinea.)**
Lisbon: Agência Geral das Colónias, 1929. 230p. map.
Includes articles by the governor of the colony, on its political economy, flora and fauna, and demography. Obviously a propaganda exercise, the book nevertheless gives insight into the state of affairs and knowledge or ignorance of the colony. There are interesting statistics on the foreign trade situation from 1910 to 1927.

94 **Guiné: finanças e economia. (Guinea: finances and economy.)**
Alfredo Loureiro da Fonseca. Lisbon: Sociedade de Geographia de Lisboa, 1912. 50p. 2 maps.
Gives a general overview of the colonial economy during the Republican administration. See also Loureiro da Fonseca's *Guiné: alguns aspectos da actual situação da colónia* (Guinea: some aspects of the present situation of the colony) (Sociedade de Geographia de Lisboa, 1915) which updates the situation and gives useful export–import statistics.

95 **'Legitimate commerce' and peanut production in Portuguese Guinea, 1840s-80s.**
Joye L. Bowman. *Journal of African History*, vol. 28, no. 1 (1987), p. 87-106.
Develops the arguments put forward by George E. Brooks (q.v.) and others regarding French control over the commercialization of peanuts, but the focus is exclusively on the Guinea-Bissau area and the Portuguese reaction to this state of affairs.

96 **Naissance de la Guiné: Portugais et Africains en Sénégambie (1841-1936).**
(The birth of Guinea: Portuguese and Africans in the Senegambia [1841-1936].)
René Pélissier, preface by Léopold Sédar Sénghor. Orgeval, France: Pélissier, 1989. 411p. 6 maps. bibliog.
A master-work by the noted French historian of lusophone Africa, the volume begins in the period of greatest Luso-African and Cape Verdean influence. It focuses, however, on the wars of 'pacification' fought to establish Portuguese rule over the area. In an introductory note, the author states that one of his objectives is to put an end to the myth of five centuries of Portuguese colonialism. This he does from the very first chapters where the accent is on the tenuousness of Portuguese influence in the face of continual French pressure. As it reaches 1878 onwards, the focus of the narrative shifts to the resistance of Guineans to Portuguese occupation. It is a facinating and remarkably detailed history with charts and maps which allow the reader to understand the chronology and motivations of resistance, as well as the politico-military situation, at a glance. The last chapter places Guinean rebellion in a comparative context with that of Mozambique and Angola. There is also an excellent annotated bibliography.

97　**No governo da Guiné.** (Inside the government of Guinea.)
M. M. Sarmento Rodrigues.　Lisbon: Ministério das Colónias, 1949.
535p.

A collection of speeches by the former governor of the colony, the text offers an interesting insight into the mentality of one of the more progressive colonial administrators. It is useful also for its data on infrastructure or, rather, the lack of infrastructure.

98　**Oração inaugural.** (Opening speech.)
Marcelo Caetano.　*Boletim da Sociedade de Geografia de Lisboa*, vol. 64, nos 5 and 6 (1946), p. 351-8.

In his position as Minister of the Colonies, Caetano opened the celebration held in Bissau of the 500th anniversary of the 'discovery' of Guinea. In his speech, Caetano recalls the close links between Guinea-Bissau and Cape Verde but he puts his emphasis on those things that in his eyes made Guinea *Portuguese*. The commemorative congress dealt with all aspects and problems of the colony and the published papers are well worth consulting – *Congresso comemorativo do quinto centenário do descobrimento da Guiné*, Lisbon: Sociedade de Geografia de Lisboa, 1946 (q.v.).

99　**Orçamento geral para o ano económico de 1973.** (General budget for 1973.)
Província da Guiné.　Bolama: Imprensa Nacional da Guiné, 1974.
266p.

Lists all government expenses for this last year of colonization. The Public Library of Guinea-Bissau has the budgets for the years 1941-73 under this listing. Under a separate listing – *Orçamento da receita e tabelas de despesa ordinária e extraordinária* – it has the budgets for 1923-38.

100　**Organic law of the Portuguese Overseas Provinces.**
Lisbon: Agência-Geral do Ultramar, 1963, 62p.

Provides the legal framework (*Lei Orgânica*) for the colonies. It established the institutions by which they were governed locally. The specific charter for Guinea-Bissau was the *Estatuto político-administrativo da Província da Guiné* (Political and administrative statute for the Province of Guinea) (q.v.), a statute which has been revised numerous times.

101　**Panorâmico energético do Ultramar.** (The energy scene in the Overseas Provinces.)
J. A. Leite de Araújo.　*Boletim Geral do Ultramar*, vol. 42, nos 487-88 (1966), p. 141-51.

Surveys the sources of energy in existence as well as potential ones. Bissau had 72 per cent of all the resources. Araújo describes the installations there and in the provincial towns of Farim, Cacheu, Safim and Quínhamel. While demand for electricity was constantly rising – at a rate of 35 per cent from 1958 to 1960 – the growth in installations had been only 2 per cent per annum from 1959 to 1964. Araújo notes that there is hydro-electric potential that has not yet been exploited, a situation that still exists today.

102 **Political and administrative statute of the Province of Guinea.**
Agência-Geral do Ultramar.   Lisbon: Ministry of the Overseas Provinces, 1963. 40p.

This is the 1963 revision of the statute for the province. It is a handy guide to the political organization of the colony in its last years. There are earlier and later versions of the statute published in Portuguese by the Agência-Geral do Ultramar under the title, *Estatuto político-administrativo da Guiné*. The overall legal framework for colonialism can be found in *Political constitution of the Portuguese Republic* (S.N.I. Books, Lisbon, 1948). It contains the Colonial Act which was adopted with the constitution in 1933 and then amended several times.

103 **Portugal and its empire: the truth.**
António de Figueiredo.   London: Gollancz, 1961. 159p. bibliog.

A member of the opposition to the Salazar régime, the author engages in demystifying the significance of the New State in Africa on the eve of the nationalist struggles.

104 **Portugal in Africa: the last hundred years.**
Malyn Newitt.   London: C. Hurst, 1981. 248p. 6 maps. bibliog.

This is an excellent overview of Portuguese colonialism in Africa. Newitt's attention is mainly on Mozambique and Angola because they had priority on the colonial agenda. Neglect formed an important part of Guinea's history and took the form of a lack of state investment in infrastructure as well as a paucity of direct foreign investment. The book is very helpful for placing Guinea in the larger African context and for understanding the impact of Salazar's New State colonial policies. James Duffy's *Portuguese Africa* (Harvard University Press, 1959), is another standard reference work.

105 **Portugal Overseas Provinces: facts and figures.**
Agência-Geral do Ultramar.   Lisbon: Agência-Geral do Ultramar, 1965. 175p. 9 maps.

Obviously a propaganda exercise, chapter two describes Guinea-Bissau's history as a colony and administrative set-up. An appendix gives its population statistics as of 1960.

106 **Portugal's stand in Africa.**
Adriano Moreira.   New York: University Publishers, 1962. 219p.

Written while he was Minister of the Overseas Provinces, Moreira defends Portuguese colonial policy against what he sees as an ideological threat. He also sees the struggle in Africa as a battle for the 'hearts and minds' of people. Moreira was minister when the Indigenous statute was abolished and reform legislation introduced. Another very important work by the professor is *Política Ultramarina* (Overseas policy) which was published by the Junta de Investigações do Ultramar (Lisbon, 1956). These are his lectures during the 1955-56 academic year at the Instituto Superior de Estudos Ultramarinos, the school for colonial administrators. They are interesting because they include material on the question of race and human rights (chapter 1) and on the legislation concerning the colonies (chapter 3). Moreira also compares French, British and Belgian régimes with the Portuguese.

107 **Portuguese Africa.**
Ronald H. Chilcote. Englewood Cliffs, New Jersey: Prentice-Hall, 1967. 128p. 4 maps. bibliog.

In one of the earliest texts by an American author on the subject, Chilcote explores the differing concepts of nationalism and development held by the Portuguese administration and the nationalists of the five African colonies. He captures well the 'developmental nationalism' of the African movements for independence. Chilcote asserts that the future of Portugal in Africa depends upon internal domestic developments, developments within the colonies and external pressures from the United Nations, the United States and its NATO allies. A very perspicacious and timely study, the book has an excellent extensive bibliography. It is very useful for placing the Guinean national liberation movement in a larger context.

108 **Por uma Guiné melhor.** (For a better Guinea.)
António de Spínola. Lisbon: Agência-Geral do Ultramar, 1970. 393p.

This is a collection of speeches by one of the last governors of the colony and a man destined to play a historic role in the transformation of Portugal itself. Spínola demonstrates in this book that he understood well that the battle in Guinea was not for territory but for the hearts and minds of the people in Guinea, in Portugal and among their respective allies. He portrays the PAIGC as an arm of Soviet imperialism and offers a counter-offensive strategy of economic and social development.

109 **Problemas do trabalho indígena na colónia da Guiné.** (Problems of native labour in the colony of Guinea.)
António Carreira. *Boletim Geral das Colónias*, no. 282 (1948), p. 35-62.

Analyses the problem of forced labour which in Guinea-Bissau was used for public works such as road-building. Carreira shows that this and other colonial practices were at the origin of mass migrations. He sees a customary basis for compulsory labour and recommends compulsory *paid* labour for various 'development' schemes. Portugal was under suspicion and, at times, attack for its practices. In the late 1950s, Guinea-Conakry lodged a general complaint against Portugal with the International Labour Organization (ILO) which sent a mission to report on labour conditions. The mission did not visit Guinea-Bissau because there were no *specific* charges brought. The Salazar régime had presumably abolished forced labour with the Native Labour Code passed on 6 December 1928 (see ILO, *Legislative Series, Vol. IX-1928*, 1931). In 1935, the régime published the legislative decree no. 938 of 16 November 1935 which established regulations for employing 'native workers' in Guinea (see 'Portuguese Guinea, Legislative Decrees: Native Labour' *Legislative Series, Vol. XVI-1935* [Geneva, Switzerland: ILO, 1938]). In 1962, Portugal published a new labour code replacing the Native Labour Code. Four years later, the US Department of Labor, Bureau of Labor Statistics listed the wages for various categories of workers in Guinea and did not report any case of forced labour (see 'Labor Conditions in Portuguese Guinea', *Labor Digests on Countries in Africa* [Washington, DC: Bureau of Labor Statistics, 1966]).

110 **Relatório da inspecção do comércio bancário referente ao ano de 1963.**
(Report of the inspection of commercial banking in 1963.)
Zeferino Monteiro de Macedo. Bissau: Província da Guiné, 1964.
82p.
This is an excellent source of general data on the colony's exports dating from 1939 to
1962. There is also a general survey of the economy and the balance of payments
account for 1962. For very specific data, see Jesus Nunes dos Santos, 'Estatística:
aspectos gerais do comércio externo. II-Guiné' (Statistics: general aspects of foreign
trade. II-Guinea). *Boletim Geral das Colónias*, vol. 26, nos 312-13, vol. 27; nos 315-19
(1951-52). The five articles give altogether a detailed analysis of aggregate and dis-
aggregated foreign trade figures from 1939 to 1949.

111 **Relatório do governador Ricardo Vaz Monteiro.** (Governor Ricardo
Vaz Monteiro's report.)
R. Vaz Monteiro. Bissau: Colónia da Guiné, 1944. 282p.
Gives the annual report of all the affairs of the colony in 1943. There are a number of
other such reports recorded in various bibliographies such as that of P. Inácio de
Gouveia published in 1883, F. Teixeira da Silva published in 1889, J. G. Correia e
Lança published in 1890, and J. F. Velez Caroço published in 1923.

112 **The Balde family of Fuladu.**
B. K. Sidibe. Banjul, The Gambia: Oral History Division, Vice
President's Office, 1984. 22p.
Records the role of the Balde in the fall of Kaabu and the rise of Fuladu, including
their relationship with the British and the French. Joye Bowman Hawkins (q.v.) gives
more of the story as it relates to the Portuguese in their drive to conquer Guinea-
Bissau.

113 **The Bijouga or Bissagos Islands, West Africa.**
Edward Stallibras. *Proceedings of the Royal Geographical Society*,
vol. 11, no. 10 (1889), p. 595-601.
Describes the Portuguese administration of the colony as disastrous and the colony's
economy as non-existent. This is not a scientific report but rather an account of a
journey to the islands via Bissau and Bolama. It is of historical interest. Another
document of approximately the same period is *Exploration géographique et commerciale
de la Guinée Portugaise: projet présenté au Gouvernement Portugais par la Société de
Géographie de Lisbonne* (Geographical and commercial exploration of Portuguese
Guinea: a project presented to the Portuguese Government by the Sociedade de
Geografia de Lisboa), 1878. This document showed how little was known about the
territory and also gave an exaggerated view of what might be found. Both documents
show the area being exploited by French, Belgian, United States and British
merchants.

114 **The colonial period in Guiné.**
James Cunningham. *Tarikh*, vol. 6, no. 4 (1980), p. 31-48.
Outlines colonial policies and describes African resistance to them.

115 **The problem of Portuguese Guinea.**
António de Spínola. Lisbon: Agência-Geral do Ultramar, 1970. 29p.
Presents the viewpoint of the then governor of the colony on the war for independence. This was a speech given to a delegation of Portuguese parliamentarians on a visit to Guinea in July 1970 at the height of the struggle. Spínola realistically characterizes the war as a 'political struggle of a revolutionary nature based on grounds of a social kind', yet he interpreted it as a fight against Communism. His political counter-offensive, which he called a 'social counter-revolution', included concrete social and economic programmes. He admits that 'the Guineans are fighting to obtain concrete advantages, they want to live a better life in peace . . .'. And he admits such errors of colonial administration as 'excess of paternalism, too much bureaucracy and routine'.

116 **The Third Portuguese Empire, 1825-1975: a study in economic imperialism.**
Gervase Clarence-Smith. Manchester, England: Manchester University Press, 1985. 221p. 8 maps. bibliog.
Demonstrates the economic rationality of the Portuguese presence in Guinea-Bissau and its other colonies. The book is indispensable to understanding the role of Guinea-Bissau in the lusophone world economy established by Salazar.

117 **Trends in Portuguese overseas legislation for Africa.**
Alfredo Héctor Wilensky, translated from the Spanish by Frank R. Holliday. Braga, Portugal: Editora Rex, 1971. 255p.
A handy reference work, this is a dissertation on the legal framework of colonialism mainly during the Salazar period.

Congresso comemorativo do quinto centenário do descobrimento da Guiné.
See item no. 1.

Guiné: apontamentos inéditos.
See item no. 5.

Guiné Portuguesa.
See item no. 6.

Guiné Portuguesa.
See item no. 7.

Guiné-Bissau: História I and II.
See item no. 35.

História: a Guiné e as ilhas de Cabo Verde.
See item no. 37.

História da Guiné 1418-1918.
See item no. 38.

La Guinée Portugaise au XXe siècle.
See item no. 39.

31

History. The period of the national liberation struggle

UNESCO general history of Africa.
See item no. 42.

Monjur: o Gabú e a sua história.
See item no. 47.

Luso-African commerce and settlement in the Gambia and Guinea-Bissau region.
See item no. 66.

Subsídios para a história de Cabo Verde e Guiné.
See item no. 75.

The establishment of the colonial economy in Guinea-Bissau: the colonial state, trade and agriculture, 1815-1925: a historical outline
See item no. 76.

The period of the national liberation struggle

118 **A/AC.108 and A/AC. 109 documents.**
    United Nations General Assembly.   New York: UN, Special
    Committee on Territories under Portuguese Administration, 1962.

This is a series of documents which includes statements by important nationalist groups and by Portuguese nationals. From them one can distinguish the PAIGC position from that of rival groups. A/AC.108/L.7 is the background paper prepared by the UN Secretariat, 'General Policies in Territories under Portuguese Administration'. Chilcote (q.v.) lists some of the more important documents by name and number, while Valimamad (q.v.) also includes an extensive listing of other UN documents.

119 **Africa in the United Nations system.**
    Wellington W. Nyangoni.   Cranbury, New Jersey: Associated
    University Presses, 1985. 255p. bibliog.

Plots the involvement of the United Nations in the decolonization process of the lusophone African countries which began with the resolution of December 1960 that Portuguese-administered territories were non-self-governing and that therefore Portugal was bound to give information about them. For more detail, consult UN Public Information Office, *A principle in torment: the UN and Portuguese administered territories* (New York: UN, 1970) and *The United Nations and decolonization: highlights of thirty years of United Nations efforts on behalf of colonial countries and peoples* (New York: UN, 1977). The study by Wohlgemuth (q.v.) is also of interest.

120 **A luta pela libertação nacional na Guiné-Bissau e a revolução em Portugal.** (The national liberation struggle in Guinea-Bissau and the revolution in Portugal.)
John Woollacott. *Análise Social*, vol. 19, nos 77-79 (1983), p. 1131-55.

Recounts the process of decolonization in Guinea including the period involving negotiations with the post-revolutionary government of General Spínola. The author is of the opinion that the PAIGC and the war had an enormous impact on the events that led to the overthrow of the Caetano government and on the decolonization process in general.

121 **Armed struggle in Africa: with the guerrillas in 'Portuguese' Guinea.**
Gérard Chaliand, translated by David Rattray, Robert Leonhardt.
New York; London: Monthly Review Press, 1969. 142p. map. bibliog.

Gives an exciting and immediate account of the bush war. Most memorable are the lengthy interviews with peasants on the impact of the war on their villages and their willingness to make sacrifices for the liberation of their area from colonialism. There are interviews also with such heroes of the war as Osvaldo Vieira and Francísco Mendes. In chapter two of *Revolution in the Third World: myths and prospects* (Hassocks, Sussex, England: Harvester Press, 1977), Chaliand concludes that the success of the PAIGC lay in Cabral's not overestimating peasant spontaneity.

122 **Circuitos económicos exteriores do Ultramar Guiné.** (Foreign trade circuits of Overseas Guinea.)
António F. Mendes Jorge. *Boletim Geral do Ultramar*, vol. 44, no. 515 (1968), p. 37-48 and nos 517-18 (1968), p. 43-51.

Records the dramatic drop in the colony's exports after 1961. The drop in 1965 was 50 per cent and in 1966 75 per cent. This was due both to war and to smuggling because of higher prices in Senegal. The colony was running a balance-of-trade deficit during the 1960s generally. By 1966, the deficit was five times that of 1961. Notable among imports was rice, the staple of the country: in 1964 and 1965 it represented about seven per cent of the total value of exports. In the second part of the article, the author delineates the origins of imports and the destiny of the major exports. One hundred per cent of the export of groundnuts went to Portugal while West Germany took most of the palm kernel. Portugal also dominated imports; it supplied around 70 per cent of the total value between 1961 and 1966.

123 **Collective decolonisation and the UN committee of 24.**
James Mittleman. *Journal of Modern African Studies*, vol. 14, no. 1 (1976), p. 41-64.

Gives an overall view of the process of decolonization and the role of the Committee of 24. Guinea-Bissau is cited as an example of the work of the Committee. Mittleman focuses on the decision of the Committee to send a special mission to the liberated areas. A report of this mission can be found in UN document A/AC. 109/L. 804 (July 1972) (q.v.).

124 **Conséquences démographiques des révoltes en Afrique portugaise (1961-70): essai d'interprétation.** (Demographic consequences of the Portuguese African revolt [1961-70]: an interpretation.)
René Pélissier. *Revue Française d'Histoire d'Outre-Mer*, vol. 61, no. 222 (1974), p. 34-73.

Using the population censuses for 1950, 1960 and 1970 as well as other data, Pélissier concludes that the Africans under nationalist control were many fewer than claimed. He states that nearly 20 per cent of the Guinean population had gone into exile, with about 83,000 in Senegal alone.

125 **Crónica da libertação.** (Chronicle of the liberation.)
Luís Cabral. Lisbon: Edições 'O Jornal', 1984. 445p.

This is the first volume of the memoirs of the first President of the independent nation. It covers his youth, the founding of the PAIGC and the early years of armed struggle. The book is full of interesting and sometimes idealized details of his own life and that of his half-brother, Amílcar.

126 **Em 'chão papel' na terra da Guiné.** (In the land of the Papel in Guinea.)
Amândio César. Lisbon: Agência-Geral do Ultramar, 1967. 195p.

Dedicated to a fallen soldier in the battle against 'terrorism', this book tries to legitimize the Portuguese presence in the country by documenting such cultural activities as a book fair, the country's only high school, the new mosque in Bissau and so on. A pathetic attempt to cover up the truth of the situation, the book is important in that it shows what official Portugal wanted people to believe about the situation in Guinea.

127 **Fighting two colonialisms: women in Guinea-Bissau.**
Stephanie Urdang. New York: Monthly Review Press, 1979. 314p.

Records the war, but focuses mainly on women's roles. The author spent two months inside the liberated zones in 1974 and interviewed ordinary people as well as leaders. She came into daily contact with their lives and reports what they fought for. She shows that most people believed that national liberation was a process that would take many years to accomplish. Urdang lets the women speak in their own voices.

128 **Guinea-Bissau and the Cape Verde islands: the transition from war to independence.**
Basil Davidson. *Africa Today*, vol. 21, no. 4 (1974), p. 5-22.

Gives an eye-witness account mainly of Guinea-Bissau at independence. The interviews with the government leaders are very interesting.

129 **Guinea-Bissau: toward final victory!**
Introduced by Ole Gjerstad. Richmond, British Columbia, Canada: Liberation Support Movement Press, 1974. 95p. map.

Presents selected speeches by Amílcar Cabral as well as the PAIGC programme and documents from the final years of the national liberation struggle.

130 **Guinea-Bissau: 24 September 1973 and beyond.**
Richard Lobban. *Africa Today*, vol. 21, no. 1 (1974), p. 15-24.
Describes Guinea-Bissau on the eve of independence and discusses US foreign policy in relation to the question of recognition of the country's sovereignty.

131 **L'épineuse décolonisation de la Guinée-Bissau.** (Guinea-Bissau's thorny decolonization.)
Jeanne Makedonsky. *Le Mois en Afrique*, vol. 9, no. 105 (1974), p. 43-55.
Brings to light some interesting information on the attempt by FLING (Frente para a Libertação e Independência da Guiné Portuguesa Guiné Bissau), which was inactive during most of the liberation struggle, to manoeuvre for a place at the negotiating table with the PAIGC.

132 **La naissance de l'état par le guerre de libération nationale: le cas de la Guiné-Bissau.** (The birth of a state through a national liberation war: the case of Guinea-Bissau.)
P. P. Mathy. Paris: UNESCO, 1980. 155p.
This is a somewhat idealized account of the national liberation struggle. Mathy characterizes it as a battle to re-establish international law, the rights of man and peace. The last chapter is on the principles orienting the foreign policy of the country.

133 **Nationalist politics, war and statehood: Guinea-Bissau, 1953-73.**
E. D. Valimamad. DPhil thesis, University of Oxford, 1984. 239p.
11 maps. bibliog.
This is one of the most complete records of the military situation during the liberation struggle. It is also a good source of information about the many nationalist groupings in Guinea before the establishment of the PAIGC and the politics among these groups. There is a wealth of detail about the development of party strategy during the war and important information about Amílcar Cabral's role. Valimamad takes as his task answering the question of how the PAIGC came to oust the Portuguese from Guinea-Bissau. He concludes that the party with Cabral as its main spokesperson and diplomat was heavily dependent upon foreign assistance. This is a non-romantic view of the struggle. Valimamad strips away the revolutionary rhetoric and sees it as a nationalist movement led by pragmatists.

134 **No fist is big enough to hide the sky: the liberation of Guinea-Bissau and Cape Verde.**
Basil Davidson, foreword by Amílcar Cabral, preface by Aristides Pereira. London: Zed Press, 1981. 187p. map. bibliog.
This is an enlarged version of the 1969 Penguin edition, *The Liberation of Guiné*. Most of the book covers the period of the struggle but there are four new chapters which cover the period after Cabral's assassination and Luís Cabral's régime. The author begins to indicate problems of governance for the post-independence PAIGC. Davidson generally sides with Aristides Pereira's version of internal party conflict during 1980-81. Pélissier suggests the reader also consult Amândio César's *Guiné 1965: contra-ataque* (Guinea 1965: counter-attack) and Armor Pires Mota's *Guiné: sol e sangue* (Guinea: sun and blood) (q.v.) to counterbalance Davidson's coverage of the period of the struggle.

35

History. The period of the national liberation struggle

135 **No regresso vinham todos.** (On the way back all came home.)
Vasco Lourenço. Lisbon: Portugalia Editora, 1975. 128p.
Recounts the story of the Portuguese commander of 2549 Company which fought in
Guinea-Bissau during 1969-71. The author later became a member of the Armed
Forces Movement that seized power in April 1974 and eventually put an end to the
war. Of all the colonial wars, the one in Guinea most marked the Portuguese. This
book shows how one such person was affected.

136 **People's war in Angola, Mozambique and Guinea-Bissau.**
Thomas H. Henriksen. *Journal of Modern African Studies*, vol. 14,
no. 3 (1976), p. 377-99.
Comments on the differences in the insurgency strategies of the three leading
nationalist movements in Angola, Mozambique and Guinea-Bissau. Henriksen sees
both the PAIGC and the MPLA (Movimento Popular de Libertação de Angola) as
having their origins in European communist movements whereas the FRELIMO
(Frente de Libertação de Moçambique) leaders were influenced by Chinese Marxism.
However, he emphasizes that all were adaptations and not satellite parties. Another
work which compares the three movements is Bonnie K. Campbell's *Libération
nationale et construction de socialisme en Afrique (Angola, Guinée-Bissau, Mozambique)* (National liberation and the building of socialism in Africa [Angola, Guinea-
Bissau, Mozambique]) (Montreal, 1977). In 1986, Henriksen looked again at the three
parties and governments in the three countries in 'Lusophone Africa: Angola,
Mozambique and Guinea-Bissau', *Politics and Government in African States 1960-85*,
edited by Peter Duignan and R. H. Jackson (London and Sydney: Croom Helm,
1986).

137 **People's war, state formation and revolution in Africa: a comparative
analysis of Mozambique, Guinea-Bissau and Angola.**
Patrick Chabal. *Journal of Commonwealth and Comparative Politics*,
vol. 21, no. 3 (1983), p. 104-25.
Represents a re-working of the material in the last chapter of his book on Amílcar
Cabral (q.v.). Chabal defines the terms 'revolution' and 'people's war' in order to
determine whether a people's war is necessary for revolution. Chabal concludes that
while there may not be a causal relationship, revolutions can still occur.

138 **PIDE and SDECE: plotting in Guinea.**
Ken Lawrence. In: *Dirty work 2: the CIA in Africa*, edited by Ellen
Ray, W. Schaap, K. Van Meter, L. Wolf, preface by Sean MacBride.
London: Zed Press, 1980. p. 140-5.
Documents the collaboration of the Portuguese secret police (PIDE) and the French
intelligence agency (SDECE) in two covert operations to topple Sékou Touré who
hosted the PAIGC in Conakry. The first was in 1970 and the second immediately
following Amílcar Cabral's death. The second plot depended upon a split within the
PAIGC between Cape Verdean and anti-Cape Verdean factions. According to the
author, it was foiled by the 25 April 1974 seizure of power by the Armed Forces
Movement in Portugal. The author warns that the network of conspirators might still
be in place.

139 **Portugal's guerrilla war: the campaign for Africa.**
Al J. Venter.   Cape Town, South Africa: John Malherbe Party, 1973.
196p. map.
Venter is openly on the side of Portugal but he tries to portray both sides of the
conflict. This is a first-hand account of the war as experienced by the author in 1971.
There is an informative interview with General Spínola, then governor of Guinea-
Bissau. See also his *Portugal's war in Guinea-Bissau* published by the California
Institute of Technology in *Munger Africana Library Notes* in the same year.

140 **Portugal's wars in Africa.**
Ruth First.   London: Christian Action Publications, 1971. 28p.
One of several tracts publicizing the state of Portuguese colonialism in Africa, this
pamphlet brings out evidence showing not only NATO, US and British support for
Portugal but also South African and Rhodesian direct involvement. A work on the
same theme is Arslan Humbaraci and Nicole Muchnik, *Portugal's African Wars
(London: Macmillan, 1974)*.

41 **Portuguese Africa and the West.**
William Minter.   Harmondsworth, England: Penguin, 1972. 160p.
4 maps. bibliog.
Documents and attacks US government support for Portugal. This is one of a series of
books and pamphlets written to alert the US and British publics to the little-known
wars in Africa. See also B. Davidson and Ruth First. Another such book from a
different point of view is the much-cited *Portuguese Africa* edited by David Abshire
and Michael A. Samuels (Pall Mall Press, London, 1969). It presents a wealth of
information on the colonies from a pro-Portuguese point of view. There is also an
ample bibliography.

142 **Portuguese Africa: nailing a lie.**
John Biggs-Davison, MP.   London: Congo Africa Publications, 1970.
44p.
Meant as a reply to Basil Davidson's writings on the war, this pamphlet is a running
commentary of the MP's visit to Guinea. Biggs-Davison was escorted by the military
governor, General Spínola. The narrative speaks for itself.

143 **Portuguese Guinea: a crucial struggle.**
Richard Pattee.   *South Africa International*, vol. 4, no. 3 (1974),
p. 132-48.
Contests the news reports, the UN mission report and other accounts that the PAIGC
controlled the majority of the population. The author, who visited Guinea in 1973,
calls the PAIGC Marxist terrorists and argues that the Portuguese have had a bad
press.

History. The period of the national liberation struggle

144 **Portuguese Guinean refugees in Senegal.**
I. W. Zartman. In: *Refugees south of the Sahara: an African dilemma*, edited by H. C. Brooks, Y. El-Ayouty. Westport, Connecticut: Negro Universities Press, 1970, p. 143-61.

Records 60,000 refugees as of 1966, whom the author describes as lacking a nationalist consciousness. Zartman speculates on whether they would be mobilized by the various nationalist groups including the PAIGC operating in Dakar and the southern Casamance.

145 **Record of the month, June 1968: Special Committee of Twenty-Four.**
UN Monthly Chronicle, vol. v, no. 7 (1968). p. 32-42.

Records the debate surrounding the resolution of the Committee condemning Portugal for its colonial war and urging it to withdraw and its allies in the North Atlantic Treaty Organization (NATO) to withhold military aid and support. The text of the resolution is given. See also Mittleman.

146 **Record of the month, November 1969: territories under Portuguese administration.**
UN Monthly Chronicle, vol. 6, no. 11 (1969), p. 23-33.

Records the debate surrounding the adoption by the General Assembly of a resolution (no. 2507 (XXIV)) reaffirming the legitimacy of the struggle of the PAIGC, FRELIMO and MPLA movements and their right to independence. The resolution also condemned Portugal and its immediate allies, South Africa and Southern Rhodesia and it invited the Security Council to intervene. The text of the resolution is given.

147 **Record of the month, December 1970, complaint by Guinea.**
UN Monthly Chronicle, vol. 8, no. 1 (1971) p. 3-19.

Records the action by the Security Council upon receipt of the report of the special mission to Guinea-Bissau (q.v.). The Council endorsed the conclusions of the report, declared the Portuguese presence in Guinea-Bissau as a threat to international security and strongly condemned Portugal for its invasion of Conakry in November 1970. Further action of the United Nations on the war was reported in the *Chronicles* of August–September, October and December 1971; May, June and August–September issues of 1972; February, March, June, November and December issues of 1973 and the October 1974 issue which recorded Guinea-Bissau's admission to the United Nations. For earlier UN action, see Wohlgemuth, Mittleman and Nyangoni, and consult the yearly indexes of the *Chronicle*. Chilcote (q.v.) has a large listing of UN documents from as far back as 1952. Valimamad has an exhaustive listing of UN documents in the UN depository at Oxford University.

148 **Report of a visit to the liberated areas of Guinea-Bissau.**
International Union of Students and National Union of Finnish Students. Helsinki: IUS/SYL, 1971. 48p.

Mainly describes the international context of the liberation struggle. The mission report also includes statements from Amílcar Cabral, João Bernardo 'Nino' Vieira and a FARP (People's Revolutionary Armed Forces) soldier. It gives a portrait of life in the liberated zones.

149 **Report of the United Nations special mission to Guinea (Bissau).**
United Nations. New York: UN, 1972. 14p. map. (A/AC.109/L.)
Contains the record of the three-man mission to the liberated zones of Guinea and
their observation of life in these regions.

150 **Report on Portuguese Guinea and the liberation movement.**
US Congress, House of Representatives, Committee on Foreign
Affairs. Washington, DC: US Government Printing Office, 1970. 25p.
Contains the statement of Amílcar Cabral before the Committee as well as a speech by
the then Prime Minister of Portugal, Marcelo Caetano. There is also a report to the
Organization of African Unity (OAU) by Cabral.

151 **Sistemas políticos acéfalos e libertação nacional.** ('Stateless' political
systems and national liberation.)
Christian Sigrist. *Economia e Socialismo*, vol. 5, no. 50 (1980),
p. 43-58.
Sustains the thesis of Laura and Paul Bohannan that decentralized political structures
are positively correlated with a tendency towards rebellion. Sigrist utilizes this
hypothesis to explain the adherence of the Balanta Brassa to the PAIGC cause.

152 **The bush rebels.**
Barbara Cornwall. New York: Holt, Rinehart and Winston, 1972.
252p.
Describes the wars in Mozambique and Guinea-Bissau as she experienced them as a
journalist in the 1960s. The account is very generalized but there are interviews with
the militants including João Bernardo (Nino) Vieira.

153 **The politics of decolonization in Portuguese Africa.**
Joseph C. Miller. *African Affairs*, vol. 74, no. 295 (1975), p. 135-47.
Reviews in a very general way the overall implications for a number of countries of
independence in lusophone Africa. The countries he touches upon are Portugal, the
United States, the Soviet Union, China, South Africa, Rhodesia, Zaire, and other
African states.

154 **The Portuguese in Guinea.**
George Martelli. *The World Today*, vol. 21, no. 8 (1965), p. 345-51.
The first foreign journalist to travel inside Guinea after the outbreak of the war,
Martelli writes not only of what he saw but also of some of the major issues raised by
the war for his British and US readers. Thus he touches upon the strategic importance
of the war to the Portuguese and of the interest of the US military in the airstrip in Sal,
Cape Verde. He was taken around Guinea by the Portuguese military and found the
land mainly under their control: he quotes the figure as 80 per cent. See also Zartman
on this period. It would be good to contrast Martelli's view with Neil Bruce's
'Portugal's African wars', *Conflict Studies*, no. 34 (March 1973), which also notes the
strategic importance of the lusophone African countries for the West eight years later.
He worries about the expansion of the Soviet Navy in the Atlantic and Indian oceans.
Bruce gives a decidely unsympathetic and misleading account of the PAIGC's struggle.

155 **The Portuguese territories and the United Nations.**
Patricia Wohlgemuth. New York: Carnegie Endowment for
International Peace, 1963. 59p. (International Conciliation no. 545).

Lists all the UN resolutions on the matter from December 1960 to December 1963,
including the General Assembly, Security Council, Committee of 24, ECOSOC (UN
Economic and Social Council) and the Economic Commission for Africa. To follow the
continuing debate, readers are advised to consult the *UN Monthly Chronicle*.

156 **The United Nations and Portugal: a study of anti-colonialism.**
Franco Nogueira. London: Sidgwick and Jackson, 1963. 188p.

Defends Portugal's colonial policies in the context of the United Nations. There is an
analysis of the evolution of the anti-colonial policy within the United Nations.
Portugal's position was that the Overseas Provinces were not juridically separate from
Portugal itself.

157 **The war of maps: Portugal versus PAIGC.**
Michael H. Glantz. *Pan-African Journal*, vol. 6, no. 3 (1973),
p. 285-96.

Shows the military situation as of 1972 through a skilful comparison of maps put out by
both the Portuguese and the PAIGC. The author locates the areas which each side
claimed to control, those under contest, the location of the strategic hamlets and the
areas under PAIGC mortar and missile attacks. He concludes that it is difficult to
assess the verity of the various claims and that there are no clear-cut winners or losers.

158 **Three revolutions: Angola, Mozambique, Portuguese Guinea: special
issue on Portuguese Africa.**
Edited by John A. Marcum. *Africa Report*, vol. 12, no. 8 (1967).

Contains three articles of interest: J. A. Marcum, 'Three revolutions'; W. A. Hance,
'Three economies'; and I. W. Zartman, 'Guinea: the quiet war goes on'. The latter
summarizes the various nationalist movements in the country and in exile in the early
1960s. There is a handy chart of the groups with the names of their principal leaders
and their ideological orientation. Zartman outlines the history of these organizations
and their interactions.

159 **Un bureau du F.L.I.N.G. à Dakar.** (A headquarters for FLING in
Dakar.)
J.-B. A. *Afrique Nouvelle*, no. 1089 (20-26 June 1968), p. 7.

Announces the establishment of an office of the Front de Libération de la Guinée
'Portugaise' under the leadership of B. Pinto Bull. This was one of the prime rival
groups to the PAIGC. Whereas the PAIGC was headquartered in Conakry under the
sponsorship of Sékou Touré, the FLING received the support of the President of
Senegal, Léopold Sédar Sénghor.

Guiné-Bissau: História I and II.
See item no. 35.

Guiné-Bissau: zwischen Weltwirtschaft und Subsistenz.
See item no. 36.

História: a Guiné e as ilhas de Cabo Verde.
See item no. 37.

La Guinée Portugaise au XXe siècle.
See item no. 39.

Population

160 **Censo da população de 1950.** (1950 population census.)
Província da Guiné. Lisbon: Junta de Investigações do Ultramar,
Centro de Estudos Políticos e Sociais, 1959. 2 vols.
Presents a demographic analysis of the colony. Volume 1 treats those who were
considered 'civilized' while volume 2 deals with the 'non-civilized' or indigenous
population.

161 **Guiné-Bissau: População-I.** (Guinea-Bissau: Population-I.)
Lisbon: Centro de Informação e Documentação, Amílcar Cabral
(CIDAC), 1990.
Contains two works on Balantas and some other miscellaneous ethnographic and other
materials.

162 **Recenseamento geral da população e da habitação, 16 de Abril de 1979.**
(General population and housing census, 16 April 1979.)
Ministério da Coordenação Económica e Plano. Bissau:
Departamento Central de Recenseamento, 1982. 8 vols.
Volume five presents a summary and general analysis of the census data. Each of the
other volumes is devoted to a specific topic. Volume one discusses the methodology
used; volume two is a list of the localities surveyed; volume three is on population;
volume four on housing; volume six gives household data; volume seven is on
education; and volume eight on economic activity.

163 **IX recenseamento geral da população, 1960: resumo geral.** (Ninth
general population census, 1960: general summary.)
Província da Guiné. Lisbon: Ministério dos Negócios Estrangeiros,
1978. 69p.
Presents in tabular form the overall resuits of the 1960 census.

164 **The demography of the Portuguese territories: Angola, Mozambique and Portuguese Guinea.**
Don F. Heisel. In: *The demography of tropical Africa*, edited by William Brass. Princeton, New Jersey: Princeton University Press, 1968, p. 440-61.
Analyses the census data from 1940 and 1950 of all three countries.

165 **The uprooted of the Western Sahel: migrants' quest for cash in the Senegambia.**
Lucie Gallistel Colvin, Cheikh Ba, Boubacar Barry, Jacques Faye, Alice Hamer, Moussa Soumah, Fatou Sow. New York: Praeger Special Studies, 1981. 343p. 25 maps. bibliog.
This is an excellent source of information on the economic realities and continuing vitality of the Senegambia region from precolonial times to the 1980s. Although there is no specific chapter on Guinea-Bissau, the text shows that Guineans migrate to the Casamance and to Dakar. The chapters by L. G. Colvin and B. Barry are the most relevant.

Introdução a geografia económica da Guiné-Bissau.
See item no. 8.

Guiné.
See item no. 93.

Portugal Overseas Provinces: facts and figures.
See item no. 105.

Ecological perspectives on Mande population movements, commercial networks and settlement patterns from the Atlantic Wet Phase (ca 5500-2500 BC) to the present.
See item no. 191.

Ethnic Groups

General

166 **A habitação indígena na Guiné Portuguesa.** (Native housing in
Portuguese Guinea.)
Edited by A. Teixeira da Mota, M. Ventim Neves. Bissau: Centro de
Estudos da Guiné Portuguesa, 1948. 538p. 2 maps.
This is a collection of essays on the housing and village constructions of the major
ethnic groups by the leading authorities of the day. Teixeira da Mota wrote the
introductory essay, which classifies the various societies and documents the development of housing patterns. The map locates the various groups. Teixeira da Mota
identifies two major groupings according to location – the coastal groups and the
savannah or sudanese groups. They situate their housing according to the type of
agriculture practices – either paddy rice cultivation or upland rain-fed cultivation.
Teixeira da Mota also notes the exceptions and attempts to explain them.

167 **Antroponímia da Guiné Portuguesa.** (Naming in Portuguese Guinea.)
António Carreira, Fernando Rogado Quintino. Lisbon: Junta de
Investigações do Ultramar, 1966. 187p.
Gives a list of names used by the different ethnic groups and the meanings of these
names.

168 **Äthiopien des Westens: Forschungsreisen in Portugiesisch-Guinea.**
(Ethiopia of the West: expeditions in Portuguese Guinea.)
Hugo A. Bernatzik. Vienna: Seiden und Sohn, 1932-33. 2 vols. map.
Volume 1 surveys Balantas, Manjacos, Banhans, Felupes, Papéis, Mancanhas
(Brames), Bijagós and some smaller groups. Volume 2 consists of photographs of
domestic life among the groups.

169 **Babel negra: etnografia, arte e cultura dos indígenas da Guiné.** (Black
Babel: ethnography, art and culture of the Guinean natives.)
Landerset Simões, preface by General Norton de Mattos. Porto,
Portugal: author's edition, 1935. [n.p.].
There is a little bit of everything in this compendium of random knowledge about the
major ethnic groups of Guinea. There is a brief description of the social organization
of each group and a short dictionary of each language. There are photographs and
drawings of people, houses, works of art, dance, cloths, and there is a section with
stories, songs and proverbs.

170 **Contribuição para o estudo do estado de nutrição dos povos da Guiné
Portuguesa. II.** (Contribution to the study of the nutritional state of the
peoples of Portuguese Guinea. II.)
G. Jorge Lanz, C. Santos Reis, F. Coutinho Costa, M. Oliveira
Lecuona, A. Reimão Pinto, A. Ruas, J. Pacheco Viana, J. Pereira da
Silva. *Anais do Instituto de Medicina Tropical*, vol. 20, nos 1-4
(1963), p. 43-60.
The text is as much ethnographic as it is medical. It contains information on what the
various groups eat, how many times they eat, how they prepare meals, conserve food,
the utensils used, the meals for sick people, ceremonies connected with food and so
on. There is an extensive bibliography.

171 **Development strategy's impact on ethnically-based political violence:
a theoretical framework with comparative applications to Zambia,
Guiné-Bissau and Moçambique.**
Virginia L. Bollinger. PhD thesis, University of Colorado at Boulder,
1984. 395p. bibliog.
Bollinger's hypothesis is that development strategy induces ethnic-based conflict in
various societies. She uses a systems analysis to describe strategies. The author admits
weakness in her database on Guinea-Bissau and Mozambique and this is telling in her
description of events in Guinea. She relies heavily on ideological pronouncements by
Amílcar Cabral and other party leaders rather than on deeds or actions in her
description of Guinean strategy. For example, she states that government policy is 'to
move rural production in the direction of a decentralized but communally-based
pattern'. However, the PAIGC abandoned communal production in the 1970s even
though Amílcar Cabral continued to urge it until he was murdered in 1973. In order to
support her thesis, Bollinger turns the 'civilized' category into an ethnic group. It
functioned, however, as a status group and was composed of a mixture of peoples. She
describes the 1980 coup as a conflict between indigenous 'blacks' and Cape Verdeans
and 'mulattoes'. This was only one aspect of a much more complex event.

172 **Inquérito etnográfico.** (An ethnographic survey.)
A. Teixeira da Mota. Bissau: Governo da Colónia da Guiné
Portuguesa, 1947. 163p. (Publicação Comemorativa do Quinto
Centenário da Descoberta da Guiné).
Presents the elements of an ethnographic survey carried out in 1946 by colonial
administrators. In the introduction, Teixeira da Mota lists the previous surveys carried

out by the Portuguese. One of the distinguishing factors of the 1946 survey is its focus on language and oral history.

173 **Notas sobre os movimentos migratórios da população natural da Guiné Portuguesa.** (Notes on migration of indigenous peoples of Portuguese Guinea.)
António Carreira, A. Martins de Meireles. *Boletim Cultural da Guiné Portuguesa*, vol 14, no. 53 (1959), p. 7-19.

Based on the 1950 population census, the authors show that the following groups lost significant population to both internal and external migration: Fula, 5.9%; Mandinga, 8.5%; Balanta, 42.7%; Manjaco, 14.7%; Papel, 16.5%; Brame, 48.8% and Bijagó, 20.2%. The major reasons had to do with economic and social factors related to colonialism, such as forced labour.

174 **Transición histórica y etnicidad en Guinea-Bissau.** (Ethnicity and the historical transition in Guinea-Bissau.)
Carlos Lopes. *Estudios de Asia y África*, vol. 22, no. 2 (1987), p. 231-9.

Adapts and applies the interpretation of ethnicity put forward by Jean Loup Amselle in *Au cour de l'ethnie* (Paris, 1985) to the case of Guinea-Bissau. Lopes argues that it is a mistake to see ethnicities as a primary political factor in the struggle for state power. It is the class struggle which is most important.

175 **Uma jornada científica na Guiné Portuguesa.** (A scientific sojourn in Portuguese Guinea.)
António Mendes Corrêa. Lisbon: Agência Geral das Colónias, 1947. 193p.

More a diary of a trip through Guinea than a scientific work, the first part of this book gives a chatty overall description of the colony. The second part, however, consists of two articles on population movements and a classification of ethnicities and languages. The third part outlines preliminary work and plans for future work in physical anthropology.

Congresso comemorativo do quinto centenário do descobrimento da Guiné.
See item no. 1.

Paysanneries en attente: Guinée-Bissau.
See item no. 11.

Esmeraldo de situ orbis.
See item no. 57.

The voyages of Cadamosto and other documents on Western Africa in the second half of the fifteenth century.
See item no. 77.

Tratado breve dos Rios de Guiné.
See item no. 78.

Annuário da Província da Guiné do anno de 1925.
See item no. 83.

Anuário da Guiné Portuguesa.
See item no. 84.

Guiné.
See item no. 93.

Mito, religion y pensamiento filosófico da Guinea-Bissau.
See item no. 238.

A descent into African psychiatry.
See item no. 245.

Ethnie, état et rapports de pouvoir en Guinée-Bissau.
See item no. 302.

Historical dictionary of the Republic of Guinea-Bissau.
See item no. 572.

Balanta

176 **African peasants and revolution.**
Basil Davidson. *Journal of Peasant Studies*, vol. 1, no. 3 (1974),
p. 269-90.
Argues the revolutionary importance of the peasant uprisings in lusophone Africa.
Davidson describes the example of the peoples of Como including their system of self-
governance during the national liberation struggle.

177 **Contribution à l'étude des coutumes de Balantes de Sédhiou.** (Contri-
bution to the study of the customs of the Balantas of Sedhiou.)
Diagne Mapaté. *Outre-Mer*, vol. 5, no. 1 (1933), p. 16-42.
The most numerous group in Guinea-Bissau, the Balantas also live in the Casamance
along the river of the same name. This article tells about the group living in Sédhiou
across the river from Tanaff which is linked by road to Farim in northern Guinea-
Bissau. The article describes family life and social, political and legal organization.
Mapaté speculates that the Balantas were originally warriors who divided into
independent clans which then regrouped into four distinct categories during the period
of colonization. Three of the four groups reside in Guinea-Bissau.

178 **L'eau et la riziculture Balante: étude de la riziculture de Cantone.**
(Water and Balanta rice cultivation: a study of the rice cultivation of
Cantone.)
Eric Denis.   Paris: Education et Développement Interculturels (EDI-
IRFED), 1986. 250p. 13 maps. bibliog.
The study is valuable for its minute analysis of the agronomic and social conditions of
rice culture in the southwest of the country. It presents a detailed study of Balanta rice
cultivation which is described mainly in terms of environmental and technical aspects.
The author appreciates the Balantas' profound knowledge of the environment and
recognizes their ability to manipulate it. The chief physical limiting factor, of recent
years, has been the irregular pattern and duration of rainfall. There are also problems
of land tenure and labour supply. The author feels that the Balanta should be
encouraged to conserve and utilize the techniques developed over the years and should
be helped to overcome the socio-economic constraints mentioned above. There are a
number of other studies on the Balanta and rice-growing in *Soronda: Revista de
Estudos Guineenses.*

179 **Nature et fonctionnement du pouvoir chez les Balanta Brassa.** (The
nature and function of power among the Balanta Brassa.)
Diana Lima Handem.   Bissau: INEP, 1986. 239p. 3 maps. bibliog.
The author distinguishes two main groups of Balantas: Balanta Batcha and Balanta
Brassa. (N'Diaye-Correard [q.v.] says that they call themselves Bejáa and Brassa.)
This classification contests the five categories denominated by colonial ethnographers.
Handem's theme is the concept of power among the Balanta Brassa, the most
numerous group of people in Guinea. She describes them as egalitarianistic rather than
egalitarian. In other words, there is a minimum of hierarchy, and the power that rests
in the elders of a village is exercised with the community in mind, in a spirit of
collegiality, conciliation and survival rather than force or coercion. Since this book was
written, there has been a grass roots movement (the Jangue-Jangue [q.v.]) among the
Balanta directly challenging this structure of power.

Paysanneries en attente: Guinée-Bissau.
See item no. 11.

Sistemas políticos acéfalos e libertação nacional.
See item no. 151.

Jangue Jangue: la politique par le bas en Guinée-Bissau.
See item no. 314.

Land tenure, agriculture and gender in Guinea-Bissau.
See item no. 346.

**Causas da queda de produção de arroz na Guiné-Bissau (a situação no sector
de Tite-região Quínara).**
See item no. 431.

Bijagó

180 **Dossier sur l'artisanat utilitaire, de service et de production dans l'île du Bubaque.** (Dossier on utilitarian handicrafts, of service and production, on the island of Bubaque.)
Robert Corneau, Dominique Leblond. Bissau: Programme Études et Projets de Développement Rural, Centre des Études et Coopération Internationale, 1987. 37p.

This working paper for the above-cited Canadian non-governmental agency is very useful for information on the construction of housing and storage facilities, on the work of blacksmiths and on the extraction of palm oil on the island of Bubaque.

181 **Dynamique de l'art Bidjogo (Guinée-Bissau): contribution à une anthropologie de l'art des sociétés africaines.** (The dynamic of Bijagó art (Guinea-Bissau): contribution to an anthropology of African art.)
Danielle Gallois Duquette. Lisbon: Instituto de Investigação Científica Tropical, 1983. 236p. 3 maps. bibliog.

More than simply a study of art, this is a work on the society of the Bijagós and the place of aesthetics in it. Included are dance, music, chants and mime as well as the plastic arts. There are 152 photographs mainly of the sculpture for which the Bijagós are justly renowned.

182 **Im Reich der Bidjogo.** (In the empire of the Bijagó.)
Hugo. A. Bernatzik. Berlin: Verlag Ullstein, 1960. 158p. map.

One of the early general works on the islanders, it covers a number of the islands and comments on the social structure.

183 **La problématique du changement de la structure familiale chez les Bidjogos.** (The problematic of change in the family structure of the Bijagós.)
Raul Mendes Fernandes. Master's thesis, University of Paris VIII, Saint-Denis, 1984. 129p. 2 maps. bibliog.

Describes the transformation of the Bijagós from a society of warriors to an agricultural society and the impact of the change on the family. Fernandes argues that society has evolved from a matrilineal-matrilocal to a matrilineal-patrilocal one, with corresponding tensions between husbands and brothers-in-law. There are also antagonistic relations between the sexes in regard to relations of production. While men are being integrated into commercial activities, women are left with the bulk of the agricultural work.

184 **Note de recherche sur le comput du temps chez les Bijogo de Bubaque (Guinée-Bissau).** (Research note on the calculation of time among the Bijagós of Bubaque [Guinea-Bissau].)
Christine Henry. *Systèmes de pensée en Afrique Noire*, cahier 7 (1984), p. 141-8.

Describes how the Bijagós of the island of Bubaque count time. They use a double lunar and solar system. The Bijagós have a lunar calendar with the year beginning at the onset of the rainy season. In another article, 'Le soupçon', *Systèmes de pensée en Afrique Noire*, cahier 9 (1986), Henry recounts the mysterious death of a woman and the efforts of the villagers to find out who is responsible.

185 **Organização económica e social dos Bijagós.** (The Bijagós and their economic and social organization.)
Augusto J. Santos Lima, introduction by A. Teixeira da Mota. Bissau: Centro de Estudos da Guiné Portuguesa, 1947. 143p. map. bibliog.

Gives an introductory description of the political, economic and social structure of the society as seen through the eyes of the then colonial administrator.

186 **Sobrevivências da cultura etiopica no ocidente Africano.** (Surviving traces of Ethiopian culture in West Africa.)
Fernando R. Rogado Quintino. *Boletim Cultural da Guiné Portuguesa*, vol. 17, no. 65 (1962), p. 5-40; vol. 17, no. 66 (1962), p. 281-343; vol. 19, no. 73 (1964), p. 5-35; vol. 21, no. 81 (1966), p. 5-27.

Sustains the original theory that there are similarities between the Bijagós and the ancient Ethiopians. Rogado Quintino feels that the ancestors of the Bijagós as well as the Ethiopians lived in the Sahara and moved because of climatic changes. He uses photographs of sculptures and paintings to prove the point of a common cultural background.

187 **Woman power and initiation in the Bissagos islands.**
Danielle Gallois Duquette. *African Arts*, vol. 12, no. 3 (1979), p. 31-5.

Controverts Augusto Santos Lima's assertion (q.v.) that women's initiation ceremonies are copied from male ceremonies by women who want to assert themselves. Duquette maintains that women's rituals have an intermediary function between God and certain defunct male spirits.

Esculturas e objectos decorados da Guiné Portuguesa no Museu de Etnologia do Ultramar.
See item no. 490.

Traditional Bijagó statuary.
See item no. 507.

Fula

188   **Fulas do Gabú.** (Fulas of Gabú.)
Jose Mendes Moreira.   Bissau: Centro de Estudos da Guiné
Portuguesa, 1948. 322p. bibliog.
Gives a socio-economic-linguistic analysis of the Fula peoples residing in the eastern
region of Gabú.

189   **The villages of Gabú region and the situation of women and children: an
anthropological study of the environmental and social conditions of
village life.**
Pablo B. Eyzaguirre.   Bissau: UNICEF, 1987. 124p. 2 maps.
Studies the situation particularly of women and children in the north-eastern region
sharing a border with both Senegal and the Republic of Guinea. A savannah region, it
is sparsely populated mainly by the Islamized Fula and Mandinga peoples. Women in
both these groups are generally known to be subordinate to men in these relatively
highly stratified societies but Eyzaguirre shows differences depending upon groups and
upon the wealth of the family. The survey covers such areas as the organization of the
society, its government, family life, economy, religion, education, communications,
health care and cultural life. It is oriented towards ways in which UNICEF (United
Nations Children's Fund) and other international agencies, in collaboration with the
government, can assist the region. Eyzaguirre particularly recommends assistance to
women in food production as the best way to raise their income and better their health
and that of their children.

190   **Usos e costumes jurídicos dos Fulas da Guiné-Bissau.** (Legal customs
and practices among the Fulas of Guinea-Bissau.)
Artur Augusto da Silva.   Bissau: Imprensa Nacional, 1980. 3rd ed.
125p.
This is a reference work for the legal practices among the Fulas; it treats the penal
code, family law, inheritance and so on.

Paysanneries en attente: Guinée-Bissau.
See item no. 11.

**Fulas e Beafadas no Rio Grande no século XV: achegas para a etnohistória de
África Ocidental.**
See item no. 45.

Monjur: o Gabú e a sua história.
See item no. 47.

**Conflict, interaction and change in Guinea-Bissau: Fulbe expansion and its
impact, 1850-1900.**
See item no. 89.

The Balde family of Fuladu.
See item no. 112.

Mandinga

191 **Ecological perspectives on Mande population movements, commercial networks, and settlement patterns from the Atlantic wet phase (ca 5500-2500 BC) to the present.**
George E. Brooks. *History in Africa*, vol. 16 (1989), p. 23-40.
Argues that climate and geography were crucial in determining the migration, trade and settlement of Mande-speaking groups.

192 **Inquérito sócio-económico: sector de Mansabá.** (A socio-economic survey: Mansabá sector.)
Bente Topsøe-Jensen. Bissau: Programa de Desenvolvimento Rural Integrado de Zona I, 1988. 16p. map.
Presents a picture of seventy-nine villages in the sector of Mansabá in the region of Oio. There are data on population, religion, language, history, production patterns, artisanry, commerce, social infrastructure and the like. Data from the oral history of the area, populated mainly by Mandingas, show that the present sites of villages were chosen on the basis of the fertility of the area and that the motivation for re-location was a search for new lands to clear for agriculture. Most of the villages are of a mixed ethnic population. There is heavy seasonal migration, some within the country, but mainly to Senegal during the dry season.

193 **Manding: focus on an African civilization.**
International Conference on Manding Studies. London: School of Oriental and African Studies, University of London, 1972. 5 vols.
Provides the proceedings of the conference which has papers on the art, language, literature, games, social organization, religion, history and foreign relations of the Mandingas.

194 **Mandingas da Guiné Portuguesa.** (Mandingas of Portuguese Guinea.)
António Carreira. Bissau: Centro de Estudos da Guiné Portuguesa, 1947. 324p. map.
Describes the social, economic and political organization as interpreted by the then colonial administrator of one of the districts in which Mandingas lived. There are photographs and a grammar and dictionary of the Mandinga language.

195 **Usos e costumes jurídicos dos Mandingas.** (Mandinga legal customs and norms.)
Arturo Augusto da Silva. Bissau: Centro de Estudos da Guiné Portuguesa, 1969. 130p.
Describes the basic social and legal structures of Mandingas, including the organization of the family, the economy, property relations, inheritance and criminal law.

Paysanneries en attente: Guinée-Bissau.
See item no. 11.

Les Kaabunke: structures politiques et mutations.
See item no. 46.

Monjur: ୦ Gabú e a sua história.
See item no. 47.

The epic of Kelefa Saane as a guide to the nature of precolonial Senegambia society – and vice versa.
See item no. 48.

Portuguese adaptation to trade patterns: Guinea to Angola (1443-1640).
See item no. 70.

Conflict, interaction and change in Guinea-Bissau: Fulbe expansion and its impact, 1850-1900.
See item no. 89.

The villages of Gabú region and the situation of women and children.
See item no. 189.

A situação das mulheres Manjacas e Mandingas.
See item no. 198.

Manjaco

196 **Instituições de direito penal consuetudinário dos Manjacos de Caió.**
(Customary criminal law institutions among Caió Manjacos.)
Artur Martins de Meireles.   In: *Conferência Internacional dos Africanistas Ocidentais*, vol. 5. Lisbon: Junta de Investigações Coloniais, 1952, p. 393-429.
Surveys the notions of crime and punishment in Manjaco society in Caió which is in the region of Cacheu. Martins de Miereles collected his data through oral sources.

197 **La diaspora manjak en France: historique et organisation des caisses de villages.** (The Manjaco diaspora in France: history and organization of the village funds.)
A. Moustapha Diop.   *Présence Africaine*, nos 133-4 (1985), p. 203-13.
Delineates the integration of the Manjacos into the world economy beginning with the Atlantic trade. A map shows the strategic location of these people from the Cacheu region. Since the end of World War I they have immigrated to France. There have been three such waves of immigration since the end of World War II. The first stop for many before embarking for France is Senegal where communities of Guinean Manjacos live. P. Pélissier, in *Les paysans du Sénégal* (St-Yriex, 1966), discusses their situation. There are between 15,000 and 20,000 immigrants in France. Diop also focuses on two mutual funds set up for social security purposes and for funerals. See

also the author's thesis, *Tradition et adaptation dans un réseau de migration sénégalais: la communauté Manjak en France* (Tradition and adaptation in a pocket of Senegalese migration: the Manjaco community in France) (Paris, 1981).

198 **Situação das mulheres Manjacas e Mandingas.** (Situation of Manjaco and Mandinga women.)
Marianne Bull, preface by Prudence Woodford-Berger. Stockholm: University of Stockholm, 1987. 57p. 2 maps. bibliog.
The result of fieldwork in two *tabancas* (villages), this report covers a number of interesting areas including a description of agricultural practices, a typical woman's work-day, how women perceive their work, emigration and the political influence of women. The women of both ethnicities find their lives very hard because of the exhausting work-load. They share a number of common health problems, including spontaneous abortion.

199 **The land as body: an essay on the interpretation of ritual among the Manjaks of Guinea Bissau.**
Wim Van Binsbergen. *Medical Anthropology Quarterly*, vol. 2, no. 4 (1988), p. 386-401.
Explores the medical and therapeutic effectiveness of certain religious rituals. This is a fascinating attempt to understand the social significance of religion in the Manjaco community and to suggest an interpetation in terms of political economy.

200 **Vida social dos Manjacos.** (Manjaco social life.)
António Carreira. Bissau: Centro de Estudos da Guiné Portuguesa, 1947. 185p. map.
Carreira was also administrator of the district of Cacheu, an area which is populated mainly by Manjacos. This is his description of their social–economic organization. It includes photographs and drawings of many aspects of Manjaco life. Although dated and of uncertain accuracy, texts such as those written in the 1940s by colonial administrators and published by the Centro de Estudos da Guiné Portuguesa are still an important starting point for research. They must, however, be read with a critical eye.

Paysanneries en attente: Guinée-Bissau.
See item no. 11.

Panaria: cabo verdeano-guineense.
See item no. 505.

Others

201 **A família Cassanga.** (The Cassanga family.)
A. Nogueira. *Boletim Cultural da Guiné Portuguesa*, vol. 3, no. 10 (1948), p. 359-94.
An excerpt from the ethnographic survey (q.v.), this article describes family life near the Cassangas, a small group living near the border with the Casamance in Senegal.

202 **Apontamentos etnográficos sobre os Felupes de Suzana.** (Ethnographic notes on the Felupes of Suzana.)
António da Cunha Taborda. *Boletim Cultural da Guiné Portuguesa*, vol. 5, no. 18 (1950), p. 187-223; vol. 5, no. 20 (1950), p. 511-61.
Presents an ethnographic picture of the Felupes of the area of Suzana on the north-western border with Senegal. There were about 8,000 divided among 15 widely dispersed villages. Their basic diet was rice and fish, but they practised agriculture and livestock raising which meant that they were able to vary their diet. Land ownership was individualized and property passed through the male line. Many more details are offered.

203 **Arte Nalu.** (Nalu art.)
Artur Augusto da Silva. *Boletim Cultural da Guiné Portuguesa*, vol. 11, no. 44 (1956), p. 27-47.
Originally animists, the Nalus have become Islamized and this has affected their artwork. The sculpture for which they were duly renowned is giving way to decoration of the home. The main theme of the article is the connection between art, religion, the natural and the supernatural among these southernmost coastal peoples.

204 **Costumi e credenze dei Nalú.** (Religious habits and beliefs among the Nalu.)
M. Faccioli. *Missioni Cattoliche* (June 1958), p. 180-2.
Outlines very briefly some of the animist religious practices of the Nalu.

205 **Etno-história dos Banhans de Guiné.** (Ethno-history of the Banhans of Guinea.)
José D. Lampreia. *Garcia de Orta*, vol. 14, no. 4 (1966), p. 475-82.
Gives an overview of this small ethnic group which has been extinguishing itself through intermarriage. The English spelling of Banhan is Banyun.

206 **Rites et coutumes des Floup.** (Rituals and customs of the Felupes.)
J. Suyeux. *Connaissance du Monde*, vol. 40 (1962), p. 44-53.
Concentrates on initiation rites, including circumcision, and on practices associated with death among these peoples who live in north-western Guinea, along the coast and in the Casamance.

207 **Usos e costumes jurídicos dos Felupes da Guiné.** (Legal customs and practices among the Felupes of Guinea.)
Artur Augusto da Silva. *Boletim Cultural da Guiné Portuguesa*, vol. 15, no. 57 (1960), p. 7-52.

Studies such institutions as the family, royalty, property, inheritance, obligation, and the penal code among these northernmost peoples.

208 **Vida material dos Brames.** (Material life of the Brames.)
Francísco Mendes. *Boletim Cultural da Guiné Portuguesa*, vol. 3, no. 9 (1948), p. 81-113.

Extracted from the ethnographic survey of the colony (q.v.), this article gives much detail about the housing, clothing, industries and agriculture of these people who live in the southern part of the Cacheu region and elsewhere. The Brame, often referred to as Mancanha, immigrated significantly during colonial times (see also Cunningham).

209 **Who are the 'Cunantes' of Portuguese Guinea?**
W. A. A. Wilson. *Boletim da Sociedade de Geografia de Lisboa*, vol. 79, nos 4-6 (1961), p. 157-62.

Describes what little is known of the Mansoancas or Suas (the name they call themselves) who live near the town of Mansôa. There are two small groups, one of whom appears to be of Mandinga origin. Wilson thinks that they recently migrated from Gabú to Mansôa. The second group do not have a tradition of migration. According to Wilson, they resemble the Balanta. He gives maps denoting the territories and villages where they live.

Paysanneries en attente: Guinée-Bissau.
See item no. 11.

Dinah Salifou: roi des Nalous.
See item no. 44.

Fulas e Beafadas no Rio Grande no século XV: achegas para a etnohistória de África Ocidental.
See item no. 45.

Conflict, interaction and change in Guinea-Bissau: Fulbe expansion and its impact, 1850-1900.
See item no. 89.

Languages

General

210 Biafada, Pajade, and the 'Polyglotta'.
W. A. A. Wilson. *Journal of West African Languages*, vol. 14, no. 2 (1984), p. 61-80.

The *Polyglotta Africana* was a book written in 1854 by S. W. Koelle and relates to languages spoken along the West African coast. Wilson sees a remarkable similarity between how Beafada and Pajade, two closely related languages, are spoken today in Guinea-Bissau and how they were annotated in Koelle's book. He also relates them to two other languages, Konyagi and Tanda.

211 Cape Verde, Guinea-Bissau and São Tomé and Príncipe: the linguistic situation.
Jorge Morais-Barbosa. In: *Miscelânea Luso-Africana*, edited by Marius F. Valkhoff. Lisbon: Junta de Investigações Científicas do Ultramar, 1975, p. 133-51.

Argues that the *crioulo* of Guinea had a separate origin from that of Cape Verde; that it arose out of primary contacts between Guineans and Portuguese. This thesis contradicts that of Baltasar Lopes da Silva who attributes the primary influence to Cape Verdean and other colonists. It also contradicts that of Teixeira da Mota who suggests that Guinean and Cape Verdean creoles developed simultaneousiy.

212 Crioulos: estudos linguísticos. (Crioulos: linguistic studies.)
Edited by J. Morais-Barbosa. Lisbon: Academia Internacional da Cultura Portuguesa, 1967. 447p. bibliog.

This is a re-edition of articles published in the *Boletim da Sociedade de Geografia de Lisboa*. The first essay (p. 1-234) by F. Adolfo Coelho has remarks on Guinean *crioulo*. He places the language in a comparative context.

213 **Guiné-Bissau: Língua (Crioulo)-I.** (Guinea-Bissau: Language (Crioulo)-I.
Lisbon: Centro de Informação e Documentação, Amílcar Cabral
(CIDAC), 1990.
Contains a number of very important works on creole including B. Pinto Bull, *Le créole de la Guinée-Bissau* (Dakar, 1975); W. A. A. Wilson, *The crioulo of Guiné* (Johannesburg, 1962) (q.v.); Luigi Scantamburlo, *Gramática e dicionário da língua Criol da Guiné-Bissau* (Bologna, 1981) and *Gramática do crioulo da Guiné-Bissau* (Detroit, 1977).

214 **Nasality in Kriol: the marked case?**
Alain Kihm. *Journal of Pidgin and Creole Languages*, vol. 1, no. 1 (1986), p. 81-107.
Takes issue with Naro's hypothesis on the origins of Guinean crioulo and maintains that pidginization was by no means a necessary prerequisite for its formation. What follows is a technical discussion on the origins of the language. Kihm notes that the national liberation struggle acted as a stimulant to the diffusion of the language from towns into the countryside. Since the war, urbanization has accelerated its usage. In 1984, Kihm published 'Is there anything like de-creolization?' in the *York Papers in Linguistics*, no. 11 and 'Verbes et noms en kriol et en général', *Modèles Linguistiques*, vol. 6, no. 1.

215 **Notes sur le verbe FCA.** (Notes on the FCA verb.)
Geneviève N'Diaye-Correard. *Annales de la faculté des lettres et sciences humaines* (Université de Dakar), vol. 3 (1973), p. 177-92.
Discusses verb forms in Balanta. There are four forms: infinitive, subjunctive, indicative and conditional.

216 **O crioulo da Guiné-Bissau: filosofia e sabedoria.** (The creole of Guinea-Bissau: philosophy and wisdom.)
Benjamin Pinto Bull. Lisbon: Instituto de Cultura e Língua Portuguesa and Instituto Nacional de Estudos e Pesquisa, 1989. 352p. map.
In this work, the most complete study of the creole language of Guinea to date, the exposition is situated in a social, historical and cultural context and makes very interesting reading. Apart from a description of the evolution of the language, there is an entertaining collection of proverbs and stories as well as an important glossary of nearly 3,000 words and their translation into Portuguese and French.

217 **Outline of the Balanta language.**
W. A. A. Wilson. *African Language Studies*, vol. 2 (1961), p. 139-68.
Outlines Balanta which is a concord operating class language listed by Westermann among the West Atlantic group. There are a number of dialects, and the article is based on the one spoken in the north of the country. See D. Westermann and M. A. Bryan, *The languages of West Africa* (q.v.).

218   **Pequeno vocabulário do dialecto Pepel.** (A short dictionary of Papel.)
Henrique Lopes Cardoso.   *Boletim da Sociedade de Geografia de
Lisboa*, vol. 20, no. 10 (1902), p. 121-8.
Briefly describes the phonology and morphology of the language of the Papel who live
on the island of Bissau. There is a four-page dictionary of Papel–Portuguese.

219   **Portuguese creole dialects in West Africa.**
Nelson E. Cabral.   *International Social Science Journal*, vol. 36, no. 1
(1984), p. 76-85.
Links the three variants of Cape Verdean, Guinean and Casamance creole and
maintains that, despite their socio-geographical differences, they may be evolving
jointly. The article includes a good bibliography.

220   **Some sociolinguistic aspects of the crioulo variant in West Africa.**
Matthias Perl.   *Zeitschrift für Phonetik, Sprachwissenschaft und
Kommunikationsforschung*, vol. 37, no. 5 (1984), p. 606-10.
Outlines what is known about the origins of creole and programmes of research on the
language.

221   **Subsídios para o estudo da língua Manjáca.** (Notes for a study of the
Manjaco language.)
António Carreira, João Basso Marques, preface by Edmundo Correia
Lopes.   Bissau: Centro de Estudos da Guiné Portuguesa, 1947. 175p.
Presents a linguistic study of the Manjaco language and includes a Manjaco–Portuguese
dictionary.

222   **Talking drums in Guiné.**
W. A. A. Wilson.   *Estudos sobre a etnologia do Ultramar Português*,
vol. 3.   Lisbon: Junta de Investigações do Ultramar, 1963, p. 199-213.
Describes the language of the drums of Guinea, particularly the *bombolom* used by the
Manjacos, Balantas and others. The word means drum in *crioulo*.

223   **The crioulo of Guiné.**
W. A. A. Wilson.   Johannesburg, South Africa: Witwatersrand
University Press, 1962. 48p.
Analyses the vocabulary, phonology and syntax of the language. Wilson describes
three main dialects and sustains the argument that *crioulo* is a West African language
and not merely a corruption of Portuguese and African languages.

224   **The languages of West Africa.**
D. Westermann, M. A. Bryan.   London: Oxford University Press,
1952. 177p. bibliog.
Chapters one and two on the West Atlantic and Mande languages are the most
relevant. The authors group Manjaco, Papel, Brame, Beafada and Bijagó together
under one language group, Mandyak or Manjaco, because they see them as closely
related in structure and vocabulary. Banhan and Balanta are also classified as language

groups while Nalu and Fula are seen as a single unit. However, with the exception of Fula, the authors query these classifications.

225   **The use of African languages in Afro-European contacts in Guinea, 1440-1560.**
P. E. H. Hair.   *Sierra Leone Language Review*, vol. 5 (1966), p. 5-26.
Describes the Portuguese attitude toward African languages and their use of African interpreters in their trading relations with the peoples of the Upper Guinea Coast. Hair makes the point that the Portuguese had a linguistic advantage over other European powers by the sixteenth century.

226   **Uma primeira interrogação em crioulo à cultura popular oral.** (A first enquiry in crioulo into oral popular culture.)
Teresa Montenegro, Carlos de Morais.   *África, Literatura, Arte e Cultura*, vol. 2, no. 6 (1979), p. 3-13.
Defends creole as a language and as a means of identifying a culture. The authors explain their methodolgy in collecting stories, riddles, oral history and literature. There are excerpts from their book *'N sta li 'n sta la* (q.v.).

Dictionaries

227   **Lexique Mandinka–Français.** (Mandinga–French dictionary.)
Denis Creissels, S. Jaata, K. Jobaate.   *Mandekan*, no. 3 (1982), p. 1-207.
Also includes an introductory section on phonology and grammar. There is a map indicating the areas where the language is spoken.

228   **Petit dictionnaire étymologique du Kriol de Guinée-Bissau et Casamance.** (A small etymological dictionary of the creole of Guinea-Bissau and the Casamance.)
Jean-Louis Rougé.   Lisbon: INEP, 1988. 161p. bibliog. (Colecção 'Kacu Martel' no. 5)
This is an excellent addition to the research being carried out on the creole of Guinea-Bissau and the southern region of Senegal, the Casamance, which is closely connected in history and culture to Guinea. The dictionary traces the origins of the vocabulary of the language, while the introductory essay surveys the history, morphology, syntax and grammar. One of the first dictionaries of creole to appear was that by Luigi Scantamburlo, *Gramática e dicionário da língua Criol da Guiné-Bissau* (Bologna: Editrice Missionaria Italiana, 1981).

Mandingas da Guiné Portuguesa
See item no. 194.

O crioulo da Guiné-Bissau: filosofia e sabedoria.
See item no. 216.

Pequeno vocabulário do dialecto Pepel.
See item no. 218.

Subsídios para o estudo da língua Manjáca.
See item no. 221.

Grammar

229 **A Manjako grammar with special reference to the nominal group.**
Jan Karlik.   PhD thesis, School of Oriental and African Studies,
University of London, 1972. 309p. map. bibliog.
Outlines the phonology, orthography and grammar of the Manjaco language, one of
the North-West Atlantic group of languages. According to the author who cites
Bertrand Bocandé, the word Manjaco means 'I told you' in the language and was
repeated so often in conversation that foreigners identified speakers with this term.
The author also cites the work by Carreira and Basso Marques (q.v.), which he states
is full of mistakes and which he corrects. He also cites J. L. Doneux who compares
Manjaco phonology with that of Papel and Mancanha. The peoples speaking these
three languages have been considered to belong to a single group. Doneux's work, 'Le
manjaku, classes nominales et questions sur l'alternance consonantique', appears in *La
classification nominale dans les langues négro-africaines* (CNRS, Paris, 1967). Bertrand
Bocandé's work appears in *Bulletin de la Société de Géographie de Paris*, ser. 3, nos 11
and 12, 1849.

Mandingas da Guiné Portuguesa.
See item no. 194.

Religion

230 **A análise duma infelicidade: religião e interpretações pessoalistas.**
(Analysing a misfortune: religion and individualistic interpretations.)
Eve Crowley. *Soronda*, vol. 3 (1987), p. 112-26.
Analyses the various interpretations of a fatal road accident.

231 **As viagens do Bispo D. Frei Vitoriano Portuense a Guiné e a
cristianização dos reis de Bissau.** (The voyages of Bishop Vitoriano
Portuense and the Christianization of the kings of Bissau.)
Avelino Teixeira da Mota.   Lisbon: Junta de Investigações Científicas
do Ultramar, 1974. 188p. 9 maps.
Treats the Christianization of Bissau and the work of the missionaries. Some original
documents are included.

232 **Atlas missionário português.** (A Portuguese missionary atlas.)
Missão para o Estudo da Missionologia Africana, Centro de Estudos
Políticos e Sociais.   Lisbon: Junta de Investigações do Ultramar, 1962.
180p. 41 maps.
Presents graphs on all the various religions in all of the Portuguese colonies. The
statistics on Guinea are 26,000 Catholics, 182,000 Muslims and 237,000
animists. A second edition published in 1964 under the same title was written by A. da
Silva Rego and E. dos Santos.

233 **Colonisation et religion, depuis la première évangélisation jusqu'à la colonisation des peuples de Guinée-Bissau.** (Colonization and religion from the first missionary activities to the colonization of the peoples of Guinea-Bissau.)
Vasco Cabral. *Mondes en Développement*, vol. 17, no. 65 (1989), p. 233-7.

Maintains that Christian missionaries actively worked hand-in-glove with Portuguese attempts at colonizing Africa. In Guinea-Bissau, however, their efforts were in vain because of cultural resistance. Islam, on the other hand, posed problems for Portuguese penetration.

234 **Crenças e costumes dos indígenas da ilha de Bissau no século XVIII.** (Beliefs and customs of the peoples of the island of Bissau in the 18th century.)
António J. Dias, OFM. *Portugal em Africa*, vol. 2, no. 9 (1945), p. 159-65; no. 10 (1945), p. 223-9.

Based on an unpublished manuscript of a Franciscan priest, the text recalls the Franciscan missionary work in Bissau and other Portuguese enclaves. They were sent there from the monastery established in Cape Verde. Dias believes that the customs and beliefs related in the manuscript were still current among the Papéis in the 1940s. He describes ceremonies connected with the agricultural year, with war, with the death of a chief and so on.

235 **Di una breve relazione sulle missioni in terra di Guinea all'inizio de 1600.** (From a brief report on the missions in the land of Guinea at the beginning of the 17th century.)
Teobaldo Filesi. *Africa*, vol. 20, no. 1 (1965), p. 40-53.

Writes of the Jesuit attempt to Christianize the peoples of the Upper Guinea Coast in the early 1600s based on a manuscript by Fernam Guerreiro published in Lisbon in 1605. Guerreiro observes with trepidation the spread of Islam in these lands. Filesi notes the similarity of this manuscript with another in the Vatican archives. The two paint a portrait of the early missionary efforts. P. E. H. Hair says that he has translated certain of Guerreiro's documents into English, 'Jesuit documents on the Guinea of Cape Verde and the Cape Verde Islands', *History in Africa*, vol. 16 (1989).

236 **Guinea-Bissau: 44 estado africano que llega a la independencia.** (Guinea-Bissau: the 44th African state to become independent.)
Angel Santos Hernandez, SJ. *Revista de Politica Internacional*, no. 140 (1975), p. 191-223.

Although the text reviews the colonial past and national independence struggle, the main focus is on past missionary work, beginning with that of the Franciscans in 1460. Father Santos details the work of the Jesuits and all other following religious orders including contemporary ones. There is an impressive bibliography.

237 **História das missões católicas da Guiné.** (History of the Catholic missions in Guinea.)
Henrique Pinto Rema, OFM.   Braga, Portugal: Editorial Franciscana, 1982. 963p.

Goes into great detail regarding parochial matters. This is a comprehensive, monumental work on the Church in both colonial and postcolonial periods. It provides much historical and sociological insight.

238 **Mito, religion y pensamiento filosófico de Guinea-Bissau.** (Myth, religion and philosophical thought in Guinea-Bissau.)
Carlos Cardoso. *Enfoques*, no. 15 (1989), p. 1-77.

Confronts the question of how to classify the consciousness or systems of thought of Guineans. Cardoso explores such concepts as magic, myth, religion and philosophy which have alternately been applied by various writers to explain the ways in which the ethnic groups (there are more than twenty of them) think. He analyses and synthesizes all the bibliographies on the subject. He sees his purpose as bringing to light and systematizing as much information as possible on a topic which he believes to be of vital importance for understanding social reality in the country and for beginning to transform it.

239 **Monumenta missionária africana: África Ocidental.** (African missionary memorial: West Africa.)
Padre António Brásio.   Lisbon: Agência-Geral do Ultramar, 1952-88. 15 vols.

Compiles and annotates records and documents relating to Portuguese discoveries, settlements and missionary work. The first volume (published in 1952) begins in the year 1471 with the founding of the mission in Mina – in today's Ghana. In 1958, Brásio began a second series of volumes. Volume 1 of that series deals with the period 1342-1499 and the 'discoveries' and settlements of Cape Verde and Guinea-Bissau. There are documents pertaining to Guinea-Bissau spread throughout the fifteen volumes. Volumes 13-15 were published by the Academia Portuguesa da História and the Calouste Gulbenkian Foundation.

240 **No segredo das crenças: das instituições religiosas na Guiné Portuguesa.** (In the heart of beliefs: religious institutions in Portuguese Guinea.)
F. R. Rogado Quintino.   *Boletim Cultural da Guiné Portuguesa*, vol. 4, no. 15 (1949), p. 419-88.

Maintains that there is a unity of thought in Guinean animism and explains what he means by this. Rogado Quintino also compares some of the animist beliefs to European practices and superstitions. He states that Islam is growing and has converted nearly 50 per cent of the population. The Mandinga and Fula peoples are mainly responsible for the conversions of the Nalu and Beafada. The Christian population is mainly urban and assimilated.

241 **O islamismo na Guiné Portuguesa.** (Islam in Portuguese Guinea.)
José Júlio Gonçalves.   Lisbon: Agência-Geral do Ultramar, 1961.
215p. map. bibliog.
Presents an overview of the influence of Islam in the colony. The three major religions
are animism, Islam and Christianity. Gonçalves found that 63.5 per cent of the
population was animist, 36 per cent were Muslims and less than 1 per cent are Roman
Catholic. He predicted the eventual demise of animism in favour of Islam, Christianity
or atheism. He also noted the collaboration of Muslims with the Portuguese
administration. It is now estimated that more than 40 per cent of the population is
Muslim.

242 **O totemismo na Guiné Portuguesa.** (Totems in Portuguese Guinea.)
Fernando R. Rogado Quintino.   *Boletim Cultural da Guiné*
Portuguesa, vol. 19, no. 74 (1964), p. 117-28.
Describes animist beliefs in general and the use and meaning of totems in particular.

243 **The observance of All Souls' Day in the Guinea-Bissau region: a**
Christian holy day, an African harvest festival, an African New Year's
celebration, or all of the above (?)
George E. Brooks.   *History in Africa*, no. 11 (1984), p. 1-34.
Puts forward the important thesis that Guinean celebration of this and other
'European' festivals indicates a shared heritage of African and European beliefs that
antedates Christianity. The article describes in great detail creole society in the region.

The land as body: an essay on the interpretation of ritual among the Manjaks
of Guinea Bissau.
See item no. 199.

Arte Nalu.
See item no. 203.

Costumi e credenze dei Nalú.
See item no. 204.

Social Services, Health and Welfare

244 **Actividade da missão de combate as tripanosomiases da Guiné.**
(Activities of the mission to fight trypanosomiasis in Guinea.)
M. de Oliveira Lecuona. *Boletim Geral do Ultramar*, vol. 43, no. 501
(1967), p. 53-66.
Reports on the work of this public health service in the colony. It consisted of a
campaign against sleeping sickness, which reached approximately 75,000 people, and
against malaria, river blindness, leprosy and tuberculosis.

245 **A descent into African psychiatry.**
Joop T. V. M. de Jong. Amsterdam: Royal Tropical Institute, 1987.
214p. bibliog.
Describes not only the day-to-day experiences of this practising psychiatrist during his
stay in Guinea-Bissau but also outlines a mental health programme. Jong was in charge
of preparing such a programme for the country. He describes the state of medical
services in general. The book is also an exciting entry into the medical beliefs and
practices of a number of local cultures and an argument for interaction between
Western and local systems. Jong believes that a national system should be built upon
local services. He tells of building a small psychiatric centre which treats patients in
relation to their social setting. He supports his arguments by citing current schools of
anthropology 'which focus on an encounter with other cultures as a dialectic process
thereby enhancing western scientific discourse and possibly formulating criticism
concerning one's own society'.

246 **Anémias gravídicas nas indígenas da Guiné Portuguesa: inquérito nas tribos do interior.** (Anaemias in native pregnant women of Portuguese Guinea: survey of the savannah peoples.)
C. Trincão, L. T. de Almeida Franco, E. Gouveia. *Anais do Instituto de Medicina Tropical*, vol. 13, nos 1-2, (1956), p. 41-9.

Compares the number of anaemic pregnant women of the savannah areas with those of coastal regions and finds that 81.8 per cent of the savannah women are anaemic whereas 92 per cent of coastal women are. The difference is explained by basic diet since maize, the staple food of the interior, has more iron than rice, the basic food of the littoral peoples. The same authors worked with a study team of haematologists who made an extensive report of their work (especially on the RH(D) blood group) in the *Anais*, vol. 10, no. 2 (1953). In vol. 13, no. 1, the first case of river blindness is reported. In the same issue, there is an article on tapeworm and its treatment by M. de Oliveira Lecuona.

247 **Anthropometry and subsequent mortality in groups of children aged 6-59 months in Guinea-Bissau.**
L. Smedman, G. Sterky, L. Mellander, S. Wall. *American Journal of Clinical Nutrition*, vol. 46, no. 2 (1987), p. 369-73.

Studies of 2,228 children between the ages of 6 and 59 months from all over the country found a positive correlation between height and survival in Guinea-Bissau. Relatively short stature was linked to high mortality. Mortality due to an outbreak of measles was found to be twice as high in Bandim (Bissau) than in the rural areas. It is also to be noted that the rural areas surveyed did not have village health centres. See also L. Smedman, *The survival and growth of children: a community study in Guinea-Bissau* (Stockholm: Karolinska Institutet, 1986).

248 **A review of the distribution of snail hosts of bilharziasis in West Africa.**
M. A. Odei. *Journal of Tropical Medicine and Hygiene*, vol. 64, no. 4 (1961), p. 88-97.

Describes previous findings of the disease in the northern areas of Guinea-Bissau and Liberia. The author felt that it did not present a problem in Guinea at the time. The morbidity was low. There is a chart which outlines the suspected and known hosts in all countries in West Africa.

249 **Contribuição para o estudo do estado de nutrição dos povos da Guiné Portuguesa. III.** (Contribution to the study of the state of nutrition of the peoples of Portuguese Guinea. III.)
Carlos Santos Reis. *Anais do Instituto de Medicina Tropical*, vol. 21, nos 1-2 (1964), p. 123-30.

Studies the diets of mothers and children, in particular those of pregnant and breast-feeding mothers. The author administered a questionnaire which he reproduces in the article and gives the overall findings. He also describes the work of the Mother–Child Centre in Bissau during 1959. Other work by the author on student populations and on newborn infants is reported in volume 16 of the *Anais*.

Social Services, Health and Welfare

250 **Estudos sobre o tifo murino na Guiné Portuguesa.** (Studies on typhus in Portuguese Guinea.)
João Tendeiro. Bissau: Centro de Estudos da Guiné Portuguesa, 1950. 200p. bibliog. (Number 13).

This is one of a number of studies on diseases in the colony sponsored by the Centro de Estudos da Guiné Portuguesa. Another by the same author is on Q fever (1952). A third by Fernando da Cruz Ferreira is on sleeping sickness (1948). A fourth study by Carlos Lehmann de Almeida is *Filaríase e elefantíase na Guiné Portuguesa* (Filariasis and elephantiasis in Portuguese Guinea), 1952.

251 **Guiné-Bissau: Saúde-I and II.** (Guinea-Bissau: Health-I and II.)
Lisbon: Centro de Informação e Documentação, Amílcar Cabral (CIDAC), 1990.

Contains early government documents on health policy and projects including several statements by Dr Manuel Boal, the influential Minister of Health until the early 1980s. The second dossier collects miscellaneous official documents from the 1980s, including the proceedings of an interesting meeting between the Ministry of Public Health and 'traditional healers' in January–February 1989.

252 **Guiné Portuguesa: taxas regionais de natalidade e de mortalidade infantil.** (Portuguese Guinea: regional birth rates and infant mortality rates.)
António Carreira. *Boletim Cultural da Guiné Portuguesa*, vol. 7, no. 27 (1952), p. 533-44.

Notes the high incidence of infant mortality in the region of Cacheu, largely among the Manjaco population. The observation period was 31 months and was based on official registration records. The birth rate was 64.1 per 1000 inhabitants; the mortality rate for infants from 0 to 11 months old was 35 per cent, a figure which counteracted the high birth rate.

253 **Malnourished or overinfected: an analysis of the determinants of acute measles mortality.**
Peter Aaby. Copenhagen: Laegeforeningens Forlag, 1988. 28p.

Concludes that the clustering of measles cases and intensive exposure are the factors most involved in severe measles leading to death. Aaby argues also that there is no empirical evidence that severe malnutrition causes measles infection. The studies were mainly conducted in the Bandim section of Bissau and in Quínhamel in the Biombo region. The results of the study were published in *Boletim de Informação Sócio-económica*, vol. 5, no. 2 (1989). See also P. Aaby, J. Bukh, I. M. Lisse and A. J. Smits, 'Measles, mortality, state of nutrition and family structure: a community study from Guinea-Bissau', *Journal of Infectious Diseases*, vol. 147 (1983).

254 **Medicine in the service of colonialism: medical care in Portuguese Africa, 1885-1974.**
Martin Frederick Shapiro. PhD thesis, University of California, Los Angeles, 1983. 405p. bibliog.

Maintains that medical care was a tool of domination and social control in the Portuguese colonies. It was only after World War II, when criticized for the inadequacy of health care, that Portugal undertook some improvements including a vaccination campaign and a campaign to eliminate trypanosomiasis (see report by M. de Oliveira Lecuona). The author, a medical doctor as well as historian, critically describes the Portuguese efforts.

255   **O controlo do paludismo na ilha de Bissau: Guiné Portuguesa.** (The control of malaria in Bissau island: Portuguese Guinea.)
Manuel Correia Gardette.   *Boletim Cultural da Guiné Portuguesa*, vol. 28, no. 110 (1973), p. 197-212.
Notes the incidence of the disease and the campaign to fight it on the island.

256   **II plano quadrienal do desenvolvimento sócio-económico: sector de saúde.** (Second four-year plan for socio-economic development: the health sector.)
Gabinete de Estudos e Planeamento de Ministério de Saúde Pública. Bissau: Ministério de Saúde Pública, 1987. 66p. bibliog.
This sectoral study for the elaboration of a second development plan gives a valuable breakdown of the health facilities in the country in 1987. It also documents international aid to the sector and prospective projects.

257   **Practiche mediche di alcune tribu della Guinea Portoghese.** (Medical practices of some tribes of Portuguese Guinea.)
Antonio Scarpa.   In: *Estudos sobre a etnologia do ultramar português*, volume 1, compiled by António de Almeida. Lisbon: Junta de Investigações do Ultramar, 1960, p. 159-80.
Surveys the practices of the Bijagós, Fulas, Manjacos, Brames, Balantas and Felupes and invites more research into the complex range of techniques and medicines that he found.

258   **Practiche mediche della Guinea Portoghese prospettate in un documentario cinematografico.** (Medical practices in Portuguese Guinea shown in a documentary film.)
A. Scarpa.   *Rivista di Antropologia*, vol. 45 (1958), p. 227-41.
Describes the documentary film he made of different techniques and practices used by the peoples of Guinea-Bissau.

259   **Primary health care is not cheap: a case study from Guinea Bissau.**
Jarl Chabot, Catriona Waddington.   *International Journal of Health Services*, vol. 17, no. 3 (1987), p. 387-409.
Reports on a community health project in the southern region of Tombali which had as its aim to make villages self-reliant in primary health care. The project adopted a 'learning process approach' which allowed it to learn from experience and make changes. This differs sharply from a blueprint approach which lays out beforehand how to accomplish goals. Villagers had an intimate role in the process as health workers (and patients) and in the construction and financing of the health centres. The article discusses project evaluation and the preliminary results obtained. It also emphasizes the role of donor agencies.

Social Services, Health and Welfare

260 **Relatório de chefe da missão de combatente as tripanosomiases referente ao ano de 1972.** (The report of the chief of the mission to combat sleeping sickness during 1972.)
Manuel Correia Gardette. *Boletim Cultural da Guiné Portuguesa*, vol. 27, no. 108 (1972), p. 677-751.
Relates the efforts of the Portuguese to fight sleeping sickness. There are extensive tables. The report of the mission to combat leprosy is reported in A. Salazar Leite, J. V. Bastos da Luz, J. Pinto Nogueira, 'Relatório da missão de combate a lepra na Província Ultramarina da Guiné', *Anais do Instituto de Medicina Tropical*, vol. 10, no. 1 (1953), p. 79-163.

261 **Subsídio para o estudo da flora medicinal da Guiné Portuguesa.** (Notes for the study of herbal medicine in Portuguese Guinea.)
Rui Álvaro Vieira. Lisbon: Agência-Geral do Ultramar, 1959. 144p. bibliog.
Presents an important survey of a number of plants used as medicine in Guinea. The study does not pretend to be exhaustive. It gives not only the scientific names of the plants but their names in *crioulo* and in the languages of the principal ethnic groups using them. It also describes in detail how they are used. The study was also reported (by the same name) in *Boletim Geral do Ultramar* in volumes 32 (1956) and 33 (1957).

262 **The deadly trade: toxic waste dumping in Africa.**
Howard Schissel. *Africa Report*, vol. 33, no. 5 (1988), p. 46-9.
Reveals the dangers to Guinea-Bissau and other African countries of accepting toxic waste from US and European companies. The government of Guinea-Bissau had accepted a contract but international pressure, especially from the European Communities, forced it to cancel.

263 **The ecology of nutrition in seven countries of southern Africa and in Portuguese Guinea.**
Jacques M. May, MD, Donna L. McLellan, preface by L. W. Trueblood. New York: Hafner, 1971. 397p. 25 maps. bibliog.
Commissioned by the US Army Natick Laboratories, the last chapter of this study is on Guinea-Bissau. There is a general overview of the country and a section on agriculture as well as a study of diets and diseases. An extensive bibliography is also included. The authors describe the basic diet in the country as vegetable. They report that, under Portuguese colonialism, the average amount of food per person per day was about 530 grams or about 1855 calories. They felt that self-sufficiency was, on the other hand, clearly possible but required a better distribution of resources, crop protection and storage, rather than increased production.

264 **The epidemiology of cryptosporidiosis and other intestinal parasitoses in children in southern Guinea-Bissau.**
H. Carstensen, H. L. Hansen, H. O. Kristiansen, G. Gomme. *Transactions of the Royal Society of Tropical Medicine and Hygiene*, vol. 81, no. 5 (1987), p. 860-4.
Studies of children in eight villages found a high incidence of hookworm but no relationship between it and anaemia. It found *Cryptosporidium* oocysts in 3.7 per cent

of the children, especially among the group which kept cattle. The team also tested for other parasites.

265 The social epidemiology of Africa's AIDS epidemic.
Ann Larson. *African Affairs*, vol. 89, no. 354 (1990), p. 5-25.
Gives recent statistics on the incidence of the virus in African countries including Guinea-Bissau, and looks at the social context surrounding the spread of the virus. See also Phyliss J. Kanke, 'Human T-lymphotropic virus type and the human immuno-deficiency virus [HIV] in West Africa', *Science*, no. 236 (1987), p. 827-31.

266 Who puts the water in the taps?: community participation in Third World drinking water, sanitation and health.
Sumi Krishna Chauhan. London; Washington, DC: International Institute for Environment and Development, 1983. 88p. 4 maps. bibliog.
Chapter five describes the methodology of the Dutch project to establish wells in the southern regions of Quínara and Tombali. Unfortunately, not much information is given.

Congresso comemorativo do quinto centenário do descobrimento da Guiné.
See item no. 1.

Guinea-Bissau: politics, economics and society.
See item no. 4.

Annúario da Província da Guiné do anno de 1925.
See item no. 83.

Anuário da Guiné Portuguesa.
See item no. 84.

No governo da Guiné.
See item no. 97.

Politics

The PAIGC

267 **A mulher na família.** (The woman in the family.)
UDEMU.   Bissau: Editora NIMBA da Direcção-Geral da Cultura,
1988. 22p.

Prepared for the second congress of the women's organization, União Democrático de Mulheres (UDEMU), held in Bissau on 4-8 December 1988, the pamphlet gives a general overview of the role of the Guinean woman in society and her particular problems.

268 **Anteprojecto do programa e estatutos do PAIGC.** (Proposal of a
programme and statutes for the PAIGC.)
PAIGC.   Bissau: Secretariado do Conselho Nacional de Guiné, [n.d.].
27p. (Cadernos do 1.o Congresso Extraordinário, 8-14 Novembre de
1981, no. 2).

Presents for adoption at the congress the organizing rules and regulations of the party, including the mass organizations as well as their programmes of action. There were no major differences between them and those adopted in 1977 at the 3rd Party Congress.

269 **Anteprojecto de teses.** (Proposal of theses.)
PAIGC.   Bissau: Secretariado do Conselho Nacional de Guiné, [n.d.].
20p. (Cadernos do 1.o Congresso Extraordinário, 8-14 Novembro de
1981, no. 1).

Presents the 'teses' of the title, which are the guidelines or organizing principles of the party, for adoption by the congress. This congress was called one year after the 1980 seizure of power by the Army and João Bernardo Vieira. The congress reaffirmed the intention of the new leaders to follow in the footsteps of Amílcar Cabral and to consolidate the party. In the matter of development strategy, the congress reiterated the principles adopted by the 3rd Party Congress in 1977.

270 **A talk with a Guinean revolutionary.**
Ufahamu, vol. 1, no. 1 (1970), p. 6-21.
This is a very down-to-earth interview with Gil Fernandes, then representative of the PAIGC in Cairo and later to be Permanent Representative of the state of Guinea-Bissau to the United Nations. The interviewer touches many points such as the educational system in the liberated areas, and foreign relations of the party with various African governments, with the Swedish government and with the United States government.

271 **Contre l'ordre du monde, les rebelles: mouvements armés de libération nationale du tiers monde.** (Rebels against world order: Third World armed national liberation movements.)
Jean Ziegler. Paris: Éditions du Seuil, 1983. 385p.
Continuing his work on national liberation movements (q.v.), Ziegler focuses on three movements including the PAIGC. He recalls in some detail the history of the party until mid-1982 and concludes that its greatest strength and, at the same time, its greatest weakness is that it never developed into a vanguard party.

272 **Development and nationalism in Brazil and Portuguese Africa.**
Ronald H. Chilcote. *Comparative Political Studies*, vol. 1, no. 4 (1969), p. 501-25.
Classifies different types of nationalist movements and relates them to different kinds of developmental goals and activities. Chilcote characterizes early Guinean resistance to the Portuguese conquest at the turn of the century as indigenous nationalism and the nationalism of the PAIGC as Jacobin or radical nationalism.

273 **Development as liberation: policy lesson from case studies.**
Denis Goulet. *World Development*, vol. 7, no. 6 (1979), p. 555-9.
Develops the case of Guinea-Bissau as an example of a liberation movement that did not lose touch with its mass support. By the time the article was published, however, this was no longer the case.

274 **Estatutos do PAIGC.** (Statutes of the PAIGC.)
Segretariado-Geral do PAIGC. Bissau: Imprensa Nacional, 1977.
19p. (Cadernos do III Congresso).
This is a fundamental revision of the version adopted in 1973, which can be found in Luisa Teotonio Pereira (q.v.). One difference is that membership is defined as well as the conditions, rights and duties of membership. Up to 1977, membership had been open with no special procedures.

275 **Guinea-Bissau: a study of political mobilization.**
Lars Rudebeck. Uppsala, Sweden: Scandinavian Institute of African Studies, 1974. 252p. map. bibliog.
Advances the theory of the PAIGC as a party-state and documents its actions in the liberated zones of Guinea during the independence struggle. This original work is the first critical analysis of the party in English. Rudebeck witnessed the events and activities he describes at first hand. He spent time with the militants in 1970 and 1972

and his work draws upon an in-depth study of Amílcar Cabral's writings as well as his own conversations with the party leader.

276 **Guinea-Bissau since independence: a decade of domestic power struggles.**
Joshua B. Forrest. *Journal of Modern African Studies*, vol. 25, no. 1 (1987), p. 95-116.
Describes the decline of party influence in the Luís Cabral government. Forrest explains the 1980 *coup d'état* in terms of three power struggles centring on the party versus the government, Cape Verdeans versus Balantas and Luís Cabral versus João Bernardo Vieira. For a contrasting view, see Chabal among others. Forrest emphasizes the personal political power and acumen of Cabral's successor, 'Nino' Vieira, particularly his ability to maintain stability in a seriously divided country. However, he incorrectly asserts that Vieira began to refurbish the PAIGC in order to mould it into an effective instrument of control over government.

277 **Guiné-Bissau: Forças Armadas-I.** (Guinea-Bissau: Armed Forces-I.)
Lisbon: Centro de Informação e Documentação, Amílcar Cabral (CIDAC), 1990.
Contains the message of the Armed Forces to the 4th Party Congress in November 1986 and the manual for political education of the troops.

278 **Guiné-Bissau: Juventude I and Mulher I.** (Guinea-Bissau: Youth I and Woman I.)
Lisbon: Centro de Informação e Documentação, Amílcar Cabral (CIDAC), 1990.
The first file has the texts presented at the first national congress of the PAIGC youth corps, the Juventude Africana Amílcar Cabral (JAAC) and the text presented by them to the 4th Party Congress. There are also some children's books in the dossier. The second contains the documents of the first and second national congress of the Democratic Union of Women (União Democrático de Mulheres, UDEMU). There are also two studies of women – in the east and on Bolama.

279 **Guiné-Bissau: Partido I-IV.** (Guinea-Bissau: Party I-IV.)
Lisbon: Centro de Informação e Documentação, Amílcar Cabral (CIDAC), 1990.
The first dossier contains the party statutes of 1973 and a number of documents relating mainly to the 1973-76 period. There are several documents written by A. Pereira as Secretary-General of the party during 1976-80 and by Amílcar Cabral including the 'Party watchwords'. A dossier on the assassination of Cabral is included. The second file has communiqués from the Party Secretariat from Conakry during 1964-73 and the *textos políticos* by Cabral. There are also statements by João Bernardo Vieira and Aristides Pereira and party documents from the 4th Party Congress. The third file has documents from the 2nd, 3rd and Extraordinary congresses of 1973, 1977 and 1981 respectively. In the fourth file are the 1960 statutes of the Partido Africano da Independência (PAI), the original name of the PAIGC; the first edition of the *Manual político* (1972); and an assortment of other documents.

280   Guiné-Bissau: Trabalho/Sindicatos-I. (Guinea-Bissau: Work/Trade
       Unions-I.)
       Lisbon: Centro de Informação e Documentação, Amílcar Cabral
       (CIDAC), 1990.
Contains documents from 1977-78 of the trade union, União Nacional dos
Trabalhadores da Guiné (UNTG).

281   Manual político do P.A.I.G.C. (Political manual of the PAIGC.)
       PAIGC. Lisbon: Edições Maria da Fonte, 1974. 2nd ed. 109p.
       (Colecção 'Libertação Nacional').
Consists mainly of 24 lessons taken from the various speeches and writings of Amílcar
Cabral. The text represents the party line on a number of crucial questions such as
whether there exist contradictions between Guinean peasants and their leaders and
whether the liberation struggle was a class struggle or simply a national independence
movement. It also represents party thinking on African unity and the African
revolution.

282   Marxism and ethno-nationalism in Guinea-Bissau.
       Judson M. Lyon. *Ethnic and Racial Studies*, vol. 3, no. 2 (1980),
       p. 156-68.
Argues that Cabral and the PAIGC leaders underestimated the strength of ethnic
attachments in the country. Lyon assesses the ethnic bases of the different nationalist
groupings.

283   O PAIGC foi, é e será o nosso guia. (The PAIGC was, is and will be
       our guide.)
       João Bernardo Vieira. Bissau: INACEP, 1985. 28p. (Edição do
       Departamento de Informação, Propaganda e Cultura do Comité
       Central do PAIGC. Série: Discursos e Reflexões).
This is the speech given by Vieira in his official role of president of the national council
of Guinea, the then highest body of the PAIGC, on the occasion of the second
extraordinary session of the council. Before November 1980, the PAIGC consisted of
two national councils, one for Guinea and the other for Cabo Verde. After the 'events'
of 14 November 1980 when Vieira seized power in Guinea, the national council of
Cabo Verde broke away to create a new party, the Partido Africano da Independência
de Cabo Verde (PAICV). In this speech given in May 1981, Vieira reaffirms the
continuity of the PAIGC in Guinea. The task of this session of the council was to take
the decisions necessary for convoking the party congress in November 1981 which
established the basis for the operation of the PAIGC exclusively in Guinea.

284   Os congressos da FRELIMO, do PAIGC e do MPLA: uma análise
       comparativa. (The congresses of FRELIMO, PAIGC and MPLA: a
       comparative analysis.)
       Luís Moita. Lisbon: CIDAC, 1979. 68p. (Colecção África em Luta –
       Nova Série 1).
Compares the 1977 party congresses of the three parties from Mozambique, Guinea-
Bissau and Angola with previous congresses and analyses their different resolutions on

objectives, the role of classes, the stages of revolution, the vanguard and development strategy. Moita quotes extensively from party documents. This is a good introduction to the study of party documents.

285 **Political mobilization for development in Guinea-Bissau.**
Lars Rudebeck. *Journal of Modern African Studies*, vol. 10, no. 1 (1972), p. 1-18.

The result of a research trip in 1970, this article describes in some detail the structure and policies of the PAIGC in the liberated areas. The author touches upon the delicate but fundamental question of confidence between the leadership and the 'masses'. He sees the PAIGC as an example of relatively successful political mobilization, a concept which he later develops in his book (q.v.).

286 **Political will: the key to Guinea-Bissau's 'alternative development strategy'.**
Denis Goulet. *International Development Review*, vol. 19, no. 4 (1977), p. 2-8.

Looks specifically at the role of the PAIGC as a mobilizer of people for 'genuine development' which Goulet distinguishes from high economic growth. Genuine development improves the lives of the majority of people. Goulet outlines the enunciated strategy of the PAIGC in this regard.

287 **Practice and theory: Guinea-Bissau and Cape Verde.**
Basil Davidson. In: *Africa: problems in the transition to socialism*, edited by Barry Munslow. London: Zed Books, 1986, p. 95-113.

Reminds the reader that the anti-colonial liberation struggle was not for socialism *per se* but rather for the improvement of material conditions and the removal of the Portuguese. Davidson feels that the struggle itself imposed a democratic practice yet it did not prepare the way for an economic transformation based on agriculture. Instead, the capital city, Bissau, swallowed the rural areas even though there were PAIGC leaders, including the Planning Commissar, Vasco Cabral, who warned that this might happen. Davidson assesses in this article what is left of the PAIGC ideals. In a very interesting article, R. Buijtenhuijs examines Davidson's concept of 'movements of maturity' and asks whether the PAIGC met its various criteria. Buijtenhuijs reviews Davidson's own analyses and that of most subsequent writers and presents a very conscientious critique. See 'People's war in Africa: the quest for "movements of maturity"', *Africa*, vol. 59, no. 3 (1989), p. 381-90.

288 **Primeiro Congresso das Mulheres para o enquadramento da mulher no desenvolvimento: estatutos e programa.** (The First Women's Congress for the integration of women in the development process: statutes and programme.)
UDEMU. Bissau: Edições Comissão Nacional das Mulheres da Guiné, 1982. 20p.

Documents the women's movement within the framework of the PAIGC and the creation of the União Democrática das Mulheres (UDEMU). The statutes set out the organization's constitution while the programme outlines its goals in terms of social, economic and civil rights.

289 **Report of the Supreme Council of the Struggle to the Third Congress of PAIGC.**
PAIGC. London: Mozambique, Angola and Guiné Information Centre, 1978. 63p. (State Papers and Party Proceedings, series 1, no. 3).
This is the fundamental document outlining party and thus government strategy for both Guinea-Bissau and Cape Verde in the early post-liberation struggle era. It was the basis for most of the positive evaluations of the PAIGC in the 1970s. The basic strategy was reaffirmed in the 1st Extraordinary Party Congress of November 1981 but drastically revised in the 4th Party Congress of November 1986.

290 **Revolutionary democracy in Africa: the case of Guinea-Bissau.**
Patrick Chabal. In: *Political domination in Africa: reflections on the limits of power*, edited by P. Chabal. Cambridge, England: Cambridge University Press, 1986, p. 84-108.
Whereas in his book on Cabral (q.v.) Chabal assesses the successes of the PAIGC, in this chapter he looks at its failures which he sees as similar to those of other postcolonial African states. These are the failures to underwrite the costs of rural development and to engage in dialogue with rural society. He posits a dichotomy between 'the state' and rural society.

291 **Segundo Congresso, UDEMU: resoluções gerais.** (Second Congress of UDEMU: general resolutions.)
UDEMU. Bissau: UDEMU, 1988. 15p.
Presents the resolutions approved by the second congress of the women's organization held in December 1988. One resolution notes the difficulty UDEMU has of receiving international aid because it is an auxiliary organization of the party rather than a governmental agency. Many of the resolutions are critical of government policy and call for changes in policy if not strategy. In the field of education, the creation of parents' associations is recommended. In the field of public health, a committee on such practices as circumcision is suggested. The protection of women's hereditary and land rights and the encouragement of women's productive and commercial associations are among the suggestions made.

292 **Statuts, revisés et approuvés par le II. Congrès du parti.** (Statutes, revised and approved by the 2nd Party Congress.)
PAIGC. Conakry, Republic of Guinea: PAIGC, Comité Executif de la Lutte, 1973. 13p.
Lists the basic statutes of the party which were adopted by the 2nd Party Congress held in July 1973. They represent a revision of the original statutes adopted in 1962. See PAIGC, 'Statuts et programme' (Conakry: PAIGC, 1962).

293 **Teses para o IV Congresso do PAIGC.** (Theses for the Fourth Congress of the PAIGC.)
Comité Central do PAIGC. Bissau: Edição do Departamento de Informação, Propaganda e Cultura do Comité Central do PAIGC, 1986. 40p.

Presents the four theses or themes of the 4th Party Congress. The first reaffirms the party as the guiding force in Guinean society and as a vanguard party. The second defines its political role. The third develops the idea of the relationship between national unity and national development and the need for internal cohesion within the party. The last spells out the development strategy of the PAIGC. There was an internal struggle over the role of the state in the economy. Those in favour of economic liberalization won.

294 **The level of political consciousness of the younger generation in Guinea-Bissau.**
E. A. Shauro. *Africa in Soviet Studies* (1983), p. 104-18.

Cites the efforts of the PAIGC to educate young people politically in the early years after independence, and assesses the results. Over a two-month period in December 1979 and January 1980 the author conducted a field survey of the political consciousness of young people. It is interesting to note that he found few people who identified socialism with people's power or ownership of the means of production. Most identified it with ending the exploitation of man by man.

295 **The PAIGC: the dilemmas of continuity.**
Patrick Chabal. *West Africa*, no. 3309 (22-29 December 1980), p. 2593-4.

Notes the efforts by the head of state, João Bernardo Vieira, and his supporters to portray themselves as the heirs of Amílcar Cabral in order to justify their seizure of power.

296 **The socialist ideal in Africa: a debate.**
Carlos Lopes, Lars Rudebeck. Uppsala, Sweden: Scandinavian Institute of African Studies, 1988. 27p. bibliog.

Consists of a polemic between Lopes and Rudebeck on the reasons why it has not been possible to construct socialism in Africa. Lopes feels that socialist ideologies in Africa have been weak, but his main point concerns the contradiction in the conditions under which the development of African societies *must* proceed. In spite of socialist goals, capitalism offers the best means for increasing food production, establishing industries, opening schools and hospitals, building houses and roads. Rudebeck challenges Lopes' pessimism about no real alternative to capitalist development in the short and medium term. He proposes an alternative development strategy, based on building people's power through a democratization of African power structures. Rudebeck argues the close connection between democracy and the development of productive forces.

297 **The state of Guinea-Bissau: African socialism or socialism in Africa?**
Peter Aaby.   Uppsala, Sweden: Scandinavian Institute of African
Studies, 1978. 35p. bibliog. (Research Report no. 45).
Looks critically at PAIGC strategy in light of the socialist ideal. Aaby concludes that
there are no specific predetermined conditions which can move a country towards
socialism but he points out a number of necessary conditions such as the state being in
the hands of a revolutionary party. Aaby sets his analysis in a critical comparative
context.

298 **Tribe, class and nation: revolution and the weapon of theory in Guinea-
Bissau.**
Jay O'Brien.   *Race and Class*, vol. 19, no. 1 (1977), p. 1-18.
Views the task before the PAIGC as one of providing proletarian leadership in a
country without a developed working class. The article is a class analysis of the
liberation struggle.

Guinea-Bissau: politics, economics and society.
See item no. 4.

Guinea-Bissau: from liberation struggle to independent statehood.
See item no. 306.

Historical dictionary of the Republic of Guinea-Bissau.
See item no. 572.

The government

299 **Assembleia Nacional Popular, Guiné-Bissau: discurso pronunciado pelo
Secretário-Geral do PAIGC, Camarada Aristides Pereira.** (National
Popular Assembly, Guinea-Bissau: speech by the Secretary-General of
the PAIGC, Comrade Aristides Pereira.)
Aristides Pereira.   [n.p.]: PAIGC, [n.d.]. 14p. (Edição do GADCG).
This is the speech given by the Party leader to open the historic first session of the
National Popular Assembly on 23 September 1973 in the liberated region of Boé, on
the border with the Republic of Guinea, before the war for national liberation had
ended. On 24 September, the Assembly declared the sovereign state of the Republic of
Guinea-Bissau. In the speech, Pereira reminds the Assembly of the reasons for the war
for independence and details the course of the struggle.

300 **Conditions of development and actual development strategy in Guinea-Bissau.**
Lars Rudebeck.   In: *Problems of socialist orientation in Africa,* edited by Mai Palmberg. Uppsala, Sweden: Scandinavian Institute of African Studies, 1978, p. 164-81.

Examines the objective economic conditions of the newly independent state and shows that it continues to depend upon food and other imports, foreign aid and credits. Rudebeck argues that in order for the government to pursue an independent strategy of development based upon agriculture it will need to create 'a political organization and a state apparatus based upon and supported by the broad masses of people'. See also 'Socialist-oriented development in Guinea-Bissau' by Rudebeck in *Socialism in sub-Saharan Africa: a new assessment,* edited by Carl G. Rosberg and T. M. Callaghy (Berkeley, California, 1979), in which h.· argues that there is a contradiction between a strategy based on internal development and the country's continued dependence on foreign help.

301 **Coup for continuity?**
Patrick Chabal.   *West Africa,* no. 3311 (12 January 1981), p. 62-3.

The third part of the series of articles on the *coup d'état* of November 1980. Chabal calls the seizure of power the 'rice coup' because of the scarcity of food in the country. This article discusses rice production and the distorted development strategy under Luís Cabral.

302 **Ethnie, état et rapports de pouvoir en Guinée-Bissau.** (Ethnicity, state and power relations in Guinea-Bissau.)
Carlos Lopes.   Geneva, Switzerland: Institut Universitaire d'Études du Développement, 1983. 2nd ed. 99p. 7 maps. bibliog. (Itinéraires, Notes et Travaux, no. 22).

Contrasts what the author calls 'ethnic rationality' with that of the modern state to explain the contradiction between the majority of people in Guinea and the PAIGC party-state. The work contains much useful general information as well as this provocative thesis.

303 **Growing from the grass roots: the state of Guinea-Bissau.**
Basil Davidson.   London: Committee for Freedom in Mozambique, Angola and Guiné, [n.d.]. 20p. map.

Documents the birth of the independent government of Guinea on 24 September 1973. This is a propaganda tract written in response to Britain's declaration of non-recognition of the new state in spite of the UN General Assembly's recognition in November 1973. The text includes the declaration of sovereignty by the National Popular Assembly and the 1973 constitution adopted by the Assembly.

304 **Guinea-Bissau.**
Amnesty International.   In: *Amnesty International Report, 1989.*
London: Amnesty International Publications, 1989, p. 57-8.

Reports on the situation of political prisoners who were tried in July 1986 with regard to their connection with the conspiracy to overthrow the government. Thirty were still reported to be in jail at the time of writing but most had been pardoned by mid-1990. There was also evidence of torture and death while in jail.

305 **Guinea-Bissau: five years of independence.**
Tony Hodges. *Africa Report*, vol. 24, no. 1 (1979), p. 4-9.
Surveys the progress of the newly independent government from 1973 to 1978 and includes some basic data on trade and other areas. See Adelino Gomes, 'Guinea-Bissau: Cabral's dream', *Africa Report*, vol. 31, no. 1 (1986), for a brief description of the political and economic trajectory of the country since independence.

306 **Guinea-Bissau: from liberation struggle to independent statehood.**
Carlos Lopes, preface by Lars Rudebeck, translated by M. Wolfers.
Boulder, Colorado; London: Westview Press and Zed Books, 1987.
185p. bibliog.
Casts the major contradiction between state and peasants in the country as a clash of mentalities or rationalities extending Amílcar Cabral's dichotomy of horizontal versus vertical societies and his emphasis on the cultural component of the national liberation struggle. Lopes offers a synopsis of Cabral's political thought and especially the concepts of nation-class and the historical role of the petty bourgeoisie. He analyses the major problems confronting the Guinean state in the late 1970s and early 1980s. In the final section he compares the Guinean experience to that of other nations.

307 **Guinea-Bissau: people's elections.**
Basil Davidson. *People's Power*, no. 6 (1977), p. 27-31.
Gives the voting statistics in the second elections in the country and describes the electoral process.

308 **Guinea-Bissau's struggle: past and present.**
Ronald H. Chilcote. *Africa Today*, vol. 24, no. 1 (1977), p. 31-9.
Interviews the new head of state, Luís Cabral, on the goals of the new nation. The interviews took place about one year after independence. Chilcote also reviews some of the early decisions of the new government. This makes very interesting reading in the light of later policies.

309 **Guiné-Bissau: Direitos Humanos-I.** (Guinea-Bissau: Human Rights-I.)
Lisbon: Centro de Informação e Documentação, Amílcar Cabral
(CIDAC), 1990.
Contains the Amnesty International report on the country of July 1986.

310 **Guiné-Bissau: Estado-I and II.** (Guinea-Bissau: State-I and II.)
Lisbon: Centro de Informação e Documentação, Amílcar Cabral
(CIDAC), 1990.
Both files contain clippings on the *coup d'état* of 14 November 1980. There are also documents relating to the event. There is a third dossier with the same title: *Guiné-Bissau: Estado I*. It contains early National Popular Assembly documents including the proclamation of statehood in September 1973. There are also speeches by Luís Cabral and A. Pereira to the I Legislature in 1973 and to the II Legislature in 1978. A number

of Council of State documents from 1976 and other miscellaneous items are included, as are two articles in English on the nature of the state by Lars Rudebeck.

311 **Guiné-Bissau: Geral-I.** (Guinea-Bissau: General-I.)
Lisbon: Centro de Informação e Documentação, Amílcar Cabral (CIDAC), 1990.

Contains eleven documents, among which are included the special issue of *Afrique-Asie*, no. 66, 23 September 1974 on the independence of Guinea-Bissau; and Jennifer Davis's pamphlet, *The Republic of Guinea-Bissau: triumph over colonialism* (New York, [n.d.]).

312 **Guiné-Bissau: três anos de independência.** (Guinea-Bissau: three years of independence.)
Luisa Teotonio Pereira, Luís Moita. Lisbon: CIDAC, 1976. 151p.
(Colecção África em Luta).

Provides an excellent source of information on the political organization of the country in the first three years of independence. The authors travelled to Guinea-Bissau on a number of visits as members of a Portuguese solidarity group, the Centro de Informação e Documentação Amílcar Cabral (CIDAC). They present a wealth of data on the economy, agriculture, infrastructure, industry, transport, health, education and foreign relations. The overall tone is highly sympathetic and optimistic, reflecting the general feeling in the country at the time. The appendices contain the PAIGC statutes; the 1973 constitution of the country; the resolutions of the National Popular Assembly; a listing of the members of the Council of State and the Commissariats; the administrative divisions within the country; and foreign embassies.

313 **Guinée-Bissau, Cape-Vert: histoire et politique.** (Guinea-Bissau, Cape Verde: history and politics.)
Patrick Chabal. *Le Mois en Afrique*, vol. 16, nos 190-1 (1981), p. 119-39.

Summarizes the history of the two newly independent states from 1974 to 1980. Chabal also examines the 1980 *coup d'état* in Guinea-Bissau and refutes the claim that it was anti-Cape Verdean or that internal party divisions were racially based. See also Bollinger and Forrest.

314 **Jangue Jangue: la politique par le bas en Guinée-Bissau.** (Jangue Jangue: politics from below in Guinea-Bissau.)
J. T. V. M. de Jong. *Politique Africaine*, vol. 28 (28 December 1987), p. 108-12.

Analyses the social import of the recent grass-roots rebellion of young, originally female, Balantas against the elder male power structure. Often characterized as a purely religious phenomenon, Jong sees the Jangue Jangue movement as also being a popular political movement and he records the government's efforts to repress it. According to on-site observers in late 1989, the movement was still active, although underground.

315 **Kandjaja, Guinea-Bissau 1976-86: observations on the political economy of an African village.**
Lars Rudebeck. *Review of African Political Economy*, vol. 41 (1988), p. 17-29.
Shows the abandonment of a village in the northern part of the country by both party and government. Rudebeck argues that the village power structure has drawn its strength and support from the pre-war social structure, and that the village is involved in a dynamic that has little to do with the transition to socialism which was part of the PAIGC ideology. There is a brief note comparing the situation in Guinea-Bissau to that of Mueda in northern Mozambique.

316 **La Guinée-Bissau: d'Amílcar Cabral à la reconstruction nationale.**
(Guinea-Bissau: from Amílcar Cabral to national reconstruction.)
Jean-Claude Andreini, Marie-Claude Lambert. Paris: Éditions l'Harmattan, 1978. 213p. map. bibliog.
One of the first evaluations of the newly independent government, this book was written by two individuals who had worked with the government in a number of capacities for more than a year and a half. It is thus an invaluable source of information on government policy in such areas as the economy, health, education and the judicial system. The first three chapters briefly survey the political organization. The authors place great emphasis on popular mobilization and political participation as a key to rural development: their view of the PAIGC in this regard is highly sympathetic, as is that of most of those writing on this early period. Readers of German might want to consult Uta Gerweck, *Guinea-Bissao: nationaler Befreiungskampf und kollectiver Fortschritt* (Guinea-Bissau: national liberation struggle and collective progress) (Nuremburg, 1974).

317 **La Guinée-Bissau indépendent et l'heritage de Cabral.** (Independent Guinea-Bissau and the Cabral legacy.)
R. Buijtenhuijs. *Kroniek van Afrika*, vol. 5, no. 2 (1975), p. 153-66.
One of the first authors to contrast the development strategy of the leaders of Guinea-Bissau with the writings and teachings of Cabral, Buijtenhuijs makes the point that Cabral had little to say about the post-independence era. Nonetheless, the author finds the early policies of Luís Cabral's régime to be progressive at best, but not revolutionary.

318 **Party politics behind Guinea-Bissau coup.**
Patrick Chabal. *West Africa*, no. 3308 (15 December 1980), p. 2554-6.
The first of a three-part series, this article looks at the splits within the PAIGC and the government, including the army, that precipitated the coup. Chabal finds that antagonism between Guineans and Cape Verdeans was not the primary cause.

319 **Party, state and socialism in Guinea-Bissau.**
Patrick Chabal. *Canadian Journal of African Studies*, vol. 17, no. 2 (1983), p. 189-210.
Discusses the difficulties of the transition to socialism in the country. Chabal measures the régime of Luís Cabral against the standard of the thoughts and ideals of Amílcar Cabral. He judges it to have failed.

320 **Problèmes de pouvoir populaire et de développement: transition difficile en Guinée-Bissau.** (Problems of popular power and development: the difficult transition in Guinea-Bissau.)
Lars Rudebeck. Uppsala, Sweden: Scandinavian Institute of African Studies, 1982. 65p. map. bibliog.

Updates the excellent analysis of the party-state in Guinea presented in his first book. This work explains the reasons behind the *coup d'état* of November 1980 and is the only critical analysis of the Extraordinary Congress of the PAIGC in November 1981, called to legitimize the sudden change of régime. Rudebeck examines such questions as the character of the state and its relationship to the majority of people in the country. He also raises the ethnic issue in relation to certain factions of the PAIGC and members of the government. Most importantly, he challenges the assumption that a progressive non-capitalist development of the country depends upon the political triumph of a 'revolutionary vanguard'. Rudebeck explores instead the concept of people's power, that is, the primacy of popular institutions over élitist and vanguard ones.

321 **Reconstruction in Guinea-Bissau: from revolutionaries and guerrillas to bureaucrats and politicians.**
Boniface I. Obichere. *A Current Bibliography on African Affairs*, vol. 8, no. 3 (1975), p. 204-19.

Outlines the pitfalls in the transition from nationalist movement to statehood including the loss of party cadres to the bureaucracy and embassies abroad; the use of Portuguese collaborators in the government; the continuation of an élitist educational system; the departure of white settlers and their expertise; the flight of capital; the resettlement of immigrants; the balance-of-payments deficits; and so on. The fact that Obichere put his finger on exactly those problems that confounded the government makes this article important reading.

322 **State, peasantry, and national power struggles in post-independence Guinea-Bissau.**
Joshua B. Forrest. PhD thesis. University of Wisconsin, Madison, Wisconsin, 1987. 792p.

Argues that while the newly independent state distanced itself politically from rural society, it still sought to 'capture' it in order to expand its power. Peasantries, however, resisted the state, and power struggles engulfed it. Forrest describes the conflicts in detail: between party and government, between the army and the party, and within the party itself. He sees conflict as having an ethnic as well as a non-ethnic basis, and he sees peasant struggle as arising from a peasant mode of production.

323 **Strategy in Guinea-Bissau.**
Luís Cabral. London: Mozambique, Angola and Guiné Information Centre, 1979. 30p. (State Papers and Party Proceedings, series 3, no. 3).

This is Cabral's state-of-the-union message to the National Popular Assembly in May 1979. Originally in creole, the text was translated into Portuguese and then into English. In it, Cabral announced the setting up of a Commission to revise the 1973 Constitution. One aspect that needed revision was the regulation of land rights. Cabral stated that some people were just taking the land and he felt that the state ought to be allowed to collect revenue from land concessions. It is interesting to note that

President Vieira also announced (in 1990) the setting up of a constitutional commission and the need for a new law governing land concessions.

324 **The 1980 coup in Guinea-Bissau.**
  Barry Munslow. *Review of African Political Economy*, no. 21 (1981), p. 109-13.
Discusses the motivations behind the 1980 seizure of power by the army. Munslow also examines the reaction of the Cape Verdeans to the events.

325 **The food crisis and the socialist state in lusophone Africa.**
  Rosemary E. Galli. *African Studies Review*, vol. 30, no. 1 (1987), p. 19-44.
Reviews and criticizes agricultural, monetary and trade policies in the five lusophone African countries and sees them as the principal causes of the decline in the economies of these countries. Galli blames the social divide between peasants and the ruling classes – which had its origins in Portuguese colonialism – for the governments' bias against smallholder agriculture, itself reinforced by the adoption of socialist agricultural policies.

326 **The peasantry, the party and the state in Guiné-Bissau.**
  Jocelyn Jones. DPhil thesis, University of Oxford, 1987. 686p.
Describes the disaffection of peasants from the PAIGC and the government from the end of the national liberation struggle up until 1980. Jones ascribes this to a differing and subsequently opposed set of material and political interests. She shows, through a detailed analysis of policies and institutions, how the interests of the urban ruling class came to dominate. This analysis was incorporated in Galli and Jones, 1987 (q.v.).

327 **The political economy of Guinea-Bissau: second thoughts.**
  Rosemary E. Galli. *Africa*, vol. 59, no. 3 (1989), p. 371-80.
Recapitulates the analysis of Galli and Jones (1987) and extends it in the light of new data and new interpretations regarding the failure of the government to move toward improving productive conditions for the majority of the country's farmers. A revised and amplified version of the article appeared in *Soronda*, no. 8 (1989) under the title 'Estado e sociedade na Guiné-Bissau' (State and society in Guinea-Bissau). In this version Galli elaborates the notion of a statist, mercantilist model of development.

328 **The Republic's motto: unity, struggle, progress.**
  Vasco Cabral. *World Marxist Review*, vol. 17, no. 2 (1974), p. 112-16.
Describes the structure and history of the new government. Vasco Cabral is one of the leading members of the PAIGC. In the same issue, Vladimir Shundeyev interviews other government officials: see 'Outlines of the New Way', p. 105-12.

Guinea-Bissau: politics, economics and society.
See item no. 4.

Transición histórica y etnicidad en Guinea-Bissau.
See item no. 174.

Historical dictionary of the Republic of Guinea-Bissau.
See item no. 572.

Legal System

329 **A constituição de 24 de Setembro de 1973 da República da Guiné-Bissau.**
(The 24 September 1973 Constitution of the Republic of Guinea-Bissau.)
António Duarte e Silva.   Final thesis for the postgraduate course in Juridical-Political Sciences, Faculty of Law, University of Lisbon, 1980. 450p.

Analyses each article of the first constitution of the state of Guinea-Bissau and also the law establishing the governing institutions after the 14 November 1980 *coup d'état*. One of the annexes presents the hotly contested constitution of 10 November 1980 which was one of the causes of the coup. Another much shorter commentary on the 1973 Constitution can be found in André Durieux, *Les institutions organiques de 1975 du Cap Vert et de la Guinée-Bissau* (Brussels: Académie Royale de Sciences d'Outre-Mer, 1980).

330 **African customary law in the former Portuguese territories, 1954-74.**
Narana Coissoro.   *Journal of African Law*, vol. 28, nos 1-2 (1984), p. 72-9.

Reviews colonial practice. Coissoro also puts into perspective the radical change in legal practices that occurred after the Native Statute was repealed in 1961 (q.v.). This meant full citizenship under the Portuguese constitution for all Africans. From that time, according to the author, African customary law was regarded as private law, and respected.

331 ***Boletim Oficial*, no. 19, 16 de Maio 1984.** (*Official Bulletin*, no. 19, 16 May 1984.)
República da Guiné-Bissau. Bissau: Direcção Geral da Função Pública, 1984, p. 9-30.

Reprints the revised Constitution of the Republic adopted by the III Legislature. Pages 1-9 list the elected deputies to the legislature.

332 **Guiné-Bissau: Justiça I.** (Guinea-Bissau: Justice I.)
Lisbon: Centro de Informação e Documentação, Amílcar Cabral
(CIDAC), 1990.
Contains ten documents, including seven law textbooks used by the School of Law of
Guinea-Bissau. There are also a number of documents on the popular tribunals.

333 **Guiné-Bissau: Legislação I.** (Guinea-Bissau: Legislation I.)
Lisbon: Centro de Informação e Documentação, Amílcar Cabral
(CIDAC), 1990.
Contains the proposed but never implemented 1980 Constitution of the Republic plus
several issues of the *Boletim Oficial* (January-May 1985).

334 **Les tribuneaux populaires en Guinée-Bissau.** (Guinea-Bissau's people's
courts.)
Alfredo Margarido, João Dantas Pereira. *Droit et Cultures*, vol. 8
(1984), p. 5-13.
Characterizes this popular institution as the principal juridical system in the country.
The courts were based upon the legal traditions of the various national groups.

Usos e costumes jurídicos dos Fulas da Guiné-Bissau.
See item no. 190.

Usos e costumes jurídicos dos Mandingas.
See item no. 195.

Instituições de direito penal consuetudinário dos Manjacos de Caió.
See item no. 196.

Usos e costumes jurídicos dos Felupes da Guiné.
See item no. 207.

Amílcar Cabral

335 A brief report on the situation of the struggle.
Amílcar Cabral.   *Ufahamu*, vol. 2, no. 3 (1972), p. 5-25.
Presents the military situation inside the country in 1971 and the effect of the war upon
Portugal. The editors update the situation on pages 26-8. *Ufahamu*, vol. 1, no. 2 (1970)
printed Cabral's statement of 26 February 1970 to the United States House Committee
on Foreign Affairs. On the occasion of the tenth anniversary of the journal, the editors
translated and printed excerpts from two of Cabral's writings: 'On the utilization of
land in Africa' and 'The contribution of the Guinean peoples to the agricultural
production of Guinea', *Ufahamu*, vol. 11, no. 1 (1981), p. 7-16.

336 Africa and the modern world.
Immanuel Wallerstein.   Trenton, New Jersey: Africa World Press,
1986. 209p.
There are two essays of interest in this anthology. They are chapter 3: 'The lessons of
the PAIGC', and chapter 9: 'The integration of the national liberation movement in
the field of international liberation'. Both of these take off from concepts elaborated
by Cabral. In the first article, Wallerstein comments on Cabral's distinction between
imperialist-colonialist history and African history, on his concept of the nation-class
and on the revolutionary petty bourgeoisie. Wallerstein himself elaborates on the
notion of the revolutionary petty bourgeoisie in the second essay. He also extends
Cabral's notion of revolution to the situation of the 1980s.

337 Allocution prononcée à l'occasion de la journée Kwame Nkrumah.
(Speech commemorating Kwame Nkrumah.)
Amílcar Cabral.   *Présence Africaine*, no. 85 (1973), p. 5-10.
Elegizes the Ghanaian leader on the occasion of his death. Cabral emphasizes the need
to struggle for the liberation and unity of the whole of Africa.

338 **Análise de alguns tipos de resistência: a resistência política, a resistência económica, a resistência cultural, a resistência armada.** (Analysis of some types of resistance: political, economic, cultural and armed struggle.)
Amílcar Cabral.   Lisbon: Editorial 'Avante' SARL, 1986. 4 vols.
(Edição do Departamento de Informação, Propaganda e Cultura do Comité Central do PAIGC, Colecção 'Cabral Ka Muri', no. 12-15).

Collects some of the lectures by Cabral to the seminar of party cadres held in November 1969. They are noteworthy for their combination of simplicity of language and profound insight. Nine other lectures from the same seminar are to be found in *Unity and struggle* (q.v.).

339 **Amílcar Cabral.**
O. Ignatiev, translated into Portuguese by G. Melmikov.   Moscow: Edições Progresso, 1984. 242p.

A biography of the revolutionary leader, this account reads like a novel. It reports conversations between Cabral and many of the other important figures of the liberation struggle. Much of the information was reported to the author by many of those closest to Cabral, a list of whom appears in the back of the book. See also *Três tiros da PIDE* (Three shots by the PIDE) (Lisbon: Prelo Editora, 1975) for more of the 'you are there' history by the Russian journalist. The scene is Amílcar Cabral's assassination. The source of the information is again certain PAIGC insiders.

340 **Amílcar Cabral and the dialectic of Portuguese colonialism.**
Cedric J. Robinson.   *Radical America*, vol. 15, no. 3 (1981), p. 39-57.

Argues that Cabral's development as a revolutionary was shaped by the contradictions inherent in the colonial situation. As an *assimilado* or person assimilated into Portuguese culture, Cabral was expected to act as an intermediary for the colonial power yet he had to suffer the humiliation of not being able to give full expression to his abilities. Robinson describes the various phases of colonialism and the place of *assimilados*, and of Cabral in particular. He then describes Cabral's theory and strategy for decolonization.

341 **Amílcar Cabral e l'indipendenza dell'Africa.** (Amílcar Cabral and the independence of Africa.)
M. Alegre, Mário de Andrade, Y. Benot, Basil Davidson, A. Entralgo, M. Glisenti, L. Luzzato, N. Ntalaja, A. Pereira, P. Pierson-Mathy, Lars Rudebeck.   Milano, Italy: Franco Angeli Editore, 1983. 195p. bibliog. (Collana IPALMO).

A compilation of articles on Cabral by the above personalities on the occasion of the international congress held in Praia, Cape Verde, on 17-20 February 1983. The bibliography refers to works by Cabral as well as those about him. The complete proceedings of the symposium were published by the PAICV in *Continuar Cabral* (Lisbon: Grafedito/Prelo-Estampa, 1984). *Latin American Perspectives*, vol. 11, no. 41 (1984) reprints in English the contributions by Ronald H. Chilcote, Basil Davidson, N. Ntalaja, Dulce Almada Duarte, Sylvia Hill and Y. Benot.

Amílcar Cabral

342 **Amílcar Cabral: essai de biographie politique.** (Amílcar Cabral: an essay on political biography.)
Mário de Andrade. Paris: François Maspero, 1980. 167p.
A eulogy of the national leader's life and an appreciation of his thought. An earlier appreciation is that by Andrade in 'Amílcar Cabral: profil d'un révolutionnaire africain (Amílcar Cabral: profile of an African revolutionary), *Présence Africaine*, no. 86 (1973). See also Aquíno de Bragança's *Amílcar Cabral* (Lisbon, 1976).

343 **Amílcar Cabral: evolution of revolutionary thought.**
Bernard Magubane. *Ufahamu*, vol. 2, no. 2 (1971), p. 71-87.
Sees Cabral as having used Marx's dialectical method in his studies of agrarian communities in Guinea-Bissau (q.v.). Magubane stresses this methodology and gives several other instances. He also underlines Cabral's insistence on socialist transformation in Guinea-Bissau.

344 **Amílcar Cabral: outstanding leader of African liberation movement.**
Yusuf M. Dadoo. *African Communist*, no. 53 (1973), p. 38-43.
A tribute to the leader on his death by the then chairman of the South African Communist Party. A similar tribute was written by the Cuban ambassador to the Republic of Guinea-Conakry at the time of Cabral's murder there. See Oscar Oramas, *Apuntes sobre a vida y el pensamiento politico de Amílcar Cabral* (Havana, 1977), a small book which is organized much like Mao's Red Book with citations from Cabral on many subjects. As he was called to the scene, he is able also to describe events after the assassination.

345 **Amílcar Cabral: pragmatic revolutionary leader shows how an African war can be successful.**
David A. Andelmàn. *Africa Report*, vol. 15, no. 5 (1970), p. 18-19.
The entire issue is devoted to a discussion of the Portuguese African wars and the role of the US and NATO as Portugal's allies. This particular article is a capsule biography of the revolutionary leader whom the author considers to be the force behind the successes of the PAIGC.

346 **Amílcar Cabral: revolutionary leader and people's war.**
Patrick Chabal. Cambridge, England: Cambridge University Press, 1983. 219p. 4 maps. bibliog.
A biography of Cabral and a brief history of the national liberation movement, the book makes fascinating reading but is heavily dependent upon interviews with Cabral's first wife, with Luís Cabral and several others, and upon the materials they made available. It centres upon Cabral's leadership which Chabal sees as the principal factor in the success of the PAIGC as a liberation movement. There is also a brief assessment of Cabral's thought. Chabal sees Cabral as essentially a man of action, a pragmatist rather than a theorist. He views the writings as falling within the Marxist tradition but he denies that Cabral was a Marxist. The book contains an important and very extensive bibliography of Cabral's writings and writings on him. Chabal first published his interpretation of Cabral in 'National liberation in Portuguese Guinea, 1956-74', *African Affairs*, vol. 80, no. 318 (1981). Chabal's 'The social and political thought of Amílcar Cabral' in *The Journal of Modern African Studies*, vol. 19, no. 1 (1981) is a revised version of chapter 6.

347 **A questão da unidade no pensamento de Amílcar Cabral.** (The question of unity in the thought of Amílcar Cabral.)
Sérgio Ribeiro, prefaces by Vasco Cabral, Alfredo Moura. Lisbon: Tricontinental Editora, 1983. 55p.

Looks at the different ways in which Cabral developed the concept of unity in his writings. Perhaps the most original and significant chapters are those concerning unity between Cape Verde and Guinea. In one chapter Ribeiro explains Cabral's rationale for proposing this development and in a later chapter his own reasons for continuing to believe in the concept even though the subject was taboo after the 1980 coup and the break in relations between PAIGC and PAICV. Ribeiro revives the idea because he considers the alternative to be the absorption of Guinea into the so-called Greater Guinea, including parts of Senegal and the Republic of Guinea.

348 **As dominantes teóricas no pensamento de Amílcar Cabral.** (The dominant concepts in Amílcar Cabral's thought.)
Carlos Lopes. *Revista Internacional de Estudos Africanos*, no. 2 (1984), p. 63-92.

Focuses on the concept of the petty bourgeoisie as outlined by Cabral and argues that, as a class, the group tends towards developing into a bourgeoisie which takes control of the state and struggles to maintains its political interests against those of workers and peasants. Lopes reminds us that Cabral thought it would be possible for at least one fraction of this class to renounce its position and work for the interests of the majority.

349 **Cabral and the African revolution.**
K. Opoku. *Présence Africaine*, nos 105-6 (1978), p. 45-60.

Analyses Cabral's ideas on social structure; on attitudes towards revolution; on party membership and leadership; on culture and national liberation; on African unity; and on the African revolution. Opoku quotes directly from Cabral's writings.

350 **Cabral's Marxism: an African strategy for development.**
Timothy W. Luke. *Studies in Comparative Communism*, vol. 14, no. 4 (1981), p. 307-30.

Argues that Cabral developed an original Marxist analysis by conceptualizing imperialism as a process of enforced modernization that ended in repression and stagnation. Luke also notes a further contradiction, that the class Cabral pinned his hopes on for modernization of Guinean society, the petty bourgeoisie, has clung to rule rather than make themselves dispensable as Cabral argued they should.

351 **Estudos agrários de Amílcar Cabral.** (Agricultural studies by Amílcar Cabral.)
Amílcar Cabral. Lisbon; Bissau: Instituto de Investigação Científica Tropical and Instituto Nacional de Estudos e Pesquisa, 1988. 781p. map. bibliog.

In this volume, the most complete compendium of Amílcar Cabral's agricultural writings, there are fifty-nine texts in all, including his works on soils and soil erosion and his research into the feasibility of sugar-beet production in Angola and Guinea. There are English and French summaries of some of the articles. There is also the important agricultural census of Guinea carried out by Cabral and his first wife, Maria

Amílcar Cabral

Helena. This was the most complete census until 1988, and it has been the reference point for much government planning. While some of the writings are strictly technical, many others demonstrate Cabral's holistic historical and socio-economic approach to agriculture. The volume includes evaluations of his work and testimonials from colleagues and professors.

352   **Éveil de la conscience nationale et stratégie révolutionnaire chez Amílcar Cabral.** (The awakening of national consciousness and revolutionary strategy in Amílcar Cabral's thought.)
Manuele Gacha. *Le Mois en Afrique*, no. 127 (July 1976), p. 69-84.

Outlines the objective economic, social and cultural conditions at the basis of Cabral's thought and describes his strategy to transform social reality. The author focuses on the role of the party.

353   **Fruits for a struggle.**
Amílcar Cabral. *Marxism Today*, vol. 17, no. 1 (1973), p. 13-21.

Denounces Portuguese racism and injustice and gives an account of the state of the struggle in the country.

354   **Guinea-Bissau: Amílcar Cabral: the meaning of an assassination.**
John Marcum. *Africa Report*, vol. 18, no. 2 (1973), p. 21-3.

Gives an unusually objective report of the military and political situation in Guinea-Bissau at the time of Cabral's assassination, offering this in partial explanation of the murder.

355   **Guiné-Bissau: Cultura I.** (Guinea-Bissau: Culture I.)
Lisbon: Centro de Informação e Documentação, Amílcar Cabral (CIDAC), 1990.

Contains five statements by Cabral on the question of culture and also some other miscellaneous items on Guinean culture.

356   **Guiné-Bissau: Pensamento político-I and Biografia-I.** (Guinea-Bissau: Political thought-I and Biography-I.)
Lisbon: Centro de Informação e Documentação, Amílcar Cabral (CIDAC), 1990.

The first dossier collects a variety of documents on Cabral's thoughts and a number of his writings including his address before the Fourth Committee of the United Nations General Assembly in October 1972. The second contains remembrances of Cabral, and two short articles giving biographies of other PAIGC leaders.

357   **Guinée-Bissau: la mort d'Amílcar Cabral.** (Guinea-Bissau: the death of Amílcar Cabral.)
R. Pélissier. *Le Mois en Afrique*, no. 86 (February 1973), p. 20-4.

In his first reaction to the murder of the leader, Pélissier reviews the probable agents of the assassination. His appraisal is noteworthy because not much more has since come to light. See also Aquíno de Bragança, 'La longue marche d'un révolutionnaire africain', *Afrique-Asie*, no. 23, 5 February-18 February 1973 and 'L'assassinat de

Cabral', *Afrique-Asie*, no. 24, 19 February-4 March 1973. Other articles and documents on the assassination have been compiled by CIDAC (q.v.).

358   **In the twilight of revolution: the political theory of Amílcar Cabral.**
Jock McCulloch.   London: Routledge & Kegan Paul, 1983. 138p.
bibliog.

Classifies and assesses the content of Cabral's writings under such categories as agronomy, class analysis, culture and personality, the state, forces of production, and imperialism. McCulloch states that Cabral's accomplishment was to give Africa a revolutionary theory, almost involuntarily. He sees Cabral essentially as a pragmatist who theorized out of necessity rather than choice and whose works lacked an overall conceptual coherency. In contrast to many other interpretations, McCulloch sees Cabral as having rejected Marxism and instead as having contributed what he calls a 'practical idealism'. He points out the tension in Cabral's work between the need for strong leadership and at the same time democratic participation in both the national liberation struggle and post-war development. McCulloch published an earlier version of Cabral and the concept of imperialism in *The Journal of Modern African Studies*, vol. 19, no. 3 (1981).

359   **Main basse sur l'Afrique: la récolonisation.** (The grab for Africa: recolonization.)
Jean Ziegler.   Paris: Éditions du Seuil, 1980. 284p. map.

Describes the national liberation of Africa and its revolutionary leaders, among them Amílcar Cabral. The section on Guinea-Bissau (p. 195-222) combines analysis with on-the-spot reporting of the independence struggle. It also contains a brief commentary on Cabral's revolutionary theory.

360   **Manuscript and other holdings about Africa.**
Amistad Research Center. New Orleans, Louisiana: Old US Mint, 1982. 36p.

The archives in this centre of the American Committee on Africa contain correspondence from, and other information on, Amílcar Cabral.

361   **On revolutionary nationalism: the legacy of Cabral.**
Basil Davidson.   *Race and Class*, vol. 27, no. 3 (1986), p. 21-45.

Evaluates the significance of Cabral's thinking and focuses particularly on his contribution to the theory of national liberation and the role of the African petty bourgeoisie. Davidson defends Cabral's use of the term 'petty bourgeoisie' in the Guinean context and explains what he meant by the notion of the need for the petty bourgeoisie to commit class suicide. He also explains Cabral's mistrust of labels to classify PAIGC ideology. Davidson enriches the discussion by referring to his own conversations with Cabral in the months preceding his assassination.

Amílcar Cabral

362 **Our people are our mountains: Amílcar Cabral on the Guinean revolution.**
Amílcar Cabral, preface by Basil Davidson.   London: Committee for Freedom in Mozambique, Angola and Guiné, [n.d.]. 40p. 2 maps.
This is the transcript of two speeches given in London in October 1971. Also included is a brief report on the situation of the armed struggle during that year.

363 **Portuguese aggression against the Special Mission of the United Nations.**
Amílcar Cabral.   [n.p.]: PAIGC, [n.d.]. 23p.
Gives a day-by-day account of the Portuguese attempts to try to stop the United Nations mission (q.v.) from visiting Guinea-Bissau.

364 **Quem é o inimigo?** (Who is the enemy?)
Aquíno de Bragança, Immanuel Wallerstein.   Lisbon: Iniciativas Editoriais, 1978. 3 vols.
This is a fasinating documentary record of national liberation movements mainly in southern and lusophone Africa. Almost all of the short articles on Guinea are pieces written by Amílcar Cabral. The original and important contribution of these three volumes is that they set Cabral's work in the larger context. They were translated into English and published by Zed Press in 1982 under the title *The African liberation reader*.

365 **Realidades.** (Realities.)
Amílcar Cabral.   *Tricontinental*, no. 33 (1973), p. 96-109.
This is an interview with the leader which touches upon several topics: the visit of the mission of the UN Special Committee, the visit of Fidel Castro, and the situation inside the country.

366 **Return to the source: selected speeches by Amílcar Cabral.**
Edited by Africa Information Service.   New York: Monthly Review Press with African Information Service, 1973. 106p. 2 maps. bibliog.
Most of these speeches were given while Cabral was in the United States, at various universities, in Harlem, and before the United Nations.

367 **Revolution in Guinea: an African people's struggle.**
Amílcar Cabral, translated and edited by Richard Handyside.
London: Stage 1, 1969. 140p. map.
Collects some of Cabral's earlier speeches and writings, the most famous and important of which are 'Brief analysis of the social structure in Guinea' and 'The weapon of theory'. Extracts also appear of Cabral's speech before the Special Committee of the United Nations in June 1962 and to the Fourth Committee of the United Nations in December 1962. Also included are an interview and an article published by *Tricontinental* in 1968 and 1969. The appendix contains the first PAIGC Party Programme.

368 **Some African theorists of culture and modernization: Fanon, Cabral, and some others.**
L. Adele Jinadu. *African Studies Review*, vol. 21, no. 1 (1978), p. 121-38.

Compares Fanon and Cabral and also such other writers as Nkrumah and Sénghor on the theme of culture and its relationship to development.

369 **State and revolution: the work of Amílcar Cabral.**
Henry Bienen. *Journal of Modern African Studies*, vol. 15, no. 4 (1977), p. 555-68.

States that Cabral, more than most African thinkers and revolutionaries, focused on the problem of the transition from liberation movement to 'the state'. Bienen also looks at Cabral's thought in relation to class struggle, violence, ethnicity and consciousness. He compares Cabral with Fanon. Others who have done the same include Jinadu (q.v.) and Robert Blackey, 'Fanon and Cabral: a contrast in theories of revolution for Africa', *Journal of Modern African Studies*, vol. 12, no. 2 (1974). The latter also looks at their concepts of leadership and political parties.

370 **The African revolution: theory and practice: the political thought of Amílcar Cabral.**
Charles McCollester. *Monthly Review*, vol. 24, no. 10 (1973), p. 10-21.

Written by a student of philosophy, the article looks at Cabral's method of analysis and theorizing. It explains that Cabral diverged from Marxist theory by seeing class struggle as the motive force in history only in a specific period. McCollester dwells upon the concepts of culture and the petty bourgeoisie in Cabral's thought. The presentation is very lucid.

371 **The poet Amílcar Cabral.**
Gerald M. Moser. *Research in African Literatures*, vol. 9, no. 2 (1978), p. 176-97.

Reproduces and analyses ten of Cabral's poems in Portuguese and translates them into English. The author gives a short biography of Cabral's literary avocation.

372 **The political thought of Amílcar Cabral.**
Ronald H. Chilcote. *Journal of Modern African Studies*, vol. 6, no. 3 (1968), p. 373-88.

This is one of the earliest assessments of the writings and speeches of the revolutionary leader. Chilcote sees Cabral's thought as being influenced by a developmental nationalism which demanded radical structural change as well as independence. Christopher Clapham, in 'The context of African political thought', *Journal of Modern African Studies*, vol. 8, no. 1 (1970), takes issue with Chilcote's interpretation. Chilcote has a forthcoming book on Cabral, including a comprehensive annotated bibliography, to be published by Lynne Rienner Publishers.

Amílcar Cabral

373 **The political thought of Amílcar Cabral: a synthesis.**
Sulayman Sheih Nyang. *Odu*, no. 13 (January 1976), p. 3-20.
Discusses Cabral's conceptualization of colonialism, the nation-class, and history. He takes issue with some of Ronald Chilcote's early interpretations (q.v.) and notes several other interpretations including John Marcum's (q.v.).

374 **The road toward effective African liberation: the cases of Ghana and Guinea-Bissau.**
Manning Marable. In: *Third World development and the myth of international cooperation*, edited by J. W. Forje. Lund, Sweden: Jowifor Publications, 1984, p. 190-209.
Cabral's writings on the role of culture in the liberation struggle are cited to support the author's argument that revolution demands more than simply the removal of the colonial administrative apparatus. It requires the development of a national culture. Cabral's strategy is contrasted with that of Nkrumah.

375 **The war in 'Portuguese' Guinea.**
Amílcar Cabral. *African Revolution*, vol. 1, no. 2 (1963), p. 103-8.
Notes with optimism the resolution of the United Nations General Assembly of 14 December 1960 demanding information from Portugal on the status of its territories in Africa and elsewhere. Cabral's message is that the Guinean struggle is part of the effort to create a new Africa, to start the African revolution. He describes Portugal's efforts to involve the NATO allies and stresses the will of the peoples of both Guinea-Bissau and Cape Verde to resist.

376 *Ufahamu*, **vol. 3, no. 3 (1973) p. 10-130.**
Edited by Teshome H. Gabriel.
The entire issue was a tribute to Amílcar Cabral who had been assassinated earlier in the year. There are translations of two of his agrarian studies as well as eulogies from a host of distinguished Africanists. Included are an assessment of the PAIGC without Cabral by G. Chaliand, and two evaluations of his thought by Eduardo de Sousa Ferreira and Maryinez L. Hubbard.

377 **Unity and struggle: speeches and writings.**
Amílcar Cabral, translated by Michael Wolfers, with biographical notes by Mário de Andrade. London: Heinemann, 1980. 298p.
A selection of writings from the most comprehensive collection, *Unité et lutte* (Paris: Maspero, 1975, 2 vols), this work contains two of Cabral's most important texts, 'The weapon of theory' and 'National liberation and culture'. There is also a summary of the agricultural census that he and his wife conducted in Guinea-Bissau in 1953, as well as the tract on Portuguese colonialism written under the pseudonym Abel Djassi. Among the noteworthy speeches are the New Year's message written shortly before his murder, the speech before the UN General Assembly in October 1972 and the speech on the eighth year of armed struggle. There is also a translation of the PAIGC watchwords written after the 1st Party Congress in 1964.

Crónica da libertação.
See item no. 125.

Amílcar Cabral and rural transformation in Guinea-Bissau: a preliminary critique.
See item no. 428.

Foreign Relations

378 **A politica externa da Guiné-Bissau.** (The foreign policy of Guinea-Bissau.)
Jorge Cabral. *Soronda: revista de estudos Guineenses*, no. 7 (1989), p. 63-84.
Retraces the various diplomatic initatives from the pre-independence period to 1989.

379 **Arbitration tribunal for the delimitation of the maritime boundary between Guinea and Guinea-Bissau: award of 14 February 1985.**
International Legal Materials, vol. 25 (March 1986), p. 251-307.
Includes the agreement between the two states to proceed to arbitration, the tribunal's award and a map showing the delimitation of the maritime boundaries. Included also are the pleadings. Guinea-Bissau submitted that the protocol signed between France and Portugal on 12 May 1886 did not establish a maritime boundary whereas Guinea-Conakry maintained that it did. The tribunal found for Guinea-Bissau.

380 **As relações económicas entre a Guiné-Bissau e os países socialistas: realidade e perspectivas.** (Economic relations between Guinea-Bissau and the socialist countries: realities and perspectives.)
Bernardino Cardoso. *Boletim de informação sócio-económica*, vol. 2, no. 3 (1986), p. 21-41.
Points out the benefits to the country of its economic relations with Cuba and Eastern Europe and surveys the possibilities of extending its relationship.

381 IX conferência dos chefes de estado de Angola, Cabo-Verde, Guiné-Bissau, Moçambique e S. Tomé e Príncipe. (Ninth conference of the heads of state of Angola, Cape-Verde, Guinea-Bissau, Mozambique and São Tomé and Príncipe.)
Praia, Cape Verde, 18-20 December 1989. [no consecutive pagination].

Contains the opening and closing speeches of the President of the Republic of Cape Verde, Aristides Pereira; the speech by Joaquim Chissano, President of the People's Republic of Mozambique; and the final communiqué of the conference which included the programme of action for 1990. The programme called for reinforcing organs of coordination of policy; concertation of foreign policy; adoption of realistic programmes of economic, cultural and political exchange; support for the Angolan government peace plan; and support for the Mozambiquan government's search for peace. The final document is the Declaration of Praia.

382 Evaluation of the technical skills training project for the Tri-Lateral Commission in Guinea-Bissau.
João Júlio Correia, Ilda Mateus dos Santos, António João Barata, Luíz Teles Grilo, James Washington, Gordon Knude. Washington, DC: Development Alternatives, 1987. 23p.

Provides an insight into the workings of an unusual development assistance arrangement whereby the United States finances a number of development projects, Portugal provides technical assistance in the form of consultants and the government of Guinea implements the projects. These three governments make up the commission in the title. The projects are designed to promote agri-business in the country.

383 From the debate.
UN Chronicle, vol. 27, no. 1 (1990), p. 19.

Guinea-Bissau called for a new international development strategy which would link developed and developing nations together in a search for guaranteed minimal standards of living for all at the 44th session of the General Assembly.

384 General debate.
UN Monthly Chronicle, vol. 13, no. 10 (1976), p. 55-6.

Records the essence of the statement of Victor Saúde Maria, Foreign Minister of the newly established Republic of Guinea-Bissau, to the 31st session of the General Assembly. He signalled support for national liberation movements in general and specifically for the Comoros, Palestine, the Western Sahara, Panama (in regard to the Canal) and Timor. Guinea-Bissau called for condemnation of South Africa's actions against Mozambique, Zambia and Botswana, and felt that all members should recognize Angola, that foreign forces should stop interfering in Cyprus and North Korea and, moreover, that Vietnam should be allowed to join the United Nations. Saúde Maria also called for the dissolution of military alliances. There were other policy statements recorded in the January, February, March and April issues of the Chronicle. The February issue of the Chronicle noted UN High Commission for Refugees assistance to those who had migrated to Senegal during the war and were now wanting to return home.

Foreign Relations

385 **General debate.**
UN Monthly Chronicle, vol. 14, no. 10 (1977), p. 62-3.

Representing the country in the 32nd session, Saúde Maria called for support for liberation movements in South Africa, Southern Rhodesia, the Western Sahara, Comoros, Palestine, East Timor and Chile and for SWAPO (South West African People's Organization). He also called for an end to the arms race and for a new international economic order. The August-September issue of the *Chronicle* noted that the first UNDP (UN Development Programme) country programme had been approved in the amount of $5.75 million.

386 **General debate. – 19 September to 13 October.**
UN Monthly Chronicle, vol. 15, no. 10 (1978), p. 82-3.

Saúde Maria spoke of the non-aligned position of Guinea-Bissau and other African countries. He also urged attention to the South African, Namibian, East Timorian and Palestinian questions. He called for an end to the arms race and hoped for a successful fifth UNCTAD (UN Conference on Trade and Development). In the same issue, the World Food Programme announced $3.6 million of assistance to the country. In July 1978, the UNDP gave special assistance.

387 **Guiné-Bissau: Cooperação Internacional I-IV.** (Guinea-Bissau: International Assistance I-IV.)
Lisbon: Centro de Informação e Documentação, Amílcar Cabral (CIDAC), 1990.

Contains the decree setting up the State Secretariat for International Assistance (the literal translation of Cooperação is Cooperation) and the papers for the Round Table meeting of donors, November 1984 and 1985. There are also the papers for the conference of Non-Governmental Organizations operating in Guinea in November 1985, the study of popular production (q.v.), CIDAC training materials for *cooperantes* (the name given to expatriates who work with the government). Also included are projects, proposals, evaluations, reports and memoirs of *cooperantes*, the article by B. Cardoso on relations with socialist countries (q.v.) and the UNDP Third Country Programme (q.v.).

388 **Guiné-Bissau: Cooperação Portugal I.** (Guinea-Bissau: Assistance from Portugal I.)
Lisbon: Centro de Informação e Documentação, Amílcar Cabral (CIDAC), 1990.

Contains documents on Portuguese assistance.

389 **Guiné-Bissau: Política Externa-I.** (Guinea-Bissau: Foreign Policy-I.)
Lisbon: Centro de Informação e Documentação, Amílcar Cabral (CIDAC), 1990.

Contains the proposals and resolutions of the 4th Party Congress on foreign policy.

390 **International Court of Justice: order in case concerning the arbitral award of 31 July 1989 (Guinea-Bissau v. Senegal).**
International Legal Materials, vol. 29, no. 3 (1990), p. 624-36.
Records the Court's refusal to advise Senegal to abstain from action in the maritime area under dispute as requested by Guinea-Bissau. The maritime boundary has been the subject of negotiations since 1977. In 1985 the two countries agreed to arbitration. Guinea-Bissau asked the arbitration tribunal whether the exchange of letters between France and Portugal on 25 April 1960 on the question of the maritime boundary had the force of law. On 31 July 1989, the tribunal decided that it did but it refused to answer Guinea-Bissau's second question regarding the line. Guinea-Bissau contends that a new dispute has therefore arisen. The International Court, however, denied Guinea-Bissau's request with only one judge dissenting.

391 **La Guinée-Bissau, république populaire en voie de libéralisation.**
(Guinea-Bissau, popular republic on the road to liberalization.)
Philippe Decraene. *L'Afrique et l'Asie Modernes*, no. 158 (1988), p. 54-62.
Presents a very general overview of some important issues facing the Guinean government such as the question of dumping toxic waste in the country, border relations with Senegal and foreign relations with France. The author notes that Cuba alone among the other socialist countries remains an important provider of assistance in the health and military sectors.

392 **118 participate in Assembly debate on Namibia question.**
UN Monthly Chronicle, vol. 15, no. 6 (1978), p. 71.
Setting out the Guinean position, Gil Fernandes, Permanent Representative to the United Nations, condemned South Africa's position not to negotiate on the question of Walvis Bay.

393 **Peiping's policy towards Africa as viewed from the independence of Guinea-Bissau and Mozambique.**
Po-t'ang Yeh. *Issues and Studies*, vol. 10, no. 15 (1974), p. 2-12.
Discusses Chinese foreign policy and aid to African national liberation movements, including the PAIGC.

394 **Portugal and Africa: the politics of re-engagement.**
Norman MacQueen. *Journal of Modern African Studies*, vol. 23, no. 1 (1985), p. 31-51.
Asserts, correctly, that Portugal's current relationship with Guinea-Bissau has symbolic value in terms of its desired relationship with the other ex-colonies, specifically Angola and Mozambique. MacQueen sees Guinea-Bissau as offering a model and as acting as a bridge towards better relations in general.

395 **President notes wide interest in global negotiations.**
UN Chronicle, vol. 18, no. 11 (1981), p. 61.
Victor Saúde Maria represented his government's views before the 36th session of the General Assembly. Kampuchea was added to the list of countries for which Guinea-Bissau expressed concern. Also new was a worry over the increase in armaments in the

101

Indian Ocean and the use of East Africa for foreign bases. Guinea-Bissau noted, however, with satisfaction the establishment of the Economic Community of West African States (ECOWAS).

396 **Representatives of 149 member states address assembly in general debate.**
UN Chronicle, vol. 17, no. 9 (1980), p. 73.

Gil Fernandes spoke to the 35th session about the situations in South Africa and Namibia. The government of Guinea-Bissau deplored Morocco's position in the Western Sahara and also great-power rivalry as it affected young states and the Israeli position in Jerusalem and Palestine. Fernandes hoped for reconciliation in Chad, between Iran and Iraq and between France and the Comoros over the island of Mayotte.

397 **Special commemorative session. 14-24 October 1984.**
UN Chronicle, vol. 22, no. 9 (1985), p. 27-8.

President João Bernardo Vieira addressed the 40th anniversary session and eulogized the United Nations for its help in allowing every nation to speak with an equal voice. He repeated the country's concern with international indebtedness and condemned South Africa.

398 **143 states take part in general debate; large numbers of heads of state welcome.**
UN Chronicle, vol. 17, no. 1 (1980), p. 138-9.

In his speech to the 34th session of the General Assembly, Saúde Maria called the situations in Namibia and Zimbabwe unacceptable and said that there was a need to create conditions for self-determination. He noted that Guinea-Bissau supported FRETILIN (Frente Revolucionário de Este Timor Independente) in its struggle over East Timor and also the Sandinista Front in Nicaragua. It welcomed the recovery of the Panama Canal and the Second Strategic Arms Limitation Treaty (SALT II) initiative. Saúde Maria noted the severe international economic crisis and condemned Israel's invasion of Southern Lebanon.

399 **Text of the proclamation of the state of Guinea-Bissau by the National Popular Assembly.**
Ufahamu, vol. 4, no. 2 (1973), p. 4-7.

The declaration on 24 September 1973 is printed in full with a commentary by George M. Houser.

400 **The general debate.**
UN Chronicle, vol. 19, no. 11 (1982), p. 16.

Speaking for Guinea-Bissau, the new foreign minister Samba Lamine Mané focused on the issues of East Timor and South Africa. In the March issue of 1982, Guinea-Bissau was again singled out for special UN foreign aid.

401 **The nations speak.**
UN Chronicle, vol. 21, no. 8 (1984), p. 28-9.
Speaking for Guinea-Bissau at the 39th session, Júlio Semedo talked about the crushing debt burden on Third World and African countries in particular. He recommended the condemnation of South Africa and Israel and urged the adoption of Security Council resolutions 554 (1984) and 435 (1978). He also mentioned support for Polisario (Frente Popular para a Liberación de Saguia el Hamra y Rio de Oro) and FRETILIN.

402 **Third country programme for the Republic of Guinea-Bissau.**
Governing Council of the United Nations Development Programme.
New York: United Nations, 1987. 22p.
Describes the plans and programmes of UN technical assistance for the 1987-91 period. The total amount to be disbursed in a number of sectors was US$ 19,306,900. There is a general description of the economic situation in the country.

Guinea-Bissau in Anglo-Portuguese relations 1860-70: a study in the diplomacy of colonial acquisition.
See item no. 60.

Histoire de la Casamanse: conquête et résistance, 1850-1920.
See item no. 61.

A questão do Casamansa e a delimitação das fronteiras da Guiné.
See item no. 86.

La naissance de l'état par le guerre de libération nationale: le cas de la Guiné-Bissau.
See item no. 132.

Nationalist politics, war and statehood: Guinea-Bissau, 1953-73.
See item no. 133.

L'aide extérieur à l'éducation et à la formation professionnelle en Guinée-Bissao en 1986 et en projet: document de travail.
See item no. 470.

Economy

General

403 **Actividades das ONGs e microrealizações na Guiné-Bissau em 1987.**
(NGO activity and small projects in Guinea Bissau in 1987.)
Bart Schaap. Bissau: SOLIDAMI, Departamento de Estudos e
Projectos, 1988. 21p. map.
Gives a comprehensive view of the activities of the then sixty, now seventy, non-
governmental organizations (NGOs) operating in the country in all sectors of the
economy including agriculture, fisheries, ~ducation, energy, transport, health, small-
scale industry, environmental protection, and so on.

404 **Analysis of the budget of Guinea-Bissau.**
A.S. International, Inc. Washington, DC: A.S. International, 1986.
76p.
Describes the budgetary process of the government during the years, 1981-85, and
analyses the various budgets. Prepared for the US Agency for International
Development (USAID) mission in Bissau, the report focuses on the 1985 budget. It
gives a positive evaluation of the policy directions indicated by the government in its
first development plan (1983-86) and recommends development assistance for the
private sector and for agro-industry.

405 **At the cross-roads: political alliances and structural adjustment, two
essays on Angola, Guinea-Bissau and Mozambique.**
Kenneth Hermele, Lars Rudebeck. Uppsala, Sweden: AKUT, 1989.
67p. 2 maps. bibliog.
The emphasis of this pamphlet is very much on Guinea-Bissau, especially in the longer
essay by Rudebeck entitled 'Structural adjustment in a West African village'.
Rudebeck looks at Kandjaja in Oio in the northeastern part of Guinea on the border
with Senegal. His findings are complementary to the study of the influence of the

liberalization of commerce and structural adjustment on the rural development in the eastern zone of the country by Galli (q.v.). Both find commerce to be greatly enhanced but the benefits to be very unevenly dispersed. While Rudebeck tentatively concludes a fall in real income for the villagers, Galli finds a more complex picture nationwide. In 1986-87, cashew producers gained in income and, after the harvest of 1988-89, rice producers also gained some ground. Both underline the lack of agricultural credit to smallholders in all regions as a major obstacle to the economic growth of the country.

406 **Development and class struggle in Guinea-Bissau.**
Lars Rudebeck. *Monthly Review*, vol. 30, no. 8 (1979), p. 14-32.
Points out the contradictions inherent in a popularly based development strategy and the dependence of the government upon massive foreign financing.

407 **Development strategy in Guinea-Bissau: the contribution of the European Economic Community.**
Rosemary E. Galli. Bissau: Delegation of the Commission of the European Communities and INEP, 1990. 165p. bibliog.
Commissioned as a study of how the structural adjustment programme affects development planning in the country as a whole and EEC (European Economic Community) investment in rural development in particular, this report synthesizes comparative macro-economic data for the years, 1986-89. It is a critique of investment programming in general which the author describes as a highly political process engaged in by government officials and donors alike. She finds that the needs and aspirations of the majority of people are the last to be satisfied in the process. In the late 1980s, in particular, the balance-of-payments support credits and loans which followed upon the structural adjustment programme have been used to create a stratum of wealthy merchants – plantation owners – officials. The last chapter looks at how this has influenced the EEC programming process in the eastern regions, Bafatá and Gabú, and suggests an alternative process and an alternative rural development strategy. The first part of the report has been revised for publication in the forthcoming *Review of African Political Economy*, no. 49 (1991) under the title 'Liberalization is not enough: structural adjustment and peasants in Guinea-Bissau'.

408 **Documento de orientação.** (Working document.)
Bissau: Conferência das Organizações não Governamentais, 1985. 58p.
In November 1985, a conference of non-governmental organizations operating in the country was called in order to attempt a coordination of their activities; to delineate a common strategy; and to improve relationships with the Ministry of Planning and the other ministries with whom they collaborate. There were around 50 such organizations at the time. There are now over 70. This was the working document of the conference. Besides outlining general information on the country, surveying the evolution of the economy and describing the first national development plan, the document analyses the work to date of the NGOs and puts forward guidelines for a strategy of cooperation. It also describes the objectives of the governmental institution, Solidami or Solidaridade e Amizade, created in 1984 to promote the strategy.

409 **Estudos de economia da República da Guiné-Bissau.** (Studies of the economy of the Republic of Guinea-Bissau.)
Unidade Pedagógica de Economia e Gestão. *Cadernos de Economia*, no. 1 (1987).

The entire issue analyses the macro-economic situation in the country. The articles are on the general economic situation by the then governor of the central bank; on the monetary situation and international trade by the studies section of the central bank; on the demographic situation; and on development perspectives by Professor Rui Costa Rodrigûes of the University of Minho.

410 **Guinea-Bissau: an introductory basic economic report.**
Maria Emilia Freire, Adelina Paiva. Washington, DC: World Bank, 1982. 3 vols.

This is indispensable reading for anyone who wants to understand the basis of World Bank thinking and strategy in the country.

411 **Guiné-Bissau: a busca da independência económica.** (Guinea-Bissau: the search for economic independence.)
Ladislau Dowbor. São Paulo, Brazil: Editora Brasilense, 1983. 120p. map. (Tudo é história, no. 77).

Critically analyses the economic options of the country. Dowbor is a Brazilian economist who in the late 1970s and early 1980s advised the Minister of Planning in Guinea-Bissau. He emphasizes the dilemma of the country which had pretensions to develop along non-capitalist lines but was under pressure from its international donors to conform to standardized models of development.

412 **Guiné-Bissau: Desenvolvimento regional I-IV.** (Guinea-Bissau: Regional development I-IV.)
Lisbon: Centro de Informação e Documentação, Amílcar Cabral (CIDAC), 1990.

Contains the informative reports on the various regions of the country by the department of regional planning in 1980-81. There are also the proposals for integrated regional development of Bolama and Boé, and some reports on the Caboxanque project.

413 **Guiné-Bissau: Economia I and II.** (Guinea-Bissau: Economy I and II.)
Lisbon: Centro de Informação e Documentação, Amílcar Cabral (CIDAC), 1990.

Contains miscellaneous government documents and two articles by Américo Ramos dos Santos on the first national development plan and by Rosemary Galli on peasant productivity (q.v.).

414 **Guiné-Bissau: evolução macro-económica (1974-85).** (Guinea- Bissau: macro-economic evolution (1974-85.)
Bernardino Cardoso. Bissau: mimeographed, 1985. 51p. bibliog.

Gives an overview of the post-independence economy up until the onset of the structural adjustment programme in 1986-87. This is a very useful document by the man who was to become Minister of Planning in 1989. The author treats such economic indicators as the evolution of prices, investment, gross domestic product (GDP) and balance of payments. There are also separate sections on foreign aid and institutional infrastructure. Cardoso notes the lack of impact of the first national development plan (1983-86) and the first stabilization programme and blames this partially on the lack of coordination between global objectives and sectoral projects which depend largely on the investment commitments of international donors. He also laments the weak preparation and dedication of civil servants and the race towards individual enrichment.

415 **Guiné-Bissau: Indústria/Energia-I.** (Guinea-Bissau: Industry/Energy-I.)
Lisbon: Centro de Informação e Documentação, Amílcar Cabral (CIDAC), 1990.
Contains mainly government documents on industrialization.

416 **Guiné-Bissau: Política económica I and II.** (Guinea-Bissau: Political economy I and II.)
Lisbon: Centro de Informação e Documentação, Amílcar Cabral (CIDAC), 1990.
Contains a number of working papers of the Comissariado de Estado de Coordenação Económica e Plano from 1979-80 on development strategy and the 4th Party Congress resolution on development. The stabilization programme of 1983-84 and the conference papers of the UN Conference on Least Developed Nations are included as is Lars Rudebeck's paper on problems of popular power and development (q.v.). In the second dossier are the first two-year development plan, 1980-81, and the second version of the stabilization plan as well as three studies by Rosemary Galli (q.v.).

417 **Guinée-Bissau: le programme de stabilisation, 1984-85, perspectives 1986-92, analyse des effets économiques, financiers, sociaux, diagnostic et propositions.** (Guinea-Bissau: the stabilization programme, 1984-85, perspectives 1986-92, analysis of the economic, financial, social effects, diagnostic and recommendations.)
Gilbert Blardone. Bissau; Geneva; INEP with the collaboration of Institut Universitaire d'Études du Développement, 1987. 72p. bibliog.
This is a preliminary analysis of the data collected by the researchers of the Instituto Nacional de Estudos e Pesquisa (INEP) between 1984 and 1986 on the socio-economic impact of the stabilization programme initiated in the country in 1984 as a result of the first national development plan. The report not only describes the economic problems which the programme aims to resolve but also raises the more fundamental question of what development strategy the country ought to pursue. Among positive effects of the programme are the raising of agricultural production through price incentives and the increase in consumer and production goods. However, the report notes that the terms of trade are still not favourable due to the capturing of producer profits by traders; it also points out the attempt to monopolize agricultural credit by large landholders (*ponteiros*). Other negative effects are the lowering of purchasing power among urban populations, especially the poorest elements; the reduction of employment in the public sector; the demoralization of workers; and the lowering of their productivity.

Economy. General

418 **Guinée-Bissau: les enjeux du développement économique.** (Guinea-Bissau: the stakes of economic development.)
Carolina Quina. *Afrique-Asie*, no. 378 (27 July 1986), p. 30-1.
Traces the general economic policy of the government after the first national development plan on the eve of what should have been the debate for the second plan (a debate which has not yet taken place and a plan which has not yet been published). The author poses the most important question facing the country which is the participation of the mass of people in the economic evolution of the country. She asks whether the PAIGC will be able to regain its former dynamism.

419 **Improving productivity.**
Howard Schissel. *West Africa*, no. 3405 (8 November 1982), p. 2883-7.
Gives a general overview of the economic situation on the eve of the adoption of the first four year plan (1983-86). The article wrongly accuses the former Minister of Planning of being the architect of the disastrous development strategy under Luís Cabral. Otherwise, it is a succint résumé of the intentions of the plan (q.v.).

420 **Índice de preços no consumidor.** (Index of consumer prices.)
Gabinete de Estudos. Bissau: Ministério do Plano, [n.d.]. 39p. bibliog.
Analyses the evolution of prices on the markets of Bissau, Bafatá, Gabú, Farim and Canchungo (the capital and major provincial towns of the north of the country) from February 1986 until April 1987. This information was important as it measured the impact of the first stages of the Structural Adjustment Programme, begun under the direction of the International Monetary Fund (IMF) in 1987. During the same period the country began to liberalize prices and privatize commerce. The study looks at ten items considered as basic primary goods. It shows that the lowest-income families spend more than half their income on two items, rice and fish. As prices rise in general, the consumption of fish and meat diminishes. Butter and sugar are consumed only occasionally. Bread is consumed normally by high-income families. The rate of inflation between February and December 1986 was over 160%. More recent data shows that general inflation was about 100% in 1987, 60% in 1988, and 100% again in 1989.

421 **L'Afrique étranglée.** (Strangled Africa.)
René Dumont, Marie-France Mottin. Paris: Éditions du Seuil, 1982. 262p. bibliog.
The section on Guinea-Bissau is short (p. 221-6) but the message is very direct and to the point. Luís Cabral's development strategy was wrong, its industrialization programme too grandiose for the size of the country and the needs of its people. The authors refer to and agree with the advice of Ladislau Dowbor (q.v.) to regionalize, decentralize and render more appropriate the technology utilized in the country.

422 **Linhas directivas e grandes orientações do II plano nacional de desenvolvimento económico e social (1987-90).** (Guidelines and overall orientations of the second national economic and social development plan [1987-90].)
Gabinete de Estudos do Ministério de Coordenação Económica, Plano e Cooperação Internacional. Bissau: Ministério de Coordenação Económica, Plano e Cooperação Internacional, [n.d.]. 29p.

This is an internal document drawn up for discussion within the Ministry in preparation for the elaboration of the second national plan. Because the plan has not yet been issued, it is the only available indication of the direction of thinking within the Ministry.

423 **Liberation economics in the post-war reconstruction of Guinea-Bissau.**
Shirley Washington. *A Current Bibliography on African Affairs*, vol. 11, no. 3 (1978-79), p. 237-52.

Describes in brief the nature of the economy in the early independence period under Luís Cabral's régime, including state control and intervention in the economy and foreign assistance. The material was adapted from the author's PhD dissertation, *Some aspects of post-war reconstruction in Guinea-Bissau*, Howard University, 1978. Washington's assessment of educational institutions in the same period is in *Black Scholar*, vol. 11, no. 5 (1980).

424 **Looking at Guinea-Bissau: a new nation's development strategy.**
Denis Goulet. Washington, DC: Overseas Development Council, 1978. 60p. map. bibliog.

Highlights the position of Amílcar Cabral and the early Luís Cabral régime on development strategy. Goulet's objective is to illuminate alternative development strategies which have as their aims meeting basic needs and creating greater social justice in the distribution of income and power. He emphasizes the crucial role of a political party as mobilizer of people to engage in decision-making and taking responsibility for improving their lives. This work is interesting from the point of view of what might have happened in Guinea-Bissau.

425 **Primeiro plano quadrienal de desenvolvimento económico e social, 1983-86.** (First four-year economic and social development plan, 1983-86.)
Secretária de Estado do Plano e Cooperação Internacional. Bissau: República da Guiné-Bissau, [n.d.]. 7 vols.

In the first development plan of the country the authors situate the major economic problems of the country in the low level of development at independence; in an unbalanced development strategy; and in the government and urban sector living beyond its means. They estimated that twelve years would be necessary for the economy to begin to develop autonomously. Since March 1987, the government has followed a structural adjustment programme under the watchful eyes of the World Bank and International Monetary Fund. Since 1984 it has been issuing annual plans, and since 1987 work has been proceeding on a second development plan.

426 **Problématique de développement de la région de Bolama (Guinée-Bissau).** (The development problematic in the Bolama region (Guinea-Bissau).)
Jacques Bernier. *Cultures et Développement*, vol. 16, no. 1 (1984), p. 75-95.

Explains the regional development strategy proposed by the researchers of the Centre for Land Management and Development (CRAD) of Laval University, Quebec. Their report is entitled *Le développement rural intégré de la région de Bolama (Guinée-Bissau)* (1982, 3 vols). The researchers were concerned with creating conditions under which the populations of the Bijagós islands could participate in their own self-defined development.

Guinea-Bissau: politics, economics and society.
See item no. 4.

Guiné Portuguesa.
See item no. 6.

Introdução a geografia económica da Guiné-Bissau.
See item no. 8.

Annuário da Província da Guiné do anno de 1925.
See item no. 83.

Anuário da Guiné Portuguesa.
See item no. 84.

Agriculture

427 **Alguns aspectos da economia da Guiné.** (Some aspects of the Guinean economy.)
Jesus Nunes dos Santos. *Boletim da Sociedade de Geografia de Lisboa*, vol. 65, nos 1-2 (1947), p. 49-71.

Explains the lack of large-scale agricultural enterprises in Guinea-Bissau by the scarcity of waged labour. Nunes dos Santos makes the fundamental point that Guinean peasants were not interested in working for others when they could work for themselves more remuneratively. He also points out the absence of infrastructure and economic and agronomic studies as incentives to capitalist investment, and shows that, as a consequence, Guinea-Bissau has always been exploited commercially.

428 **Amílcar Cabral and rural transformation in Guinea-Bissau: a preliminary critique.**
Rosemary E. Galli. *Rural Africana*, nos 25-26 (1986), p. 55-73.

Analyses the two most important rural development projects in Guinea-Bissau at the time, the Integrated Rural Development Programme (PDRI) of Zone 1 (q.v.) and the

Geba Valley rice experimentation project at Contuboel. Galli finds that both follow different lines of thought in Amílcar Cabral's writings, a modernist, technocratic line and a non-directive, participative line and she critically reviews both. An elaboration of this analysis is in Galli and Jones (q.v.).

429 **A produção popular em Guiné-Bissau.** (Popular production in Guinea-Bissau.)
Peter Torrekens, Atilano J. Mendes. Bissau: Ministério de Coordenação Económica, Plano e Cooperação Internacional with the collaboration of OXFAM-Belgium, 1985. 36p.
Presents a breakdown of the different small-scale rural industries projects and documents the kinds of technologies in use and being introduced with the assistance of international NGOs. The authors also characterize the activities as 'popular economy' or 'informal economy'.

430 **As desigualidades regionais na Guiné-Bissau.** (Regional inequalities in Guinea-Bissau.)
Milton Santos. *Estudos Áfro-Asiaticos*, no. 10 (1984), p. 73-93.
Explains some of the obstacles to rural development including the fact that the city of Bissau has benefited almost exclusively from investments. He also cites the lack of transport and communications. Santos forecasts increasing regional inequalities and also a further polarization between city and rural areas.

431 **Causas da queda de produção de arroz na Guiné-Bissau (a situação no sector de Tite-região Quínara).** (Causes of the breakdown in rice production in Guinea-Bissau [the situation in Tite sector-Quínara region].)
Carlos Rui Ribeiro. Bissau: INEP, Centro de Estudos Sócio-Económicos, 1988. 41p. bibliog.
This is a study commissioned by the Dutch government in support of its work in reconstruction of rice fields in the south of the country. The study investigates the reasons for a fall in rice cultivation among the renowned Balanta producers of the region. The author details the physical, cultural and commercial conditions of production in a historical time-frame. He demonstrates that continual commercial pressure by various governments and a parallel weakening of labour organization were at the heart of the crisis.

432 **Condições sócio-económicas para a construção de barragens em bolanhas de água salgada.** (Socio-economic conditions for constructing dikes in salt-water paddies.)
Uwe Birkholz. Bissau: Instituto Nacional de Estudos e Pesquisa (INEP), 1989. 52p. bibliog.
Studies the social and economic conditions surrounding rice production in six villages in the southern region of Tombali. The purpose of the study is to determine the best location for dikes. Construction of dikes has presented social and ecological problems since colonial times. The methodology of the study is important because the author actually interviews the farmers who would use paddies affected by dike construction.

He asks them their opinions on construction, a practice which, even though logical, is uncommon.

433 **Contribution à l'élaboration d'une stratégie de développement rizicole en Guinée Bissau.** (Contribution to the elaboration of a development strategy for rice-growing in Guinea-Bissau.)
Association pour le Développement de la Riziculture en Afrique de l'Ouest (ADRAO). Abidjan, Ivory Coast: ADRAO, 1977. 29p. 3 maps.

Presents a general overview of agriculture in the country with a specific focus on rice, the principal crop. Charts and maps show the different types of rice-growing that occur. The text discusses the problems surrounding this cultivation, pointing out the great diversity of seeds and varieties used. The report recommends certain varieties and the use of fertilization.

434 **Guiné-Bissau: Agricultura-I and II.** (Guinea-Bissau: Agriculture-I and II.)
Lisbon: Centro de Informação e Documentação, Amílcar Cabral (CIDAC), 1990.

The first dossier contains mainly Ministry of Planning documents on rural development but there are also a number of inter-ministerial committee documents on food security and Department of Agricultural Research (DEPA) reports on the Caboxanque project. Of particular interest is the bibliography of works on agriculture in the library of the Ministry of Planning (now the State Secretariat). Dossier II contains the important article by Ursula Funk on land tenure, agriculture and gender (q.v.).

435 **Guiné-Bissau: Cooperativísmo-I.** (Guinea-Bissau: Cooperativism-I.)
Lisbon: Centro de Informação e Documentação, Amílcar Cabral (CIDAC), 1990.

Contains the CIDAC pamphlet on the experimental rice project at Contuboel and a number of other documents, specifically on the integrated rural development project at Caboxanque and on the Domingos Ramos cooperative.

436 **Land tenure, agriculture and gender in Guinea-Bissau.**
Ursula Funk. In: *Agriculture, women and land: the African experience*, edited by Jean Davison. Boulder, Colorado; London: Westview Press, 1988, p. 33-58.

Emphasizes the vital importance of women's role in Guinean agriculture. Funk looks at the differing access to land and relations of production in Balanta-Brassa and Balanta-Mané communities in northern Guinea-Bissau. Significantly, she finds that despite an ideology of communal property, individualized rights and even private property exist. Moreover, not even family or household budgets exist but rather separate spousal budgets. Funk's research adds precision and depth to Hochet's analyses of the Oio region. In her conclusion, Funk sees the several processes of increasing population density, skewed distribution of the land and land concessions as potentially threatening women's usufruct rights. In a forthcoming article, Funk looks at coping strategies in times of food shortages in the above communities and also in urban settings. She finds that they differ, and that women are more affected than men because of the varying gender divisions of labour. Moreover she finds that such strategies take time away from opportunities to increase income and that they thus exacerbate poverty and inequalities. See 'Labor, economic power and gender: coping with food shortage in Guinea-Bissau' in *The political economy of the African famine: the class and gender basis of hunger*, edited by S. P. Rayna, D. O. Kerner, R. E. Downs (New York: Gordon and Breach, forthcoming).

437 **On peasant productivity: the case of Guinea-Bissau.**
Rosemary E. Galli. *Development and Change.* vol. 18, no. 1 (1987), p. 69-98.
Argues that Guinean peasants can be highly productive when there are reasonable terms of trade and offers historical evidence of this. Galli shows an anti-smallholder bias in much of the development literature.

438 **Os efeitos sócio-estruturais da introdução de inovações tecnológicas nos meios rurais Sahelianos (os efeitos dos projectos de recuperação de bolanhas na orzicultura salgada da Guiné-Bissau): estudo de caso.** (The socio-structural effects of the introduction of technological innovations in Sahelian rural areas [the effects of bolanha reclamation on salt-water rice cultivation in Guinea-Bissau]: a case study.)
Carlos Rui Ribeiro. Bissau: INEP, Centro de Estudos Sócio-Económicos, 1988. 36p. bibliog.
Finds that both colonial and postcolonial administrations have erroneously approached the problem of rice cultivation in several of the most important rice-growing areas of Guinea. Both understood the problem only in technical terms. Both ignored the social aspects of rice culture and focused mainly on reclaiming the fields through the construction of large-scale dikes which did not permit either individual or village regulation of water flow. This is a major factor in salt-water rice growing. 'Traditional' mud dikes allowed for village regulation but 'modern' dikes require a supra-community institution for water control, a factor which has been completely ignored. As a consequence, much of the reclaimed land has had to be abandoned for lack of proper water management.

439 **PDRI-Zona 1.** (Integrated Rural Development Programme-Zone 1.)
Jorge Oliveira. Bissau: Ministry of Rural Development and Fisheries, 1986. 9p. map.
Outlines the philosophy of rural development of the Ministry and the strategy being pursued in the Integrated Rural Development Programme of Zone 1 which includes the regions of Cacheu, Oio and Biombo. In 1986, the Programme covered 74 per cent of the families of Cacheu and Oio and was due to begin work in the region of Biombo in 1988. The document includes the plan of work for the period 1987-89. There are annual reports issued on the Programme.

Economy. Agriculture

440 **Prática e utensilagem agrícola na Guiné.** (Agricultural practices and tools in Guinea.)
F. Rogado Quintino. Lisbon: Junta de Investigações Científicas do Ultramar, 1971. 106p. 16 maps. bibliog.

Presents a comprehensive overview of the agricultural technologies practised in the colony. The presentation differs from that of most of the colonial writers in that the author does not give a strictly ethnic interpretation to agricultural practices or tools. He recognizes many similarities among the ethnic groups. Moreover, unlike most administrators, he shows an understanding of the rationality of Guinean cultivators. The book is extremely detailed and beautifully illustrated.

441 **Programa de pesquisa camponesa na região de Tombali.** (Programme of research on peasants in the Tombali region.)
Laurent Thomas, Eric Sabourin. Bissau: Ministério do Desenvolvimento Rural e Pescas, Departamento da Pesquisa Agrícola (DEPA), 1987. 178p. 6 maps.

A valuable addition to the study of agriculture in the southern region of Tombali, this work doubles as a manual for training people in agricultural research. The methodology advocated involves engaging producers in the research. However, the traditional methods of direct observation, interview and village meetings still appear to be the main means of gathering and diffusing information.

442 **Prospects and problems of the transition from agrarianism to socialism: the case of Angola, Guinea-Bissau and Mozambique.**
Tetteh A. Kofi. *World Development*, vol. 9, nos 9-10 (1981), p. 851-70.

Discusses the origins of the theory of an agricultural path to socialism in Marx and Cabral, and reviews the development of the economies of the three countries under Portuguese colonialism. This is the background for his discussion of the prerequisites for socialist transformation, one of which is that progressive elements of such classes as the petty bourgeoisie, workers and peasants must have state power. He also invokes the concept of people's power (*poder popular*) or people's rule. See also Rudebeck for an elaboration of this concept.

443 **Recenseamento agrícola de Guiné: 1960-61.** (Agricultural census of Guinea: 1960-61.)
Comissão para os Inquéritos Agrícolas no Ultramar. Lisbon: Ministério do Ultramar, Direcção Geral de Economia, 1963. 22p. 8 maps.

The original and still classic census was made by Amílcar and Maria Helena Cabral in 1953 and published in the *Boletim Cultural da Guiné Portuguesa*. It has recently been published in the *Estudos agrários de Amílcar Cabral* (q.v.). The above census was carried out under the auspices of the Food and Agriculture Organization of the United Nations (FAO). There is a large quantity of data on types of crops, where and how grown. The tables give comprehensive figures which are also broken down into zones. There are also figures on cattle-raising. The report itself casts doubt on the validity of the data but the text is useful for comparative purposes. The government carried out another census with the collaboration of the FAO in 1988 (q.v.).

444 Recensement agricole de 1988: résultats preliminaires. (Agricultural
census 1988: preliminary results.)
Ministère du Développement Rural et de l'Agriculture, Cabinet de
Planification Agricole. Bissau: République de Guinée-Bissau, 1989.
60p. map.
An agricultural census of the smallholder sector (the predominant productive sector),
this volume begins by discussing the methodology and concepts used in the survey. It
estimates the total population in Guinea at 950,985 individuals and the agricultural
population at 713,975. The male population is slightly higher (51%) than the female
population. The active population is estimated at 405,162 working 83,974 farms. These
are divided into 239,270 plots representing 95,195 hectares. Rice is the principal crop
(on 89% of all farms) followed by maize, sorghum, millet and fonio (on 81% of farms).
Approximately 40% of farms grow groundnuts, cotton and cashew trees. Yams, sweet
potatoes, and cassava are planted on about 10% of the farms. The survey is the closest
the government has got to updating the agricultural census done by Amílcar Cabral
and his associates (q.v.). Unfortunately, there are problems with the methodology and
results of the current survey.

445 Sectorial consultation on agriculture.
Ministry of Planning, Ministry of Rural Development and Fishery.
Bissau: Republic of Guinea-Bissau, 1986. 2 vols.
The 1985 Round Table meeting of major donor organizations, nations and the
government decided to organize a consultation on agriculture. The documents for the
conference were elaborated by the government with the support of the World Bank,
UNDP and FAO. The reader is warned that the English translation is faulty, but the
general information and data concerning development projects and strategy is worth
the struggle.

**446 Socialism without liberation: land reclamation projects in Guinea-
Bissau.**
Dirk Kohnert. *Sociologia Ruralis*, vol. 28, nos 2-3 (1988), p. 161-75.
Compares the land reclamation projects of the Portuguese during colonial times with
those of the independent government and arrives at the conclusion that there was little
difference in their conception, management and failure. A top-down approach ignored
the needs and social organization of the local populations and consequently much of
the reclaimed land lay idle. See Galli and Jones for a comparison of colonial and postcolonial policies in various sectors.

447 The Guinea-Bissau: a study of the food and agricultural sector.
Lorenzo Cabellero. Uppsala, Sweden: Swedish University of
Agricultural Sciences, 1987. 100p. 7 maps. bibliog. (Rural
Development Studies, no. 23).
This useful survey of the agriculture, animal husbandry and fisheries sectors includes
an introductory chapter of general information. As it covers a wide range of
information, a word of caution must be sounded regarding the reliability of the data. It
is advisable to check a second source as well. Particularly interesting are the
comparative statistics on land use and production in three time periods, 1953, 1976 and
1985.

448 **The PAIGC and the economic development of Guinea-Bissau: ideology and reality.**
F. O. E. Okafor. *Developing Economies*, vol. 26, no. 2 (1988), p. 125-40.

Reviews the development strategy of Luís Cabral's régime. The article concludes that agricultural credit is of vital importance to the Guinean peasant, a situation that has not changed and is of even greater importance since economic liberalization – see Galli, 1990. Another more comprehensive review of development strategy and particularly rural development is Thomas Paulini's *Guinea-Bissau: nachkoloniale Entwicklung eines Agrarstaates* (Guinea-Bissau: post-colonial development of an agrarian state) (Göttingen, West Germany: Edition Herodot, 1984).

449 **The soils of Portuguese Guinea.**
A. J. da Silva Teixeira. *Garcia de Orta*, vol. 8, no. 1 (1960), p. 175-92.

Presents a summary of a much larger work by the author in Portuguese of the same title (*Os solos da Guiné Portuguesa*). These are the results of the work of the Brigada de Estudos Agronómicos da Guiné. Guinean soils were provisionally classified as fersiallitic to ferrallitic, organic hydromorphic, hydromorphic and as regosols. Sand and rock banks, uncovered by the low tide, were also mapped. The article describes typical profiles of the topography, vegetation and soils of the countryside. Soil studies are currently being undertaken by the Department of Hydrology and Soils (DHAS).

Guinea-Bissau: politics, economics and society.
See item no. 4.

Guiné Portuguesa.
See item no. 6.

Paysanneries en attente: Guinée-Bissau.
See item no. 11.

Annuário da Província da Guiné do anno de 1925.
See item no. 83.

Anuário da Guiné Portuguesa.
See item no. 84.

L'eau et la riziculture Balante: étude de la riziculture de Cantone.
See item no. 178.

The food crisis and the socialist state in lusophone Africa.
See item no. 325.

Fisheries

450 **Análise do sector de pesca no ultramar: subsídios para o seu estudo.**
(Analysis of the overseas fishing sector: notes for its investigation.)
Rómulo de Figueiredo. *Boletim Geral do Ultramar*, vol. 42, no. 493
(1966), p. 123-50.
Surveys the possibilities of stimulating the fishing industry in Guinea-Bissau in
recognition of its great potential. Figueiredo describes the state of the fleet and
processing industry and the state of imports and exports. He also makes a series of
recommendations.

451 **Guinea-Bissau, Cape Verde: now the boat's come in.**
Howard Schissel. *West Africa*, no. 3455 (31 October 1983),
p. 2510-12.
Reports on the development of the fishing industry in both countries. Schissel makes
the important point that Guinea-Bissau still has not reached the level of fishing of its
neighbours. Even more important than the state of the industry is the fact that the
extent of Guinea's Exclusive Economic Zone (EEZ) is in dispute with Senegal.

Finance and banking

452 **Guinea-Bissau: a prescription for comprehensive adjustment.**
World Bank Staff. Washington, DC: World Bank, 1987. 68p. map.
(A World Bank Country Study).
Outlines several possible models for structural adjustment over different time
frameworks. This technical document analyses the advantages and disadvantages of
alternative macro-economic strategies as a basis for World Bank sponsorship of a
structural adjustment programme. The report was based on a mission to the country
and was the basis for negotiation of the current structural adjustment programme.

453 **Guinea-Bissau: economic difficulties and prospects for structural
adjustment.**
Dionisio D. Carneiro, Marcelo de P. Abreu.   Stockholm: Swedish
International Development Authority. 1989. 86p. (Studies in
Macroeconomic Management).
Evaluates the economic performance of Guinea since independence and the need for
structural adjustment. This is a useful overview but the body of the text is written for
economists. Some of the author's conclusions need further explication. For example,
they do not show how 'modernizing the state' will lead the government to attend to the
'objective social needs of the Guinean people'. Moreover, they state that the scarcity
of foreign exchange is a major constraint to the country's economic growth but they do
not analyse how the available foreign exchange is being spent. Nor do they address the
question of how to guarantee that the foreign exchange conceded by bilateral and

multilateral organizations is used for productive investment. The analysis thus does not go far enough.

454 **Programa de ajustamento estrutural 1987: relatório de execução (preliminar).** (The 1987 structural adjustment programme: preliminary report on its implementation.)
Segretária de Estado da Presidência para os Assuntos Económicos e Cooperação Internacional.   Bissau: Presidência da República da Guiné-Bissau, 1988. 22p.

Describes the macro-economic situation of the country after the first year of the first structural adjustment programme (1987-89) under the supervision of the International Monetary Fund and the World Bank. The preliminary results show positive results in terms of an increase in agricultural production and exports, a dampening of imports but negative ones also, including an inflation rate of around 100 per cent and a very large increase in the monetary supply. There were continuing problems of an overall governmental budget deficit, a rapidly growing foreign debt and thus dependency on international donors. There are many statistical tables in the annexes.

455 **Round Table follow-up meeting: economic situation in 1984, perspectives for 1985 and 1986.**
Secretary of State for the Presidency for International Cooperation (SEPCI).   Bissau: SEPCI, 1985. 44p.

This is volume 5 of the documents for the follow-up to the Round Table meeting that took place between the government and the major donors in May 1984. There is an overview of the economy in 1984 and a description of the development projects that were presented to the donors at the meeting. There is also an analysis of their status as of January 1985.

456 **Staff report on the request for a second annual arrangement under the structural adjustment facility.**
African Department.   Washington, DC: International Monetary Fund, 1989. 63p.

Reports such as this one provide recent and official data on the macro-economy of the country. This does not guarantee the reliability of the data. However, reading such reports allows one to understand the basis upon which governments, international organizations and banks decide to finance a country. This report notes the failure of the Guinean government to comply with all the agreements in the structural adjustment programme for 1987 and 1988. It lays the basis for the new programme agreed for 1989-91. It also provides an insight into the kind of political economy the financiers are aiming to promote in the country.

Trade

457 **Avaliação do projecto de assistência técnica a reforma das estruturas comerciais: relatório final.** (Evaluation of the project of technical assistance for commercial reform: final report.)
João Vilela, José Lencart. Bissau: Delegação de Comissão das Comunidades Européias de Bissau and República da Guiné-Bissau, 1989. 99p.
Shows that the liberalization of trade had still not eliminated the dominant position of the then state-owned Armazéns do Povo in the import–export business and that the new system of private trade was only partially reaching farmers. Some areas of the country were being better serviced than others while one area – Boé – was completely cut off from trade.

458 **Guinea-Bissau: shifting course.**
Daphne Topouzis. *Africa Report*, vol. 34, no. 5 (1989), p. 49-51.
Reviews, in a journalistic fashion, the trade liberalization policy and economic reform begun in 1987.

459 **Guiné-Bissau: Comércio I and II.** (Guinea-Bissau: Trade I and II.)
Lisbon: Centro de Informação e Documentação, Amílcar Cabral (CIDAC), 1990.
Contains copies of the *Boletim mensal de comércio externo* for July 1975, December 1976, January-March 1977, December 1977, January-March 1980, October-December 1980, January-March 1981, January-June 1981, January-September 1981, January-December 1981, January-March 1982, April-June 1982, September, 1982, October 1982, November 1982, December 1982 and August 1983. There is also a résumé of foreign trade statistics for 1976-80.

460 **Trade promotion in Guinea-Bissau.**
H. J. Wilson. Geneva, Switzerland: International Trade Centre, UNCTAD/GATT, 1983. 15p. bibliog.
The report of a mission sent to Guinea to discuss possibilities for the expansion of the country's exports, this document gives a good indication of the thinking at the time of the first national development plan. Although now out of date, its recommendations for long-term promotion of exports are now being put into effect: the development of cereals production, fishing, cashew-nut processing. Only one, textile finishing, is not being undertaken at this time. There are tables showing the composition of exports and imports from 1975 to 1981 and the balance of payments from 1975 to 1980.

Guinea-Bissau: politics, economics and society.
See item no. 4.

Guiné Portuguesa.
See item no. 6.

Transport

461 **Les transports en Guinée-Bissau.** (Transport in Guinea-Bissau.)
A. Lederer.   *Bulletin des Séances de l'Académie Royale des Sciences d'Outre-Mer*, vol. 29, no. 3 (1983), p. 319-32.
Gives a general overview of the difficulties of transport in the country and makes some interesting recommendations. He discusses river transport in particular. There is a summary in English and three maps.

Education

462 **Bases para a implantação do sistema nacional de educação e formação.**
(Basis for establishing a national system of education and training.)
Grupo de Coordenação. Bissau: Ministério de Educação Nacional,
1981. 53p.
A key document in the many discussions on educational reform of the country, it
argues for a reorientation of the system to make it more relevant to the development
needs of the country. One of its major contributions was to focus on the need to
integrate vocational training into the system at various levels.

463 **Dossier sobre a experiência CEPI.** (Dossier on the CEPI experiment.)
Equipa técnica CEEF no GEOP. Bissau: Ministério de Educação,
Cultura e Desportos, Centros Experimentais de Educação e Formação,
1985. [n.p.].
Evaluates the experimental educational centres, CEPI or Centros de Educação
Popular Integrada. These centres provided a fifth and sixth year of education which
complemented the four years of primary education. Their model was the PAIGC
village school set up in the liberated zones during the war for independence and their
purpose was to integrate the entire community into an innovative educational
programme. Begun in 1976, the experiment was ended in 1986 and the centres were
transformed in a number of ways. The report evaluates various aspects, including their
unique pedagogy. Galli and Jones give a general introduction (q.v.), while Paola
Belpassi Bernardi (q.v.) presents a critical analysis.

464 **Education and production in Guinea-Bissau.**
Carlos Dias. *Development Dialogue*, no. 2 (1978), p. 51-7.
Articulates well the idealism of the early post-independence years. Dias describes the
new educational system which attempted to combine work with classroom learning.
Most often the work was in school gardens. In boarding schools, the aim was to
provide a basic food supply. The overall purpose of the programme was to return

people to the source, as Cabral exhorted, that is to prevent the alienation of the educated from rural society.

465 **Education in Guinea-Bissau 1978-81: the impact of Swedish assistance.**
Edited by Roy Carr-Hill, Gunilla Rosengart. Stockholm: Swedish International Development Authority, 1982. 149p. map. bibliog.

More than simply an evaluation of Swedish assistance to the sector, this report is an excellent source of information about the development of the educational system since colonial times, in particular about the period 1954-81. Many of the observations made are still relevant because, although there is recognition that basic changes are needed, change has been slow in coming.

466 **Guinea-Bissau '79: learning by living and doing.**
Institute of Cultural Action. Geneva, Switzerland: IDAC, 1979. 51p.

This is a brief survey of educational efforts in the country in the early post-independence era by the people directly involved. The literacy campaign is the focus.

467 **Guiné-Bissau: Alfabetização/Educação de Adultos I and II.** (Guinea-Bissau: Literacy training/Adult education I and II.)
Lisbon: Centro de Informação e Documentação, Amílcar Cabral (CIDAC), 1990.

Contains many documents from the two literacy campaigns, including training manuals and materials. There is also the evaluation of the two experiences by Marcela Ballara, 'Analisis del proceso de alfabetización de adultos en Guinea-Bissau, 1976-84: estudio comparativo de dos experiencias', 1985. Another evaluation of the campaign is Linda M. Harasim's *Literacy and national reconstruction in Guinea-Bissau: a critique of the Freirean literacy campaign*, PhD thesis, University of Toronto, 1983. It concludes that the differing socio-economic conditions in Guinea-Bissau and Brazil was a major reason for the lack of success of the Freirean approach.

468 **Guiné-Bissau: Educação I-IV.** (Guinea-Bissau: Education I-IV.)
Lisbon: Centro de Informação e Documentação, Amílcar Cabral (CIDAC), 1990.

Contains important government and other documents and studies on the educational system as a whole. There are also the issues of the magazine *Bombolom* put out by the Centros de Educação Popular Integrada (CEPI). There are two evaluations of the CEPI. The third dossier contains studies by the Institute of Cultural Action (Geneva, Switzerland) which cooperated in the literacy programme. These include the study by the Darcy de Olivieras, *Guinea-Bissau: reinventing education*, 1975-76. Government documents on pre-school education are included in the dossier: Guiné-Bissau: Ensino Pre-Escolar-I; on primary education in Guiné-Bissau: Ensino Primário-I; and on secondary education: Ensino Secundário-I and -II. These last four dossiers are rich in documentation up to 1981.

469   Guiné-Bissau: Formação de Professores-I; Formação Profissional-I;
      Formação de Profissionais de Saúde-I. (Guinea-Bissau: Teacher
      training-I; Vocational training-I; Training of health workers-I.)
      Lisbon: Centro de Informação e Documentação, Amílcar Cabral
      (CIDAC), 1990.

The first dossier contains eleven documents mainly on teacher training – including
three studies by Jean-Pierre Lepri (q.v.) – and several on the literacy programme. The
second has eleven documents, most of which from the Technical Training Institute
(Instituto Técnico de Formação Profissional) and the Management Center (Centro de
Formação Administrativo). The third contains the training document for village
midwives and health workers.

470   L'aide extérieure à l'éducation et à la formation professionnelle en
      Guinée-Bissao en 1986 et en projet: document de travail.
      (Foreign aid to education and vocational training in Guinea-Bissau in
      1986 and projects in the pipeline: a working paper)
      Jean-Pierre Lepri.   Bissau: UNESCO and UNDP, 1986. 41p.

Reports the assistance of the principal donor agencies and nations to the government
for the educational sector in 1986 and prospected for 1987. Included in the list are both
governmental and non-governmental agencies.

471   Leggere e scrivere in una cultura orale: ricerche in una communità della
      Guinea-Bissau. (Reading and writing in an oral culture: research in a
      community of Guinea-Bissau.)
      Paola Belpassi Bernardi.   Urbino, Italy: Argalia Editore Urbino,
      1988. 284p. map.

Compares the process of learning, particularly in the CEPI or Centros de Educação
Popular Integrada, in Guinea-Bissau with the pedagogy of Piaget. Bernardi observes
closely a number of children from various communities throughout the country. She
particularly highlights those schools and those communities where education is seen as
a process of work and where the children learn by doing.

472   O ensino na Guiné-Bissau no ano lectivo 1984-85. (Teaching in Guinea-
      Bissau in the academic year 1984-85.)
      Jean-Pierre Lepri, translated by Maria Luísa Buscardine.   Bissau:
      Instituto Nacional para o Desenvolvimento da Educação, 1986. 7p.

Presents a breakdown of statistics on the educational system. In 1984-85, there were
93,000 students which represented a scholastic rate of 37 per cent of children between
the ages of 7 and 14. Fifteen per cent of all students were in high school. The report
estimates that 89 per cent of the population above the age of seven remained illiterate.
There was a noticeable drop in the number of adult students.

473   Para uma educação endógena em África subsariana. (Towards an
      endogenous education in sub-Saharan Africa.)
      Manuel Rambout Barcelos.   Bissau: mimeographed, 1987. 26p.

Analyses and criticizes the current educational situation throughout Africa and
proposes a new model or strategy that does not copy other ones, particularly Western

models, but is instead the product of popular research into the specific conditions and necessities of each region. Annexed to this document prepared for the Consultative Meeting on new educational policies for sub-Saharan Africa are three working documents by Jean-Pierre Lepri on the same subject in relation to Guinea-Bissau. Manuel Rambout Barcelos was Minister of Education, Culture and Sports in 1989.

474 **Pedagogia adattata e scuola: istituzioni formative e trasmissione culturale in Guinea-Bissau.** (Appropriate pedagogy and schooling: educational institutions and cultural transmission in Guinea-Bissau.) Paola Belpassi Bernardi. Milano, Italy: Franco Angeli Editore, 1983. 309p.

A very thorough critical examination of the educational system including the Centros de Educação Popular Integrada, this work focuses on educational philosophy, particularly during the early more idealistic period of the 1970s.

475 **Pedagogy in process: the letters to Guinea-Bissau.** Paulo Freire, translated by Carman St John Hunter, introduction by Jonathon Kozol. London; New York: Writers and Readers Publishing Cooperative and Seabury Press, 1978. 178p.

Freire, who is well known for his innovative work in literacy training in the northeast of Brazil, was involved in the first literacy campaign in Guinea. This is a record of that involvement and consists of a series of letters to the then Minister of Education, Mário Cabral. The campaign was not successful as it was aimed at adult literacy in Portuguese. In the final postscript of the text, Freire emphasizes the problem of the choice of language during decolonization.

476 **Projecto e estratégia de desenvolvimento do sector de educação.** (Development project and strategy for the education sector.) Ministério da Educação, Cultura e Desportos, Secretária de Estado do Ensino. Bissau: República da Guiné-Bissau, 1987. 43p.

Provides an excellent overview of the educational system and its problems from the point of view of the Ministry of Education and outlines a medium-term strategy to correct them. The objectives are to improve teaching particularly in the basic education system, to implement a system of vocational and technical training and improve the administrative framework. Sub-goals include collapsing the two-stage division of primary education in order to make a unitary one of six years and revising the basic curriculum in order to introduce notions of health, nutrition and agriculture.

477 **Quelle école pour la Guinée-Bissau?** (What school for Guinea-Bissau?) Jean-Pierre Lepri. Bissau: Ministère de l'Éducation, de la Culture et des Sports, Bureau des Études et de la Planification, 1985. 2nd ed. 88p.

This is a basic text for understanding the changes in the educational system proposed in the late 1980s. Lepri was a UNESCO (UN Educational, Scientific and Cultural Organization) consultant to the ministry. He documents in great detail, with accompanying statistics, the ineffectiveness of the system and its irrelevance to the overwhelming majority of people in the country. He criticizes the accepted wisdom that the fault lies in the lack of structures, administrators, teachers, equipment and so on, and shows that the problem lies in the élitist, Europeanist conceptualization of education. Lepri proposes a methodology for inventing a new type of schooling.

478 **Regionalizar o ensino nacional: algumas propostas.** (Regionalizing national education: some proposals.)
Jean-Pierre Lepri, translated from French by Diana Lima Handem.
Bissau: Instituto Nacional para o Desenvolvimento da Educação, 1987. 27p.

Proposes the creation of two systems of education; the conventional one for school-age children and a vocational education for young people and adults *and* a regionalization of the system so that it responds to the diffcrent needs of these populations in their specific locales. The basic idea is to involve local populations in the planning and administration of the school system.

Guinea-Bissau: politics, economics and society.
See item no. 4.

Ensino rudimentar (para indígenas) em Angola e na Guiné Portuguesa.
See item no. 91.

Environment

479 **Guiné-Bissau: Urbanismo/Ordenação do Território.** (Guinea-Bissau:
Urban planning/Environmental planning.)
Lisbon: Centro de Informação e Documentação, Amílcar Cabral
(CIDAC), 1990.
Has a map of the city of Bissau; the government statement on environmental policy of
February 1986; and the study by Júlio Davila (q.v.).

480 **Planification villageoise en Guinée Bissau: problèmes, expériences,
perspectives.** (Village planning in Guinea-Bissau: problems,
experiments, perspectives.)
Hans Geisslhofer.   Dakar, Senegal: Environnement Africain
(ENDA), 1981. 25p. 2 maps. (Études et Recherches, no. 70-81).
Outlines a methodology for regional development planning, using as a case-study the
region of Cacheu. The author argues for village-level planning in order to alleviate the
phenomenon of alienation of peasants from the land known all over the Third World
as 'rural exodus'. He notes that this phenomenon is more accelerated in Guinea-Bissau
than in the neighbouring countries.

481 **Problemática do meio ambiente em alguns países africanos.** (The
problem of the environment in some African countries.)
Edited by Carlos Lopes.   Lisbon: INEP, 1987. 142p. (Colecção 'Kacu
Martel', no. 3).
A collection of essays on the environment in such different countries as Guinea-Bissau,
Cape Verde, São Tomé e Príncipe, Equatorial Guinea and Mozambique, this volume
is the result of a seminar sponsored by the UN Environmental Programme (UNEP),
the Ministry of Rural Development and INEP. The final report of the seminar presents
a comparative picture of environmental problems in the different countries and a list of
recommendations. Such problems as water contamination, sewage collection and
removal were found to be universal whereas soil erosion, desertification and acid soil

126

were common to Guinea-Bissau and Mozambique and, with the exception of acid soils, also to Cape Verde. All the countries face the challenge of sensitizing their publics, completing an inventory of natural resources, training personnel, instituting legislation and planning in the area of conservation.

482 **Shelter, poverty and African revolutionary socialism: human settlements in Guinea-Bissau.**
Júlio D. Davila.   London: International Institute for Environment and Development, Human Settlements Programme, 1987. 89p. 2 maps. bibliog.
Only the last chapter (p. 60-89) is on housing, the first three chapters consist of very general information. The report concludes that very little has been done to improve housing conditions for the poor.

Essential problems of urbanization in the Overseas Provinces: urban structures of integration and intercourse.
See item no. 92.

Ecological perspectives on Mande population movements, commercial networks and settlement patterns from the Atlantic Wet Phase (ca 5500-2500 BC) to the present.
See item no. 191.

Literature and
the Arts

483 **A luta é a minha primavera.** (The struggle is my Spring.)
Vasco Cabral, preface by Fernando Martinho.   Lisbon: África
Editora, 1981. 106p.
Collects the poetry by the distinguished elder statesman of the PAIGC from the 1950s
to the 1970s. The poems are divided into different themes.

484 **Antologia temática de poesia africana: o canto armado.** (A thematic
anthology of African poetry: the song as weapon.)
Mário de Andrade.   Praia, Cape Verde: Instituto Caboverdeano do
Livro, 1980. 178p. vol. 2
Features the poetry of Agnello Regalla and José Carlos Schwarz.

485 **Arquitectura tradicional: Guiné-Bissau.** (Traditional architecture:
Guinea-Bissau.)
D. Błażejewicz, R. Lund, K. Schönning, S. Steincke.   Stockholm:
Swedish International Development Authority, 1983. 2nd ed. 271p.
22 maps. bibliog.
Gives an overall view of the architecture in seventeen villages throughout mainland
Guinea. There are beautiful, detailed drawings and photographs of compounds and
such village constructions as houses, storage facilities, fencing, animal shelters and so
on. The villages represent the following ethnic groups: Balanta, Papel, Manjaco,
Brame, Nalu, Beafada and Fula. This fascinating study concludes with a taxonomy of
the different types of housing.

486 **Bronzes antígos da Guiné.** (Antique Guinean bronzes.)
A. Teixeira da Mota. In: *Actas do Congresso Internacional de Etnografia*, vol. 4. Porto, Portugal: Colóquio de Etnografia Comparada, 1963, p. 149-54.

Describes, with photographs, the ancient bronzes called 'sonos' which may have been from the Malian empire. A map shows that they have been found all over northeastern and central areas in the country. Teixeira da Mota links them with the Soninque peoples.

487 **Catálogo-inventário da secção de etnografia do Museu da Guiné Portuguesa.** (Inventory-catalogue of the ethnographic section of the Museum of Portuguese Guinea.)
José D. Lampreia. Lisbon: Junta de Investigações do Ultramar, 1962. 89p. bibliog.

Catalogues the works of art in this museum.

488 **Colonialism and literary production in Guinea-Bissau.**
James H. Kennedy. *A Current Bibliography on African Affairs*, vol. 17, no. 2 (1984-85), p. 155-65.

Maintains that colonial policies prevented the flourishing of a written literature in Guinea-Bissau in comparison to what can be found in other lusophone African countries. Kennedy cites particularly the lack of a widespread educational system. On this point, see also Joan E. Collemacine, 'A look at African literature in the Portuguese language', *Africa* (Rome), vol. 32, no. 2 (1977). Gerald Moser makes some of the same arguments in 'African literature in Portuguese: the first written, the last discovered', *African Forum*, vol. 2, no. 4 (1967). Moser mentions the novel *Auá* (1934) on Fulas in Guinea-Bissau by the Cape-Verdean-born Fausto Duarte. Kennedy discusses António Baticã Ferreira, the only published Guinean poet before independence. He also notes the efforts of the postcolonial government to stimulate artistic creativity including the establishment of a writers' union.

489 **Critical perspectives on lusophone literature from Africa.**
Edited by Donald Burness. Washington, DC: Three Continents Press, 1981. 307p. bibliog.

Two of the essays discuss literature from Guinea-Bissau and the relative lack of it: G. Moser, 'The lusophone literatures of Africa since independence' and R. Hamilton, 'Cape Verdean poetry and the PAIGC'.

490 **Esculturas e objectos decorados da Guiné Portuguesa no Museu de Etnologia do Ultramar.** (Sculptures and decorative art from Portuguese Guinea in the Overseas Ethnology Museum.)
Fernando Galhano. Lisbon: Junta de Investigações do Ultramar, 1971. 120p. bibliog.

Contains drawings of noteworthy pieces of art found in this museum. Bijagó sculpture takes pride of place but there are also examples of Fula and Mandinga handicrafts, particularly jewellery, and Nalu sculptures and masks. The reader is advised to consult Carreira's *Panaria* (q.v.) for examples of the artwork of Manjacos and Papéis.

Literature and the Arts

491 **Guiné-Bissau: Literatura-I.** (Guinea-Bissau: Literature-I.)
Lisbon: Centro de Documentção e Informação, Amílcar Cabral
(CIDAC), 1990.
Contains a poem by Amílcar Cabral; the anthology of young poets published in 1978;
and three stories in *crioulo*.

492 **Guiné: sol e sangue.** (Guinea: sun and blood.)
Armor Pires Mota. Braga, Portugal: Editora Pax, 1968. 162p.
These are short stories by a Portuguese soldier recounting fighting experiences during
the national liberation struggle in the 1960s.

493 **José Carlos Schwartz: bard of popular mobilization in Guinea-Bissau.**
James H. Kennedy. *Présence Africaine*, nos 137-8 (1986), p. 91-101.
Focuses on the life and work of the well-loved poet, much of whose work was set to
music and song in order to capture the widest possible audience in this mostly illiterate
country. Kennedy likens Schwartz to the *griots* or minstrels of Malian ancestry.
Schwartz's work was highly political and his last poem openly critical of the
opportunism of some public officials.

494 **Junbai: storias de Bolama e do outro mundo.** (Junbai: stories of Bolama
and the other world.)
Teresa Montenegro, Carlos de Morais. Bolama, Guinea-Bissau:
Imprensa Nacional, 1979. 97p. map.
Collects *crioulo* stories in a *crioulo*–Portuguese edition which includes very beautiful
woodcuts depicting scenes from the stories.

495 **Kaabu and Fuladu: historical narratives of the Gambian Mandinka.**
Gordon Innes. London: School of Oriental and African Studies,
University of London, 1976. 297p. map. bibliog.
Although recorded in The Gambia, the five narratives relate the history of two
important states that existed in the northern part of Guinea-Bissau from the thirteenth
to the nineteenth century. The first two texts, which are sung by the bards or *griots*
throughout the Senegambia, record the fall of Kaabu at Kansala (in Guinea-Bissau) at
the hands of the Fula populations.

496 **Les littératures Africaines de langue Portugaise: à la recherche de
l'identité individuelle et nationale.** (Lusophone African literature: the
search for individual and national identity.)
Paris: Fondation Calouste Gulbenkian, 1985. 570p.
Gives the proceedings of the international meeting of the same name held in Paris
from 28 November to 1 December 1984. Representatives of the five African countries
and members of the international academic community attended. Those who spoke on
Guinea-Bissau were Carlos Lopes – who talked on the concept of power and national
identity, B. Pinto-Bull who spoke on Fausto Duarte; Patrick Chabal who discussed
Amílcar Cabral; and H. J. de Dianoux who spoke on Guinean literature written in
Portuguese.

497   **Literatura africana, literatura necessária: Moçambique, Cabo Verde, Guiné-Bissau, São Tomé e Príncipe.** (African literature, necessary literature: Mozambique, Cape Verde, Guinea-Bissau, São Tomé and Príncipe.)
Russell G. Hamilton.   Lisbon: Edições 70, 1984. 273p. bibliog.

Evaluates this still young literary tradition in a comparative context. The essay on Guinean authors is only eighteen pages in length but is extremely informative. It covers the known published works in the first ten years of independence and compares those written in Portuguese (mainly poetry) with those in *crioulo*. An invaluable source of information and commentary.

498   **Mantenhas para quem luta: a nova poesia da Guiné-Bissau.** (Cheers for the fighters: the new poetry of Guinea-Bissau.)
Conselho Nacional de Cultura.   Bissau: República da Guiné-Bissau, 1977. 103p.

Features poetry on the national liberation struggle. This was the first such book published by the new government. A second anthology was *Antologia dos jovens poetas*, 1978.

499   **Não posso adiar a palavra.** (I can't put off speaking.)
Helder Proença, preface by Manuel Ferreira.   Lisbon: Sa da Costa, 1982. 89p.

Collects the work of the young poet who was first published in *Mantenhas para quem luta* (q.v.).

500   **No reino de Caliban.** (In the kingdom of Caliban.)
Edited by Manuel Ferreira.   Lisbon: Seara Nova, 1975. vol. 1. 328p.

Focuses on one poet, António Baticã Ferreira, in the ten pages dedicated to the poetry of Guinea-Bissau.

501   **Notas sobre a musica indígena da Guiné.** (Notes on indigenous Guinean music.)
Abilio Gomes.   *Boletim Cultural da Guiné Portuguesa*, vol. 5, no. 19 (1950), p. 411-24.

Describes the musical instruments used among the principal groups in Guinea-Bissau.

502   **'N sta li 'N sta la: livro de adivinhas.** ('N sta li 'N sta la: book of riddles.)
Bolama, Guinea-Bissau: Cooperativa Domingos Badinca, 1979. 77p.

Edited for children in the International Year of the Child, this beautiful book of riddles in *crioulo* was set by hand. It was the first book edited in the language by the Imprensa Nacional (National Printing Office).

503   **Os continuadores da revolução e a recordação do passado recente.**
(Those who continue the revolution and the remembrance of the recent past.)
Departamento de Edição, Difusão do Livro e do Disco. Bolama,
Guinea-Bissau: Imprensa Nacional Empresa Pública, [n.d.]. 90p.
Published in the International Year of the Child, this is a collection of poems from the
students of the experimental school begun during the war for independence and known
as the Escola Piloto. Mainly in Portuguese, the poems were inspired by the
independence
struggle.

504   **Os 10 poemas da Vasco Cabral: uma leitura.** (Ten poems by Vasco
Cabral: a reading.)
Maria Teresa Brocardo.   *África, Literatura, Arte e Cultura*, vol. 11,
no. 8 (1980), p. 367-74.
Traces the common thread in ten poems of the PAIGC leader. The recurring symbols
include peace, hope, liberty, revolt and struggle. More of his poetry is in *A luta é a
minha primavera* (q.v.).

505   **Panaria: cabo verdeano-guineense.** (Textiles: Cape Verdean-Guinean.)
António Carreira. Lisbon: Instituto Caboverdeano do Livro, 1983. 2nd
ed. 226p. map. bibliog.
Both an economic and an art history of cotton growing and weaving in Guinea-Bissau
and Cape Verde, Carreira traces the cycle of cotton growing and textiles before
Portuguese colonization and after. He traces the Portuguese influence on Cape
Verdean textiles in particular and also notes the similarities in the crafts in Guinea and
Cape Verde. There are numerous photographs.

506   **Subsídios para o estudo da tecelagem na Guiné Portuguesa.** (Notes for a
study of weaving in Portuguese Guinea.)
Maria Emília de Castro e Almeida, Miguel Vieira.   *Estudos sobre a
etnologia do Ultramar português*, vol. 3. Lisbon: Junta de Investigações
do Ultramar, 1963, p. 19-87.
Describes weaving techniques in Guinea-Bissau, especially among the Manjacos.

507   **Traditional Bijagó statuary.**
Robert C. Helmholz.   *African Arts*, vol. 6, no. 1 (autumn 1972),
p. 52-7.
Summarizes what little had already been published on the uses of statuary among the
Bijagós. According to the author, there were two main functions: as a repository for
the spirits of ancestors (*irãs*) and as a medium for consulting God.

508 **Voices from an empire: a history of Afro-Portuguese literature.**
Russell G. Hamilton.   Minneapolis, Minnesota: University of
Minnesota
Press. 1975. 450p. bibliog.
Covers *pre-independence* Afro-Portuguese literature. Hamilton places the authors in a
social and historical context. There are some translations of the various authors' work.

509 **When bullets begin to flower: poems of resistance from Angola,
Mozambique and Guiné.**
Selected and translated by Margaret Dickinson.   Nairobi: East Africa
Publishing House, 1972, 129p.
Features the works of two Guinean poets, Mário Cissoko and Mindelense. The
anthology also includes works by Cape Verdean poets belonging, at the time, to the
PAIGC.

Babel negra: etnografia, arte e cultura dos indígenas da Guiné.
See item no. 169.

**Dynamique de l'art Bidjogo (Guinée-Bissau): contribution à une anthropologie
de l'art des sociétés africaines.**
See item no. 181.

Manding: focus on an African civilization.
See item no. 193.

Arte Nalu.
See item no. 203.

Statistics

510 **Anuário estatístico.** (Statistical yearbook.)
Bissau: Direcção Geral de Estatística, Comissariado de Estado de
Desenvolvimento Económico e Planificação, 1974- . annual.

The publication is supposed to be annual but the volume for 1974 was published in 1977. The same department also began publishing a quarterly bulletin, *Boletim trimestral de estatística*, and a monthly bulletin of foreign trade, *Boletim mensal de comércio externo*, both with long delays.

511 **Anuário estatístico, vol. II: territórios ultramarinos.** (Statistical
yearbook, vol. II: overseas territories.)
Lisbon: Instituto Nacional de Estatística, 1947-74.

Gives data from the last few years of colonial administration on a wide variety of subjects including demography, trade, health, education, agriculture, industry, energy, and so on. There was also a monthly bulletin, *Boletim mensal de estatística*, which began publishing in 1926; in 1974 it ceased publishing statistics on Guinea-Bissau. Mary Jane Gibson (q.v.) lists an *Anuário estatístico* published in Bissau by the Repartição Provincial dos Serviços from 1947 and a quarterly, *Boletim trimestral de estatística*, from 1938. The School of Oriental and African Studies library, London, has copies of the yearbook for the years 1947-51.

512 **Anuário Estatístico da Educação.** (Education Statistics Yearbook.)
Bissau: Gabinete de Estudos e Plano, Ministério de Educação, 1979- .
annual.

The annual record of the activities of the Ministry of Education. The March 1989 edition analyses the data for 1987-88 in a comparative context, beginning with data for the academic year of 1981-82.

513 **Estatísticas do comércio externo.** (Foreign trade statistics.)
Lisbon: Instituto Nacional de Estatística, 1863-1967. annual.
The data were arranged by commodities. In 1967, the yearbook stopped reporting data for Guinea-Bissau.

514 **FAO Yearbook: Commerce, 1988.**
Rome: FAO, 1942- . annual.
Records imports and exports of principal crops and livestock production.

515 **FAO Yearbook: Production.**
Rome: Food and Agriculture Organization of the United Nations, 1947- . annual.
Gives statistics on land, population, crops, livestock and so on. Since 1952, FAO also publishes a *Monthly Bulletin of Agricultural and Economic Statistics.*

516 **Guiné-Bissau: Dados Estatísticos-I and II.** (Guinea-Bissau: Statistics I and II.
Lisbon: Centro de Informação e Documentação, Amílcar Cabral (CIDAC), 1990.
Contains the *Anuário estatístico* (1977) and the following issues of the *Boletim trimestral de estatística*: third quarter, 1979; third and fourth quarters, 1980; all four quarters, 1981; and all four quarters, 1982. Dossier II contains documents from the population census of 1979.

517 **Monthly Bulletin of Statistics.**
New York: United Nations, Statistical Office, 1947- . monthly.
The same kinds of data as the yearbook, only published on a monthly basis.

518 **Statistical Yearbook.**
New York: United Nations, Statistical Office, 1947- . annual.
Provides comparative data for most countries on a range of subjects including population, trade, agriculture, education, and health. The reliability of most UN data is a problem.

519 **The statesman's year-book: statistical and historical annual of the states of the world for the year 1989-90.**
Edited by John Paxton. London: Macmillan Reference Books, 1864- . annual.
This is a handy quick guide to some very basic data.

520 **UNESCO Statistical Yearbook.**
Paris: UNESCO, 1963- . annual.
Contains comparative data on population, education, libraries, publishing, radio, television, cinema, and so on.

Statistics

521 **World Bank atlas.**
Washington, DC: World Bank, 1966- . annual.

Shows comparative statistics on population, per capita product and growth rates. For reports specifically on Guinea-Bissau, the reader should consult the introductory basic economic report (q.v.) and such other published works as *Guinea-Bissau: a prescription for comprehensive structural adjustment* (1987) (q.v.).

522 **World debt tables, 1989-90.**
Washington, DC: World Bank, 1977- . annual. 2 vols.

Volume 1 analyses the data and presents general tables, while volume 2 presents financial tables specific to each country.

523 **World tables.**
Baltimore; London: Johns Hopkins University Press for the World Bank, 1971- . annual.

Covers both economic and social indicators, including financial, payments and trade data; manufacturing and agricultural data; demographic, educational and employment data.

Para uma leitura sociológica da Guiné-Bissau.
See item no. 10.

Periodicals

524   **África confidencial.** (Confidential Africa.)
      Lisbon: InformÁfrica Publicações, 1987- . bi-weekly.
This is a scandal sheet with short features on Guinea-Bissau on a more or less regular basis. Its focus is mainly on Angola. Because it had a name similar to the more noted and respectable *Africa Confidential* of London, the journal changed its name in 1989 to *InformÁfrica*.

525   **África, literatura, arte, cultura.** (Africa, literature, art, culture.)
      Lisbon: A.L.A.C. 1978- . quarterly.
Presents articles on the artistic activity in lusophone Africa. The journal suspended publication but appears to be publishing at present.

526   **Anais.** (Annals.)
      Lisbon: Junta das Missões Geográficas e de Investigações Coloniais, 1946-. annual.
The reports of the various colonial missions were published in this journal. In 1947, more than one issue began to be published to accommodate the reports of the various missions. In 1948, the name of the Junta was changed to Junta de Investigações Coloniais but the name of the journal stayed the same. In 1952 it changed again to Junta de Investigações do Ultramar, in 1961 to Junta de Investigações Científicas do Ultramar. In 1983 it became known as the Instituto de Investigação Científica Tropical. It is said that the name may change yet again.

Periodicals

527   **Boletim cultural da Guiné Portuguesa.** (Cultural bulletin of Portuguese Guinea.)
Bissau: Centro de Estudos da Guiné Portuguesa, 1946-73. quarterly.

The best source of social science investigation of the colony. All of the most known students of Guinea, whether foreign or Portuguese, wrote for the journal, including Amílcar Cabral.

528   **Boletim de informação científica e técnica.** (Bulletin of scientific and technical information.)
Bissau: Centro de Estudos de Tecnologia Apropriada do INEP, 1988- . quarterly.

The objective of this journal is to discuss appropriate technology in the Guinean context. The editorial of the first issue describes the aim as promoting scientific debate on the country's development.

529   **Boletim de informação sócio-económica.** (Bulletin of socio-economic information.)
Bissau: Centro de Estudos Sócio-Económicos (CESE) of INEP, 1985- . quarterly.

An invaluable source of information, the bulletin reports the latest socio-economic research on the country by nationals and foreigners.

530   **Boletim de Sociedade de Geografia de Lisboa.** (Bulletin of the Geographical Society of Lisbon.)
Lisbon: Sociedade de Geografia de Lisboa, 1876- . monthly, then quarterly, now twice a year.

Published articles of general and scientific interest until the country's independence.

531   **Boletim geral das colónias.** (General bulletin of the colonies.)
Lisbon: Agência Geral das Colónias, 1924-74. monthly.

This was an official journal which reported general news about the colonies as well as speeches by Salazar, Caetano and other high government officials. Its name changed to *Boletim Geral do Ultramar* in 1951.

532   **Boletim oficial da Guiné.** (Official bulletin of Guinea.)
Bolama, Guinea-Bissau: Imprensa Nacional da Guiné, 1880-1974. weekly.

The official journal of the colonial administration. The School of Oriental and African Studies, University of London, has a collection from 1964 to 1974 when the bulletin was printed in Bissau. The *Boletim Oficial* continues to be published by the República da Guiné-Bissau (q.v.).

138

533 **Country report: Senegal, The Gambia, Guinea-Bissau, Cape Verde.**
London: Economist Intelligence Unit, 1978- . quarterly with an annual supplement.
Gives an overall and timely, if brief, sketch of economic and political activity. The annual supplement is entitled *Country Profile*. In 1978, the first report on Guinea-Bissau was included with the *Quarterly Economic Review of Angola, Mozambique*, no. 1 (1978). Then it was issued with the *Quarterly Economic Review of Angola, Guinea-Bissau, Cape Verde, São Tomé and Príncipe*, until 1985 when it was published under the title *Quarterly Economic Review of Senegal, The Gambia, Guinea-Bissau, Cape Verde*.

534 **Garcia de Orta.**
Lisbon: Instituto de Investigação Científica Tropical, 1953- . trimestral.
Formerly, the journal of the Junta de Investigações do Ultramar, it covers all of the lusophone African countries. It includes a broad range of subjects in the so-called hard sciences but also ethnographic materials. A second series was begun in 1973 and the issues now appear more sporadically. There are eight different topics covered by the journal from agronomic studies to anthropology.

535 **Marchés tropicaux et méditerranéens.** (Tropical and Mediterranean markets.)
Paris: Marchés Tropicaux et Méditerranéens, 1945- . weekly.
An excellent source for current economic events in the country.

536 **Nô pintcha.** (Forward!)
Bissau: PAIGC, 1975- . thrice weekly.
This is the official newspaper of the country. It was originally printed three times a week and now only occasionally. There are problems getting newsprint, and spare parts for the machinery which is old and frequently breaks down. When published, it is often a good source of news in the country generally from the point of view of the urban educated public. In 1990, the government announced that it would be getting new machinery and that it aimed at daily publication of the newspaper.

537 **Nubedadi: boletim de novidades da Biblioteca Pública.** (Nubedadi: bulletin of new acquisitions in the Public Library.)
Bissau: INEP, 1987- . quarterly.
References the books and periodicals received by the Public Library of Guinea. Volume one, number one documents all the periodicals in the collection of the library.

538 **O militante.** (The Militant.)
Bissau: PAIGC, 1977-83. monthly.
This was the journal of the National Council of Guinea-Bissau, the highest organ of the PAIGC during the Luís Cabral régime. It was a good source for party thinking.

539 **PAIGC actualités: la vie et la lutte en Guinée et Cap Vert.** (Current PAIGC affairs: life and struggle in Guinea and Cape Verde.)
Richmond, BC, Canada: Liberation Support Movement Information Centre, 1969-74. quarterly.

This information bulletin was issued monthly in French by the Commission for Propaganda and Information of the Central Committee of the PAIGC and published in Dakar. The LSM information centre began to translate it into English, edit and reprint it on a quarterly basis from 1969.

540 **People's power.**
London: Mozambique and Guiné Information Centre, 1976-82. bi-monthly.

The name of the centre changed to Mozambique, Angola and Guiné Information Centre (MAGIC). It not only published this journal which discussed issues relating to the five newly independent countries of lusophone Africa but it also translated into English many of the most important official documents of these countries. The journal went from six to four issues a year.

541 **Ponto de encontro.** (Meeting point.)
Bissau: SOLIDAMI, 1989- . quarterly.

The first number records the history of SOLIDAMI, which stands for Solidaridade e Amizade (Solidarity and Friendship), an organization which aims at coordinating the activities of the non-governmental organizations operating in Guinea. The first issue is full of information about the 70 NGOs in the country.

542 **Relatório anual de actividades do INEP.** (Annual report of the activities of the INEP.)
Bissau: Instituto Nacional de Estudos e Pesquisa (INEP). 1985- . annual.

Lists the activities of the research institute on an annual basis from October to October.

543 **Revista internacional de estudos Africanos.** (International review of African studies.)
Lisbon: Centro de Estudos Africanos e Asiaticos, Instituto de Investigação Científica Tropical, 1984- . semestral.

Presents historical, social science and cultural research on the lusophone African countries by scholars from all over the world.

544 **Soronda: revista de estudos guineenses.** (Soronda: review of Guinean studies.)
Lisbon: Instituto Nacional de Estudos e Pesquisa, 1986- . semi-annual.

Presents the latest social science and cultural research on the country by national and foreign investigators. There are also book reviews, speeches by Guinean personalities and a regular report on the activities of INEP.

545 **West Africa.**
London: West Africa Publishing Company, 1917- . weekly.
Provides up-to-date information on the country on a regular basis.

Bibliographies

546   **A bibliography for the study of African politics.**
Alan C. Solomon.   Waltham, Massachusetts: Crossroads Press, 1977.
vol. 2.
Volume I was issued in 1973 as occasional paper no. 9 of the African Studies Center of the University of California, Los Angeles and was compiled by Robert B. Shaw and Richard L. Sklar. Volume III was published in 1983 (by the same publishers as noted above) and was edited by Eric R. Siegel. This volume appears to be the last in the series. The listings are focused on government and politics.

547   **A current bibliography on African affairs.**
New York: Greenwood Periodicals for African Bibliographic Center, 1963-67. bimonthly. 1968- . monthly.
Lists books, pamphlets, documents and articles, some of which are annotated.

548   **Additions to *Materials for West African history in the archives of Belgium and Holland* by Patricia Carson, London, 1962.**
H. M. Feinberg.   *African Studies Bulletin*, vol. 10, no. 3 (December 1967), p. 48-53.
Adds new materials for the historical researcher. Feinberg published another addition in *African Studies Bulletin*, vol. 12, no. 1 (April 1969), p. 81-9.

549   **Africa bibliography 1988: works on Africa published during 1988.**
Hector Blackhurst.   Manchester, England: Manchester University Press, 1984- .
Published on an annual basis since 1984, this is the latest volume in the series. Works are cited under the name of the country.

550 **Africa index: selected articles on socio-economic development.**
Addis Ababa: United Nations Economic Commission for Africa,
1973- .
Issued quarterly, the index lists articles from such sources as the *IMF Survey*.

551 **Africa south of the Sahara: index to periodical literature.**
African Section, African and Middle Eastern Division. Washington,
DC: Library of Congress, 1971- . 4 vols.
The first four volumes cover 1900-70. There have been three supplements since then,
in 1973, 1982 and 1985. The first volume covers a wide range of articles written during
the period of Portuguese Guinea. It covers many of the articles in the *Boletim Cultural
da Guiné Portuguesa* as well as a number of articles in *Garcia de Orta* and the *Boletim
Geral das Colónias*. Some of the entries are annotated.

552 **African abstracts: quarterly review of articles appearing in current
periodicals.**
London: International African Institute, 1950-72.
Published quarterly, this was an excellent annotated resource for articles on
ethnographic, social and linguistical materials. It is especially recommended for its
annotations of many articles in the *Boletim Cultural de Guiné Portuguesa*.

553 **Africana: bibliographies sur l'Afrique luso-hispanophone (1800-1980).**
(Africana: bibliographies on Portuguese- and Spanish-speaking African
countries [1800-1980].)
René Pélissier. Orgeval, France: Éditions Pélissier, 1980. 205p.
This *annotated* bibliography is a fundamental source. It presents a critical reading of
the literature. Pélissier periodically updates the bibliography in the journal *Les Mois en
Afrique*. See for example, numbers 207-8, 209-10 (1983), numbers 237-8 (1985),
numbers 243-4 (1986) and numbers 253-4 (1987).

554 **Amílcar Cabral: a bio-bibliography of his life and thought, 1925-73.**
Ronald H. Chilcote. *Africana Journal*, vol. 5, no. 4 (winter 1974-75),
p. 289-307.
Gives a more or less comprehensive bibliography of Cabral's writings and a list of
works about Cabral. Chilcote has recently updated and annotated this work in the
forthcoming *Amílcar Cabral's revolutionary theory and practice: a critical guide*
(Boulder, Colorado: Lynne Rienner Publishers, 1991).

555 **A tentative Portuguese-African bibliography.**
Gerald M. Moser. University Park, Pennsylvania: Pennsylvania State
University Libraries, 1970. 151p.
Surveys the bibliography of Portuguese literature in Africa and African literature in
Portuguese. The work is divided into three parts: oral literature, written literature, and
literary history and criticism.

556 **Bibliografia das publicações sobre a África de língua oficial portuguesa entre Janeiro de 1975 e Janeiro de 1983.** (Bibiliography of publications on lusophone Africa between January 1975 and January 1983.)
Jill R. Dias. *Revista Internacional de Estudos Africanos*, no. 1 (1984), p. 243-303.

This is a regular feature of the journal and is in most of the following numbers. The bibliography covers books, theses and articles in several languages, including English.

557 **Bibliografia geográfica de Guiné.** (A geographical bibliography of Guinea.)
Francísco Tenreiro. *Garcia de Orta*, vol. 2, no. 1 (1954), p. 97-134.

Compiles a list of articles and books, mainly official, on the Province. There are 435 items.

558 **Catálogo da exposição cartográfica, iconográfica e documental sobre Guiné-Bissau.** (Catalogue of the exposition of maps, representations and documents on Guinea-Bissau.)
Arquivo Histórico Ultramarino. Lisbon: Instituto de Investigação Científica Tropical and Direcção-Geral da Cooperação do Ministério dos Negócios Estrangeiros, 1988. 11p.

Lists a minor part of the maps, representations and historical documents about Guinea in the historical archives in Lisbon, a major source for information on the Portuguese presence in the area. The documents bridge the period 1616-1806.

559 **Catálogo das publicações em série africanas de língua portuguesa.** (Catalogue of lusophone African periodicals.)
Lisbon: Biblioteca Nacional, 1988. 69p.

This is a guide to newspapers and periodicals published in lusophone Africa and deposited in the National Library of Portugal. The collection of Guinean periodicals concerns the colonial period. Those working on the Republican period and the first 'independence' movements will find the collection worthwhile.

560 **Catálogo de publicações.** (Publications catalogue.)
Instituto de Investigação Científica Tropical (IICT). Lisbon: IICT, 1987. 304p.

This is the most complete listing available of the works of the Instituto, formerly known as the Junta de Investigações Científicas do Ultramar, the Junta De Investigações do Ultramar, the Junta de Investigações Coloniais and the Junta das Missões Geográficas e de Investigações Coloniais.

561 **Catálogos sumários dos fundos de arquivos: administração civil de Cacheu.** (Summary catalogues of the archives of civil administration of Cacheu.)
Nelson Fernandes, François David, Carlos Alfredo, Suzette Cabral, Heidi Keita, Pé. João Vicente, Francíso Malu. Bissau: Arquivos Históricos do Instituto Nacional de Estudos e Pesquisa, 1988. 112p. (Série Catálogos, publicação no. 1).
Catalogues the public documents existing in the archives in Bissau on the region of Cacheu. Invaluable for the historian.

562 **Contribuição para uma bibliografia sobre a Guiné-Bissau.** (Contribution for a bibliography on Guinea-Bissau.)
Lisbon: Centro de Documentação e Informação, Rua Jau, 47, Lisboa, 1977. 77p. [no consecutive pagination].
Lists the collection in the centre and in the various departments of the Junta de Investigações Científicas do Ultramar, now known as the Instituto de Investigação Científica Tropical. The bibliography is broken down by subject matter. It is valuable because it lists – by subject – the articles from the *Boletim Cultural da Guiné Portuguesa* and *Garcia de Orta*, the two most informative journals of colonial time. Most of the bibliography refers to the New State period of Portuguese colonialism.

563 **Documenting Portuguese Africa.**
Compiled by R. H. Chilcote, P. Duignan, E. L. Presseien, M. Leder. *Africana Newsletter*, vol. 1, no. 3 (1963), p. 16-36.
Provides information on where to find Portuguese Africana including libraries, the press, periodicals and national archives. The coverage includes the United States, Portugal, other European countries, and lusophone Africa.

564 **Emerging nationalism in Portuguese Africa: a bibliography of documentary ephemera through 1965.**
Ronald H. Chilcote. Stanford, California: Hoover Institution on War, Revolution and Peace, Stanford University, 1969. 114p.
A very important collection of documents of the various national liberation movements in the Portuguese African colonies. Besides the early documents of the PAIGC (most of which were written by Amílcar Cabral) and the speeches by Cabral, the bibliography lists a number of statements by the FLING and MLG (Movimento da Libertação da Guiné), rival Guinean nationalist groups. The bibliography also includes published works and United Nations publications. All the works listed are on microfilm at the Hoover Institution.

565 **Guide to research and reference works on sub-Saharan Africa.**
Peter Duignan. Stanford, California: Hoover Institution Press, 1971. 941p.
This is an annotated bibliography of publications on Africa.

566   **Guide to the sources of the history of Africa.**
International Council on Archives.   Zug, Switzerland: UNESCO, 1971. 8 vols.

Presents a guide to the archives of Italy, West Germany, Spain, France, the Vatican, and Scandinavian countries. There will be eleven volumes in all including those on Belgium, the United Kingdom and the United States.

567   **Guinea-Bissau: a bibliography covering the rural sector with emphasis on the period after 1975.**
Lorenzo Cabellero, Katarina Carlqvist.   Uppsala, Sweden: Sveriges Lantbruksuniversitet (Swedish University of Agricultural Sciences, International Rural Development Centre), 1984. 27p.

Divided into sections covering related subject matter, this bibliography covers works relating mainly to rural development.

568   **Guinea-Bissau and Cape Verde islands: a comprehensive bibliography.**
Joseph M. McCarthy.   New York; London: Garland Publishing, 1977. 196p.

There are over 2,500 items on both countries, ranging over a number of topics. Most of the items on Guinea-Bissau are historical, and the liberation struggle is featured. Sources in Portuguese, English and French are cited.

569   **Guinea-Bissau: an historiographical essay of post-1960 literature.**
Joye Bowman Hawkins.   Bad Homburg, Germany: International Colloquium on Portuguese-speaking Africa, 1980. 39p.

Comments on the gaps in the literature as well as on major works with special emphasis on historical texts between 1960 and 1980. It is an excellent example of an annotated bibliography, and has been published in *A Current Bibliography on African Affairs*, vol. 17, no. 3, 1985, p. 219-42.

570   **Guiné-Bissau, conhece?: 1100 referências para pesquisa em ciências sociais (1960-1980).** (Do you know Guinea-Bissau?: 1100 references for social science research [1960-80].)
Carlos Lopes.   Geneva, Switzerland: Centre de Documentation, Institut Universitaire d'Études du Développement, 1985. 2nd ed. 97p.

Lists books, journal and magazine articles – and even pertinent newspaper articles – by subject. It covers works in English, Portuguese, French, Italian and German.

571   **Historical abstracts: bibliography of the world's historical literature.**
American Bibliographical Center. Santa Barbara, California; Oxford, England: ABC-CLIO Press, 1955- . annual.

Divided into two parts, Part A covers the period 1450-1914, while Part B covers the literature from 1914 to the current year. This is an excellent source for articles on Guinea-Bissau from Russia and Eastern Europe as well as from Western Europe, the United States and elsewhere.

572 **Historical dictionary of the Republic of Guinea-Bissau.**
R. Lobban, Joshua Forrest.   Metuchen, New Jersey; London:
Scarecrow Press, 1988, 2nd ed. 211p. 2 maps. (African Historical
Dictionaries, no. 22).

A dictionary of people, places, terms and subjects, the text also contains a brief
introduction to the country, a very extensive bibliography, and a useful diagram of
ethnic groups. The treatment of the material suffers from trying to cover too much.

573 **Index africanus.**
J. O. Asamani.   Stanford, California: Hoover Institution Press, 1975.
659p. (Hoover Institution on War, Revolution and Peace,
Bibliographical Series, 53).

Lists periodicals published between 1885 and 1965.

574 **Infectious diseases in twentieth-century Africa: a bibliography of their
distribution and consequences.**
K. David Patterson.   Waltham, Massachusetts: Crossroads Press for
the African Studies Association, 1979. 209p.

This is an invaluable source of articles and books on diseases in Guinea-Bissau. The
literature is surveyed on a variety of diseases, including yellow fever, filariasis,
onchocerciasis, Guinea worm, leprosy, helminthic infections, malaria, sleeping
sickness, bilharziasis, typhoid fever, typhus and so on. Most of the articles are from the
Anais de Instituto de Medicina Tropical and the *Boletim Cultural de Guiné Portuguesa*
but there are other journals as well.

575 **International African bibliography.**
David Hall.   London: Mansell, 1970- .

Issued quarterly, this reference compiles books, papers and articles on Africa. The
works on Guinea-Bissau are listed under country and under general themes. There is
an index. Articles in *Soronda* and *Boletim de informação sócio-económica* are listed.

576 **Materials for West African history in the archives of Belgium and
Holland.**
Patricia Carson.   London: Athlone Press, 1962. 79p.

This is an important resource for those doing research on the Dutch explorations, trade
and settlements and the Dutch challenge to the Portuguese slave trade along the Upper
Guinea Coast. Carson has also written a similar book on resources in French archives
which was published by the same press in 1968. There are three other books in this
series: Richard Gray and David Chambers, *Materials for West African history in Italian
archives* (1965), A. F. C. Ryder, *Materials for West African history in Portuguese
archives* (1965) and Noel Matthews, *Materials for West African history in the archives
of the United Kingdom* (1973).

577 **Nationalist documents on Portuguese Guiné and Cape Verde Islands and Moçambique.**
Ronald H. Chilcote. *African Studies Bulletin*, vol. 10, no. 1 (April 1967), p. 22-42.

Lists documents on deposit at the Hoover Institution on War, Peace and Revolution at Stanford University. Chilcote has continued to collect material through the years (q.v.).

578 **Portugal in Africa: a bibliography of the UCLA collection.**
Gerald Bender, Tamara L. Bender, D. S. Hill, C. A. Hughs, C. T. Rosario. Los Angeles, California: African Studies Center, University of California, Los Angeles, 1972. 317p.

Lists the books and periodicals in the collection. The section on Portuguese Guinea consists mainly of historical and economic works.

579 **Portuguese Africa: a guide to official publications.**
Mary Jane Gibson. Washington, DC: Library of Congress, 1967. 192p.

This is a partial listing of official Portuguese publications concerning the African colonies from the nineteenth century up until 1964.

580 **Statistics, Africa: sources for social, economic and market research.**
Joan M. Harvey. Beckenham, Kent, England: CBD Research, 1978. 2nd ed. 342p.

Besides being a source for statistics in individual countries, the introductory section of this book gives various general and *specialist* reference works for a variety of subjects. These include minerals and mining, agriculture, commodities, industry, energy, construction, trade, population, labour, and finance.

581 **The African studies companion: a resource guide and directory.**
London: Hans Zell, 1989. 148p.

Lists all the specialist bibliographies and resource books – including guides to archival materials – in the United States, Great Britain, Europe, and Africa.

Para uma leitura sociológica da Guiné-Bissau.
See item no. 10.

Naissance de la Guiné: Portugais et Africains en Sénégambie (1841-1936).
See item no. 96.

Reference Books

582 **Africa contemporary record: annual survey and documents.**
Edited by Colin Legum, Marion E. Doro.   New York; London:
Africana Publishing Company, 1968-69- . annual.
A two-year survey with general articles and country reviews. The material is slightly
out of date by the time it is published but the coverage of political and economic issues
is very good.

583 **Africa South of the Sahara 1990.**
London: Europa Publications, 1971- . annual.
This is the best of the reference books in terms of political and economic coverage.
The information, which is generally reliable, is within six months of the publication
date and is very extensive. There are also general articles covering the continent.

584 **The Africa Review 1990.**
Saffron Walden, Essex, England: World of Information, 1977- . annual.
Originally published as *Africa Guide 1978*, the review has general articles and country
reports. The articles contain encapsulated information for the businessman and
traveller. There is a general if somewhat superficial overview of the year's events.

Indexes

There follow three separate indexes: authors (personal and corporate); titles; and subjects. Title entries are italicized and refer either to the main titles, or to other works cited in the annotations. The numbers refer to bibliographic entries, not to pages. Individual index entries are arranged in alphabetical sequence.

Index of Authors

A

A.S. International 404
Aaby, P. 253, 297
Abreu, M. de P. 453
Abshire, D. 141
Africa Information Service 366
African Department, International Monetary Fund 456
African Section, African and Middle Eastern Division, Library of Congress 551
Agência-Geral do Ultramar 102, 105
Ajayi, J. F. A. 41
Alegre, M. 341
Alfredo, C. 561
Almada Duarte, Dulce 341
Almeida, António 257
Álvares d'Almada, A. 78
Alves, M. Luisa Gomes 29
American Bibliographical Center 571
Amistad Research Center 360
Amnesty International 304
Andelman, D. A. 345
Andrade, Mário 341, 342, 484
Andreini, J-C. 316
Arquivo Histórico Ultramarino 558
Asamani, J. O. 573

Association pour le Développement de la Riziculture en Afrique de l'Ouest (ADRAO) 433

B

Ba, Cheikh 165
Bacelar, A. 32
Barata, A. J. 382
Barcellos, C. J. de Senna 75
Barcelos, M. Rambout 473
Barreto, João 38
Barros, Luíz Frederico 5
Barry, B. 165
Basso Marques, J. 221
Bastos da Luz, J. V. 260
Beaver, Philip 49
Bender, Gerald 578
Bender, T. L. 578
Benot, Y. 341
Bernardi, Paola Belpassi 471, 474
Bernatzik, H. A. 168, 182
Bernier, J. 426
Bienen, Henry 369
Biggs-Davison, J. 142
Birkholz, Uwe 432
Birmingham, D. 34
Blackey, Robert 369
Blackhurst, H. 549
Blake, J. W. 58
Blardone, G. 417
Błażejewicz, D. 485

Bocandé, Bertrand 229
Bollinger, Virginia L. 171
Boulegue, J. 41
Bourdillon de Grissac, C. 19
Bowman, Joye 80, 89, 95, 569
Boxer, C. R. 40, 71
Bragança, Aquino 342, 357, 364
Brásio, A. 239
Brass, W. 164
Brigada de Estudos Florestais da Guiné 30
Brocardo, M. Teresa 504
Brooks, George E. 51, 64, 66, 69, 79, 191, 243
Brooks, H. C. 144
Bruce, N. 154
Bryan, M. A. 217, 224
Buijtenhuijs, R. 317
Bukh, J. 253
Bull, M. 198
Burness, D. 489

C

Cabellero, L. 447, 567
Cabral, Amílcar 279, 335, 337-8, 351, 353, 362-3, 365, 367, 375, 377, 443
Cabral, Jorge 378
Cabral, Luís 125, 323
Cabral, Maria Helena 443
Cabral, Nelson E. 219
Cabral, Suzette 561

151

Index of Titles

157

159

Index of Subjects

166

169

Feinberg, H. M. 548
Felupe
  legal practices 207
  medical practices 257
  rituals 206
  social structure 202
Fernandes, Álvaro 77
Fernandes, Gil 270, 392,
  396
Fernandes, Nelson 561
Fernandes, Raul M. 183
Fernandes, Valentim 53,
  70
Ferreira Rosa, M. 91
Ferreira, António Baticã
  488, 500
Ferreira, E. de Sousa 376
Ferreira, F. da Cruz 250
Ferreira, J. de Araújo 25
Ferreira, Manuel 500
Ferreirinha, M. P. 24
Figueiredo, A. 103
Figueiredo, R. 450
Filesi, T. 235
First, Ruth 140
Fishing industry 450-1
FLING 131, 159, 564
Flora 5, 23-32, 50, 84, 93,
  261
  Afzelia africana 24, 30
  Bissolim 30
  Borassus aethiopium 30
  Chlorophora regia 24, 30
  Cola cordifolia 30
  Connaraceae 31
  Cordyla africana Lour.
    24, 30
  Daniellia oliveri 30
  Detarium senegalense 30
  Diallium guineense 30
  *Erythrophloeum
    guineense* 24, 30
  forests 27, 30
  Khaya senegalensis 30
  Lophira alata 24, 30
  Parinari excelsa 30
  Parkia biglobosa 30
  plants for medicinal
    purposes 261
  Prosopis africana 30
  Pterocarpus erinaceus
    24, 30
  Schrebera arborea 30
Fondation Calouste

Gulbenkian 496
Forced labour 109
Foreign aid 300, 400, 414,
  470
  see also Foreign relations
Foreign relations 89, 132,
  193, 270, 312, 378-402
  border disputes 379,
    390-1
  border problems 86
  declaration of
    sovereignty 303, 399
  foreign aid 380, 382,
    385-7, 391, 393, 400,
    402-8, 410-11, 429,
    431, 452-6, 465, 470
  non-alignment 386
  policy statements at UN
    General Assembly
    383-6, 392, 395-8,
    400-1
  recognition of
    sovereignty 303
  support for liberation
    movements 384-5
  Tri-Lateral Commission
    382
  with lusophone Africa
    381
  with socialist countries
    380
Forje, J. W. 374
Forrest, Joshua B. 276,
  322, 572
Frade, F. 32
France 5, 61, 86, 89, 96,
  197, 379, 390-1, 396,
  421, 553, 566
  archival materials 566
  French intelligence
    agency (SDECE) 138
  French merchants 113
  relationship with Balde
    family 112
Franco, L. T. de Almeida
  246
Freire, M. Emilia 410
Freire, Paolo 475
Freitas, M. C. 24
FRELIMO 136, 146, 284
  party congresses 284
FRETILIN 398, 401
Fula 45, 47, 173, 188-90,
  224, 240, 485, 490, 495

Firdu 47
  handicrafts 490
  language 224
  legal practices 190
  medical practices 257
  migration 45
  social structure 188-9
  women and children
    189
Fuladu 112, 495
  Balde family 112
Funk, Ursula 434, 436
Futa Djalon 45

G

Gabinete de Estudos 420
Gabinete de Estudos do
  Ministério de
  Coordenação
  Económica, Plano e
  Cooperação
  Internacional 423
Gabinete de Estudos e
  Planeamento de
  Ministério de Saúde
  Pública 256
Gabriel, T. H. 376
Gabú 47, 188, 209, 420
  see also Kaabu
Gacha, M. 352
Galhano, F. 490
Galli, Rosemary 4, 325,
  327, 405, 407, 413,
  416, 428, 437
Gama, P. 19
Gambia 56, 66, 80, 112,
  495, 533
Gamboa de Aiala,
  Gonçalo 59
Gardette, M. Correia 255,
  260
Geba Valley rice
  experimentation
  project 428, 435
Geisslhofer, Hans 480
Geography 6, 8, 13-22, 50,
  55, 191
  demographic 8
  economic 8
  geo-hydrological mission
    22
Geographic Names, US

171

Periodicals 524-45, 547, 552, 559, 563, 573, 578
Perl, M. 220
Photographs 3, 9, 19, 168-9, 181, 186, 194, 200, 485-6, 505
PIDE 138, 339
Pinto Bull, B. 159, 213, 216, 496
Pinto, A. Reimão 170
Pires Mota, A. 134, 492
Polisario 401
Political economy 4, 93, 199, 315, 324, 327, 407, 416, 436, 456
Politics 4, 133, 136-7, 153, 267-328, 394, 546
  Cape Verdean issue 171, 276, 313, 318
  class struggle 174
  comparison with Angola and Mozambique 136-7, 158
  comparisons with other countries 284, 287, 296, 306, 313, 315, 325
  decentralized political structures 151
  ethnic issue 171, 174, 276, 282, 313, 320, 322
  local power structure 315
  popular movements 314
Pombal, Marquês de 65, 67
Ponteiros 417
Population 2, 83, 105, 124, 143, 160-5, 173, 175, 191-2, 240-1, 252, 436, 444, 472, 515-16, 518, 520-1, 580
  census for 1940 163
  census for 1950 124, 160, 163, 173
  census for 1960 124, 163
  census for 1970 124
  census for 1979 162
  comparison with Angola and Mozambique 164
Populations
  children 189, 247, 264
  coastal peoples 62, 64, 166, 203, 246
  savannah peoples 64, 166, 189, 246

Portugal
  adaptation to trade patterns 70
  and France 89
  and Fulas 89
  Anglo-Portuguese relations 60
  Armed Forces Movement 135, 138
  as a chivalric warrior state 73
  Brigada de Estudos Agronomicos da Guiné 449
  Caetano government 120
  Colonial Act 102
  colonial administration 5, 7, 83-4, 88, 97, 105, 107, 111, 113-14, 118
  colonial budgets 99
  colonial ideology 106
  colonial labour conditions 109
  colonial mentality 7, 83
  colonial myths 38
  colonial policy 1
  colonial taxes 88
  colonial veterinary services 23
  empire 40, 71, 73, 103, 116
  errors of colonial administration 115
  Estatuto dos Indígenas 90
  Estatuto político-administrativo da Guiné 102
  Estatuto político-administrativo da Província da Guiné 100
  foreign aid to Guinea-Bissau 388
  government of General Spínola 120
  impact of PAIGC 120, 135
  Instituto de Investigação Científica Tropical 526, 562
  invasion of Guinea-Conakry 147
  Junta das Missões

  Geográficas e de Investigações Coloniais 560
  Junta de Investigações Científicas do Ultramar 526, 560, 562
  Junta de Investigações Coloniais 560
  Junta de Investigações do Ultramar 526, 534, 560
  Lei Orgânica 100
  military policy 1
  monopolistic commercial policies 38
  Native Labour Code 109
  neglect of Guinea 104
  Portuguese secret police (PIDE) 138
  post-independence relations with Guinea 394
  race relations in empire 71, 106
  Republican administration 82, 94
  wars of occupation 80
Portuguese Guinea 2, 5-7, 13-14, 20-1, 23-4, 26-9, 32, 39, 80-117, 143, 150, 158, 164, 166, 170, 173, 175, 209, 240, 246, 249-50, 252, 257, 261, 263, 346, 449, 487, 490, 506, 551, 578
Power 10, 47, 135, 138, 174, 179, 187, 269, 276, 283, 290, 294-6, 301-2, 307, 314-15, 320, 322, 324, 340, 396, 416-17, 424, 436, 442, 496, 540
Prian, J. R. 19
Prince Henry 73
Proença, Helder 499
Programa de Desenvolvimento Rural Integrado (PDRI) 428, 439
Property 72, 195, 202, 207, 436
Província da Guiné 16, 81,

Map of Guinea-Bissau

This map shows the more important towns and other features.

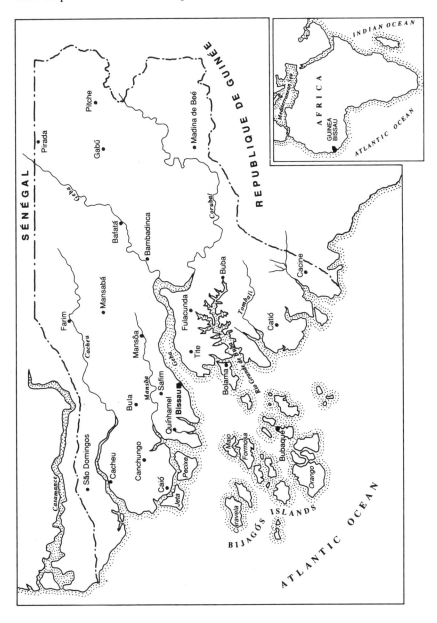